DECISION-ORIENTED EDUCATIONAL RESEARCH

Evaluation in Education and Human Services

Editors:

George F. Madaus, Boston College, Chestnut
    Hill, Massachusetts, U.S.A.
Daniel L. Stufflebeam, Western Michigan
    University, Kalamazoo, Michigan, U.S.A.

Previously published books in the series:

Decision-Oriented
Educational Research

William W. Cooley
William E. Bickel

Kluwer-Nijhoff Publishing
a member of the Kluwer Academic Publishers Group

Boston/Dordrecht/Lancaster

Distributors

for the United States and Canada: Kluwer Academic Publishers,
190 Old Derby Street, Hingham, MA, 02043, USA

for the UK and Ireland: Kluwer Academic Publishers, MTP Press
Limited, Falcon House, Queen Square, Lancaster LAI IRN, UK

for all other countries: Kluwer Academic Publishers Group,
Distribution Centre, P.O. Box 322, 3300 AH Dordrecht,
The Netherlands

Library of Congress Cataloging in Publication Data
Main entry under title:

Cooley, William W.
  Decision-oriented educational research.

  (Evaluation in education and human services)
  Bibliography: p.
  Includes index
    1. Education — Research — Pennsylvania — Pittsburgh. 2.
Educational accountability — Pennsylvania —
Pittsburgh. 3. Educational statistics. 4. Public
schools — Pennsylvania — Pittsburgh — Case studies.
I. Bickel, William E. II. Title. III. Series.

LB1028.C592   1986   370′.7′8074886   85-14828
ISBN 0-89838-201-7

Printed in the United States of America

To Richard C. Wallace, Jr.,
whose leadership and cooperation made
these explorations possible

Contents

Acknowledgments

There is always indebtedness in a project of this sort, both direct and indirect. Here is the short list of those to whom we are most directly indebted:

- our many clients in the Pittsburgh public schools, who were willing to engage in the necessary dialogue, particularly Richard Wallace, the superintendent of schools;
- the co-directors of the Learning Research and Development Center (LRDC), Robert Glaser and Lauren Resnick, who provided support and encouragement for this effort;
- our other colleagues at LRDC, particularly Gaea Leinhardt, Leslie Salmon-Cox, and Naomi Zigmond, who are fellow researchers in the schools;
- our many other colleagues in educational research who have contributed to this effort, both indirectly, as acknowledged in our references, and more directly, such as Paul Lohnes, Dan Stufflebeam, and Marvin Alkin;
- the graduate students and research assistants who worked on the tasks summarized in the case histories, especially Paul LeMahieu, who went on to become the director of testing and evaluation in the Pittsburgh school district, and who provided important substantive feedback on drafts of these chapters and cases;
- the National Institute of Education, which provided most of the funds that supported the work of the cases, and the Ford Foundation which provided support for Case 9;
- our secretaries, Terri Komar and Margaret Emmerling, who labored long and hard to help us get this manuscript to the publisher on time;
- two other special people, Cynthia Cooley and Donna Bickel, who provided intellectual and moral support that was particularly important when the going got tough, as it will in this hectic role of decision-oriented educational researcher.

Preface

Decision-Oriented Educational Research considers a form of educational research that is designed to be directly relevant to the current information requirements of those who are shaping educational policy or managing educational systems. It was written for those who plan to conduct such research, as well as for policy makers and educational administrators who might have such research conducted for them.

The book is divided into three main parts. Part I is background. Chapter 1 describes some of the basic themes that are woven throughout subsequent chapters on decision-oriented research. These themes include the importance of taking a systems view of educational research; of understanding the nature of decision and policy processes and how these influence system research; of integrating research activities into the larger system's processes; of the role of management in the research process; of researchers and managers sharing a sense of educational purposes; and of emphasizing system improvement as a basic goal of research process. Chapter 2 is a discussion of the background of the research activities that form the bases of this book. Our collaboration with the Pittsburgh public school system is described, as are the methods and structure we used to build the case histories of our work with the district.

Part II, encompassing chapters 3 through 9, addresses basic generalizations about decision-oriented educational research that we have derived from our experiences. These generaliztions include: discussions of the nature of and the need for a client orientation in this type of research (chapter 3); the importance of being methodologically eclectic so that the research can respond to a broad range of client information needs (chapter 4); the value of moving away from conceptualizing research as discrete studies of program impact and toward a view that emphasizes an ongoing process of data collection and analysis that enables policy shapers and system managers to monitor critical system indicators and to use information to tailor actions in response to system needs (chapter 5); the nature of and the critical importance of developing computer-based information systems that permit the researcher to respond to client information needs in a timely fashion (chapter 6); the benefits that can be derived from closely document-ing the development of major system innovations in order both to improve implementation processes and to develop an institutional memory that can benefit future system reform efforts (chapter 7); the role of student achieve-ment data in analyzing system performance (chapter 8); and the role of flex-ible, interactive dissemination processes involving both clients and research-ers in increasing the utilization of research results (chapter 9). In chapter 10, we summarize our conception of how decision-oriented research can be of value to policy shapers and managers in educational systems. As part of our discussion, we address the basis for generalization from our experiences to other system contexts. Finally, we describe how decision-oriented educa-tional research can make positive contributions in three broad policy areas involving technology, the preparation of system managers and researchers, and the public accountability of educational systems.

Part III (cases 1–11) provides the details of our research experiences with the Pittsburgh public schools. The case histories are central to the chapters on generalizations about decision-oriented research. The cases are a representative sample of the kinds of research activities encompassed in our work with the district. They are drawn upon in each chapter in part II to provide examples of strategies and methods we are recommending, and to offer supportive evidence as to why we take particular positions. The cases provide important evidence about what didn't work well as well as what were successful research efforts. The cases themselves range in substantive issues. They include: traditional program evaluations (cases 3, 6, 11); ex-ploratory analyses of quantitative data addressing policy questions related to achievement differences among black and white students, and among various configurations of school organizations (cases 1 and 2, respectively); and the use of acheivement and other data for analyzing administrator per-formance (case 10). Cases 5 and 9 provide specific examples of the documentation of complex educational innovations. Cases 4 and 7 describe system-wide and middle-school needs assessments, respectively. Finally, case 8 describes the nature and role of computer-based information systems in decision-oriented research.

Each case provides information on the background of the research task, the methods used, the results reported and how they were used (or not) by system personnel. While the reader will find references to cases throughout the generalization chapters in part II, it is important to note that some chapters are more closely linked to particular cases than others. In terms of a reading and teaching strategy, we recommend going back and forth between chapters and cases, perhaps with the following combinations:

Background	Chapters 1 and 2	Cases 1 and 2
Client Orientation	Chapter 3	Cases 3 and 4
Eclectic	Chapter 4	Case 7
Monitoring	Chapters 5 and 6	Case 8
Documentation	Chapter 7	Cases 5 and 9
Achievement	Chapter 8	Cases 6 and 11
Utilization	Chapter 9	Case 10

Another suggested teaching strategy would be to have the students review some of the case histories in terms of the *Standards for Evaluations of Educational Programs, Projects, and Materials* (Joint Committee, 1981). Those cases that represent the type of program evaluation to which the standards apply would be cases 3, 5, 6, 9, and 11.

It is our hope that the reader will find what follows in the chapters and cases to be stimulating and useful in thinking about how researchers, policy shapers, and managers can work together for the improvement of educational systems. We have come to believe that decision-oriented educational research has a vital role to play in this important goal.

I BACKGROUND

1 EDUCATIONAL RESEARCH AND EDUCATIONAL SYSTEMS

This book is about research — not all kinds of research, but research designed to be immediately useful to those who are responsible for educational systems, either in the role of policy setting or in administration and management. Cronbach and Suppes (1969) divided up the world of research into conclusion-oriented and decision-oriented inquiry. This book is about the latter. We call it decision-oriented educational research (DOER). It is research designed to help educators as they consider issues surrounding educational policy, as they establish priorities for improving educational systems, or as they engage in the day-to-day management of educational systems.

DOER is not research designed to clarify or defend particular theoretical notions but, rather, is a very applied research designed to inform the day-to-day guidance of educational systems. It does involve what the verb "research" implies: "to search or investigate exhaustively," but it is not what is generally considered to be scientific research. So this book is about applied, decision-oriented, educational research, the kind being done by educators who have developed research skills but who are educators more than scientists.

3

Many scientists are also studying education today from the perspective of their particular disciplines. Educational phenomena are the objects of their research, but the scientists' primary objective is to contribute to theoretical developments in their disciplines. Today there are psychologists who are studying instruction, economists who are looking at the financing of educational institutions, sociologists who are studying organizational structures in education, etc. This book is by and for people whose primary concern is educational practice and how to help educational systems do their job better. We are educators who have developed skills in generating and organizing information in ways that people who operate educational systems find useful. We have written about how that kind of research can be done, either for those conducting the research or for those who would have it done for them.

Our concern lies with research done within the context of an educational system. The focus is similar in some respects to the arena Love (1983) and others have called "internal evaluation." The "system" might be a school district or a particular school in the district, a state educational system or a regional (intermediate) system within the state, or a college or university system. The distinguishing feature is that the research is guided by the information needs of the people responsible for that system. It is usually conducted by employees of an educational system or by researchers who are working closely with such systems and who have their research agendas established by the information needs of the educational system.

Most large educational systems include people charged with the responsibility for generating information that others find useful in their decision making. A 1978 survey (Lyon, Doscher, McGranahan, and Williams, 1978) found that 90 percent of the school districts serving 50,000 or more students have such offices. The labels might differ: office of research and evaluation; institutional research; planning office; testing and evaluation; information systems; etc. We will refer to any such enterprise as the research office. Their locations vary in the organization of the educational system. In school districts, the research office might report to the superintendent or to someone further down in the administrative hierarchy, such as the assistant superintendent for curriculum and development. Similarly, in state systems or universities, the office may report to the chief administrative officer or to someone else. Just where it reports is important in determining who the primary clients of the office become, and that in turn influences the research priorities for such offices.

Size is also a variable. In a small school district the research office might consist of one part-time person responsible for the standardized testing program. In a large school district, dozens of people might be involved. For example, in 1984 the Philadelphia school district employed 51 professionals in its office of planning, research and evaluation (Lytle, 1984). A 1983 survey of state departments of education revealed that three-fourths of the states have research offices, with the largest employing 37 professionals (Smith, 1984).

It is important to understand the relationship between what we call "decision-oriented educational research" and the field of "evaluation." One way to distinguish the two concepts is by the typical scope of activity they encompass. Historically, the latter has tended to imply a more specific undertaking largely dominated by program evaluation. A program evaluation is a discrete study of a particular program. The type of research that we are talking about here includes program evaluation, but it is broader than that. For example, it includes a type of operations research that involves a continuous activity of data collection, analysis, and feedback to policy shapers and managers of educational systems.

So in one sense DOER involves activities that are not included in how evaluation is usually defined. On the other hand, DOER emphasizes a subset of what is generally considered the scope of evaluation. For example, Scriven (1967) distinguished between formative (for program improvement) and summative (for program effectiveness) evaluation. Stufflebeam (1971) divided evaluation into proactive (for decision making) and retroactive (for accountability) evaluation. The emphasis in DOER is formative, proactive evaluation. The purpose is to guide policy development and management as it relates to improving the educational processes that are taking place within the system as they occur.

In emphasizing formative evaluation, we do not take the position that summative studies are never useful undertakings. There are indeed circumstances where the retrospective study of specific programs is desirable, perhaps even mandatory. We are saying that such research seems to have overly dominated the field of evaluation. It is our position that evaluation researchers, and system administrators who define the tasks of evaluators, would do well to re-examine the scope of research activity typically encompassed by the work of evaluators. This concept of an expanded domain of tasks and purposes, together with a formative emphasis, is already reflected in some of the more recent literature in the field of evaluation (Patton, 1978; Love, 1983; Cronbach and associates, 1980). By using the phrase decision-oriented educational research rather than evaluation research to describe our work, we hope to underscore our own commitment to an expanded vision of the role of research in educational systems.

DOER represents an important yet largely unrealized promise in contemporary education. The promise lies in the capacity of sound, well-designed research to contribute directly to effective strategies for improving current policies, programs, and practices. The promise remains largely unrealized because research which has had the objective of informing decisions has tended to take place in isolation from the policy or administrative processes. Too often, what is produced is knowledge that is little understood or used by those responsible for the direction of the various levels of the educational enterprise. This record is reflected in the numerous questions raised about evaluation research in the literature. Is evaluation research studying policy relevant issues? Are the answers sound enough to justify their use? Are policy makers willing and able to use the results of this research? The impression that prevails is a general skepticism about the utility of evaluation research.

An objective of this book is to describe ways in which educational research can become more relevant and valid. We believe that the promise DOER holds for education is genuine and realizable; educational practices can be improved through DOER. We believe that this is especially true of research that is conducted by system-based researchers.

Throughout this book we draw upon our experience in doing this type of research for the Pittsburgh public schools. Chapter 2 describes the nature of that relationship. Part III represents 11 case histories of specific requests for our services. These "real life" experiences provided a major basis for our conclusions about how to conduct DOER. The case histories provide concrete illustrations of the points we are making as the arguments develop. In chapter 10, we discuss why we believe our conclusions about DOER may be generalizable to other contexts.

Major Themes

Six themes pervade this book. The first concerns the importance of thinking about DOER as taking place within an educational system. The second involves how systems arrive at policies and decisions, and the relationship of research to these processes. The third relates to the critical importance of the integration of DOER into the policy and decision-making processes. A fourth theme concerns the responsibility of system managers and researchers to be involved in DOER. A fifth concerns the need for those involved with DOER to have a shared set of values about the goals of education. A sixth theme involves an emphasis on the improvement of processes and programs within systems and the role of research in the improvement process. Each of these themes is briefly described in the following sections and then further developed throughout the book.

Educational Systems

DOER takes place within and for an educational system. Because this notion of an educational system is extremely important, it is useful for us to consider its meaning. As Borich and Jemelka (1982) point out, systems concepts are becoming an important part of educational research. But because such concepts have evolved from a variety of fields, there is often confusion about what is meant by them.

The most basic components of an educational system include students, teachers, instructional materials, and administrators. Beyond these lie parents and the larger community. In combination, they form a network of relationships, actions, and reactions that are very interdependent. That is what we mean by system. The most dominant kind of educational system in the United States is the school district. There are over 15,000 of them, and each district is a somewhat special system in terms of how it works and what might happen if a component in the system were modified in some way.

One can also think of a particular school as an educational system. In the context of a school district, a school is a subsystem, but it can also be considered as a reasonably bounded system, in and of itself, with its special set of components and working relationships. Similarly, a school district can be thought of as a subsystem within a state system, and the 50 state systems, collectively, form a national system of public education, albeit a loosely coupled one.

There are, of course, many other educational systems besides those that are directly part of the U.S. system of public schools. A university is an educational system, and so is a private nursery school. They are also subsystems of a national educational system, with dependencies across subsystems.

In addition to recognizing that a given educational system (e.g., a school) is not isolated from other educational systems (e.g., a school district), it is also important to consider how educational systems are influenced by and in turn affect the larger social system, the economic system, the political system, etc. Boulding (1985) has produced a provocative book on that point called *The World as a Total System*.

One of the challenges in working to improve education in the United States is the vastness, complexity, and interrelatedness of it all. For example, as one works to implement change within a school district, it is soon clear that the district is not an isolated system. Innovations often run up against state codes, for instance, which can quickly frustrate the intended change. Similarly, if one chooses a school building as the system of interest and tries to evoke reforms within a school, district policy can become a serious impediment to change. This interdependence of the various components in a system, and the realization that any given system is a subsystem in some larger network of relationships, is part of what has to be taken into account when one undertakes DOER.

One characteristic of systems that is important to understand is that they at times can react to change in counter-intuitive ways. One does not have to be in education very long before noticing how a well-intentioned change within the system can "backfire." This is because of the tendency in education to try to solve an educational problem in isolation, without taking into account the context in which that problem is immersed. This failure to consider the context is what Churchman (1979) calls "the environmental fallacy," and it is a very important systems concept.

The environmental fallacy can be illustrated by referring to case 3. In this case we were asked to evaluate Project Pass, a newly implemented program designed to meet the academic needs of the large number of students failing a grade. (The school system had, prior to this, passed a resolution against the social promotion of students.) The closer we looked at the program, the more it became clear that many of the students in Pass had failed because of high truancy rates. The failing of students based upon truancy was itself the result of another recently developed board policy which allowed teachers to fail students based upon absenteeism alone. The program, aimed at improving academic skills, had no mechanism for addressing truancy; thus many of the students placed in Pass remained both truant and unexposed to the academic treatment available.

Case 3 reminds us that a school district is a complex educational system. The performance of particular subsystems cannot be improved in isolation. Board politics and policies, union contracts, bureaucratic turf, state codes, federal guidelines, and court actions (to name a few!) all influence the behavior of the system. So do the value orientations of the thousands of participants in the system. As Green (1980) pointed out so well, the behavior of the system as a whole usually frustrates the intent of particular changes in policy. Systems theory provides a framework for designing ways to improve a system. The environmental fallacy notion underscores the fact that you don't improve systems by solving problems in isolation.

Decisions and Research

Within educational systems, decisions are being made all the time. A school board member decides how to vote on a policy issue. A superintendent decides to make school closings a personal priority. A principal decides to give a second grade teacher more supervisory attention. A teacher decides to bring a student's truancy problem to the attention of the school social worker. These many decisions will vary in the degree to which they are informed by systematically collected and analyzed data. A fundamental assumption of DOER is that better decisions will be made by better informed decision makers. We take this position, however, with some important qualifications.

The phrase "decision maker" is a little troublesome in educational systems. It tends to imply that it is always possible to find someone who makes the big decisions. Take Project Pass as an example (case 3). No one person defined or shaped that project. Lots of different people made lots of little decisions that resulted in the program as actually implemented. Of course some of the "little" decisions are bigger than others. An example of a larger one was the superintendent's deciding to recommend to the board that Pass be part of a system-wide desegregation plan. But he would not have done that if Pass had not been promoted by his assistant superintendent. She would not have promoted Pass if her director of instruction, together with a group of supervisors, had not sketched out the general design for dealing with student failures. No one person was willing or able to claim to be *the* decision maker that launched Project Pass.

Rather than writing about "decision makers," Cronbach and associates (1980) used the expression "policy shaping community," recognizing that educational policy is the result of lots of different actors. The PSC (as they refer to it) is a very important and useful concept, and it is in that sense that we refer to decision makers. They are the actors in the PSC. The decisions they make affect how they think and behave as individuals. Their decisions may or may not actually affect what happens in the system.

But decisions are being made. Goals are being set. Resources are being allocated. Priorities are being established. Votes are being taken. How people decide will be influenced (in part) by the information they have. We say "in part" because individual "decisions" will always draw upon a wide range of sources of influence, including political values and resource contingencies. The task of DOER is to identify (indeed anticipate where possible) the kinds of policy and management decisions people have to be making in the system, and then generate and disseminate information relevant to those decisions. The fact that the decision process is so diffuse makes the task more difficult, but by adopting a strong client orientation, as described in chapter 3, it is possible to do it well. Also, in chapter 9 we discuss the relationship of dissemination and research utilization to these decision processes.

Let's take a brief look at an example of how information generated by research can influence decision makers. In case 2, the school board was considering a plan to move to a uniform scheme of grade organization. In the board's deliberations, it became clear that some of the board members were misinterpreting some achievement test results. Noticing this misinterpretation (through observing board meetings), the researchers worked up achievement data to show how student performance was and was not being influenced by the different grade organizations that were operating in the district. These new analyses were presented at the subsequent board meeting, and the result was a change in the dialogue regarding the pros and cons of different grade organization schemes. The misinterpretations were no longer a part of the argument against moving to district-wide middle schools. The quality of the deliberations was improved by the results of that decision-oriented research effort. While the research data represented only one type of information used, the process was informed by its availability.

Integration of DOER into Policy and Management Processes

A third perspective that pervades this book is that DOER must be closely linked to the policy and management processes in a system. The integration we are calling for has several important aspects to it. If research is to respond to the information needs of the system, then those needs must be known and understood. One aspect of integration then is meaningful access to relevant decision and policy shapers in order to assess information needs. It is important that decision-oriented researchers become "students of" and communicators with the policy and management communities in sustained ways.

A second component of integration involves the communication of and use of research results that have been generated to meet information needs. An integrated research capability is one that is closely linked to relevant action mechanisms in the larger system that have responsibility for managing and improving operational performance. This linkage with action mechanisms can occur through direct interaction between system researchers and managers of action components, or through intermediaries.

In chapter 5, "Monitoring Indicators and Tailoring Practice," the concept of linking information systems with the policy shaping community and action mechanisms is discussed in detail. In chapter 3, "Client Orientation," and chapter 9, "Utilization and the Role of Dissemination," we discuss the role of the client in both shaping the research and in integrating research information into the operations of a system.

In calling for an integration of DOER into the policy and management processes, we recognize that this may contrast sharply with the way research/evaluation is thought of in many organizational systems. One has a sense from the limited amount of literature in this area that research offices are often organizationally isolated from both the general policy process and the management contexts of specific system programs. Taking school district offices as an example, they may be viewed either as the sources of "white-coated" researchers appearing on the scene to determine program effectiveness (summative evaluation); or simply as testing offices, producing predetermined kinds of data on an annual basis for compliance or public accountability functions. While these activities may fulfill important system functions, they tend to stand as isolated research or data collection efforts, detached from ongoing system processes. In contrast to these views, we propose an alternative vision, that of a research process well integrated into the life of an educational system. As such, DOER would represent an online research resource, where data collection and dissemination are continual, linked to changing system information needs, and the action systems designed to respond to these needs.

The Responsibility of System Managers in the Research Process

A fourth theme that pervades this book concerns the responsibility of management in the research process. To date much of the literature on evaluation research has emphasized discussions of the responsibilities of researchers in the information generation process. The responsibilities of researchers are many, which we discuss in subsequent chapters. However, it is our conviction that management also has several important roles to play in the research process that are critical to its success.

Management responsibility has several aspects to it. First, it is management that ultimately has the responsibility for defining the ways in which the system's research capability is deployed. Our case history experience suggests that the range of information needs in a system can be great indeed. Managment that broadly defines the range of tasks that are the legitimate domains of research responsibility, enhances the potential value of the research resource to the system. Researchers, of course, must be in position and ready to respond to such an expanded domain. But, without the legitimization of an expanded role, the opportunity to be responsive is constrained at the outset. An important characteristic of the system's environment in which our work took place was that management broadly defined the potential arena for research activity.

A second aspect of management responsibility in the research process has already been alluded to in our discussion of the integration theme. We feel it is incumbent upon the researcher to study the system, and to communicate with policy and decision shapers about information needs and the information generated through DOER. Similarly, management has a responsibility to be accessible and responsive to such communication. We discuss in detail in chapter 3 what we mean by a mutually educational dialogue that can enhance research and utilization processes.

DOER and Shared Educational Goals

The fifth perspective that pervades this book is the importance of a sense of educational purpose, one that is shared by system managers and researchers alike. Development of some commonly held educational values is an important aspect of the dialogue that must take place between researcher and client. It is a critical feature of the incrementalist-type approach to the improvement of educational systems that we are advocating here. Fine-tuning that is simply a directionless tinkering is not our focus. The best way to avoid such a pitfall is to have client and researcher develop a shared sense of what education should accomplish in our society. That may well be the most important outcome of the researcher-client dialogue.

For example, in chapter 5 we examine the nature and extent of inequities in opportunity that occur in education. We identify a philosophy of education which can guide one's thinking about this critically important issue. A review is provided of the general approaches that have been used in dealing with this problem, as are outlines of procedures that emerged from our efforts to reduce inequities in educational opportunity. These goals were shared by management and researchers alike, and they served as important guideposts in defining a research program. Goals, of course, will vary by context. However, regardless of how shared goals may be different in different systems with different actors, the notion of researchers and managers developing some values in common remains an important component of DOER.

DOER as Improvement-Oriented Research

Our sixth and final theme concerns a commitment to system improvement as a central goal of DOER. We have already noted the distinction made by Scriven (1967) and others between summative and formative research. In a fundamental way, our perspective about DOER emphasizes a formative mission. In part, our position is one of attempting to redress an imbalance we see in the literature and in practice. It is also a position based on experience suggesting that real benefits are accrued from an improvement orientation.

There has been a preponderance of discussion of the impact mission of evaluation research among researchers, and an overemphasis of this use of research by system managers. The case history experience suggests that the deployment of a system's research capability in ways that contribute to the ongoing improvement of operations can be a powerful tool for management. Cases 5 and 9 concerning the documentation of the development of a school improvement program and a teacher center, respectively, demonstrate the payoff a district can obtain by working hard at improving the implementation of a new program as it occurs. Similarly, chapter 5 and case 4 illustrate an improvement orientation at a district level.

The improvement orientation contrasts with the more traditional, summative-style employment of research resources in several important respects. Often the summative exercise occurs after it is too late to do anything about a program's performance (for example). If the impact data are negative, the system often moves to replace an existing program with a new one. And the cycle is repeated again. What is lost is the opportunity to improve operations as they occur. Deploying research resources systematically in an improvement-oriented mode can significantly benefit system operations and can help to avoid costly cycles of innovation, judgment, and new innovations.

These six themes concerning a system's perspective to research, the nature of decision processes, the integration of system research, the responsibility of managers in the research process, the sharing of values among researchers and managers, and the improvement-orientation of DOER are key elements in the way we have come to think about DOER. They have been derived from the facts of our 11 case histories, and they serve as a basic infrastructure for our chapters in part II where we discuss specific research strategies we have found useful in decision-oriented research.

2 THE PITTSBURGH EXPERIENCE

The Context

We have been able to investigate strategies for improving the methods and uses of DOER by actually conducting research in collaboration with a large urban school district. The district did not have its own research office at the time these investigations began. Our collaboration with the Pittsburgh public schools provided the opportunity to conduct research in a school district setting in order to learn more about district information needs and to test research strategies that could increase the validity and utility of those research activities.

There are a number of other ways one might address the question of how to improve DOER. Some researchers have conducted extensive surveys of existing school district research offices or of consumers of district research (Lyon, Doscher, McGranahan, and Williams, 1978; Kennedy, Apling, and Neumann, 1980; Webster and Stufflebeam, 1978; King and Thompson, 1981). Others have done retrospective case studies of evaluation research (Alkin, Daillak, and White, 1979). Such efforts have tried to sort out effective and ineffective practices by applying utilization of the resulting information as the primary criterion. They have also had to rely on the reports of others regarding what was done, how it was done, and what was learned.

The work undertaken during our Pittsburgh collaboration encompassed a wide variety of research tasks. These ranged from studies of program impact to needs assessments designed to help district leadership establish district or program priorities. In addition, we were able to conduct methodological investigations so that we could explore the utility of research strategies that are not typically employed by system research offices. It is important to point out that we did this work as part of the research and development program of the Learning Research and Development Center (LRDC), a University of Pittsburgh-based institute that Robert Glaser started in 1964. In 1978 a small group of us began to work on the question of how to improve district-based research and how the results of local research efforts can improve school practice. The choice was made to work on how to improve school district research by doing it, as opposed to observing what existing district-based offices were doing.

Establishing and Maintaining a Working Relationship

Our first "discovery" in this work was that we had to do more than just offer to provide research services to the Pittsburgh public schools. We needed to build a working relationship with the district. We had to convince district leadership that we were ready to do their research and development, to be driven by their questions and concerns. Fortunately, we had strong support from a local community action group, the Pittsburgh Urban League, which was interested in obtaining evidence that might stimulate school improvement. In the spring of 1978 we began to establish a three-way partnership, starting with the superintendent and slowly building the trust and confidence that this kind of effort requires. We attempted to reinforce this relationship by exploring issues in the district that were useful for planning and decision making. There had been considerable skepticism about the utility of educational research among board members, district administrators, and the teachers' union. Eventually, after a year and half we had established an excellent working relationship and had begun some large evaluation projects. The school board, the superintendent, and the central district staff became our primary clients depending upon the specific research task, with the Urban League continuing to provide moral and political support as needed.

In the spring of 1980, however, things became a little untidy. The district's latest desegregation plan was rejected by the Pennsylvania Human Relations Commission; the school board chose not to renew the superintendent's contract; and the teachers' union announced that they would go on strike in the fall if their demands were not met. We began wondering where we might turn to continue working on evaluation problems. Fortunately, the teachers' contract was settled, a desegregation plan was approved, and the school board selected Richard Wallace as their new superintendent. Such ups and downs are typical of complex educational systems.

Wallace arrived on the scene the first day of September 1980, and it took a relatively short time to establish a good working relationship with him. The task was made easier because of his strong background in educational research and evaluation. He recognized and appreciated what we had begun doing in the district for his predecessor. He also began his term of office by announcing that he intended to conduct a major needs assessment in the district so that he would have a good basis for setting priorities with his board, and for himself and his administrative staff. He realized that there was too little in-house capability for such an assessment, so when we offered to help, he accepted. The details of this assessment are summarized in case 4.

The Pittsburgh Public Schools (PPS)

Because we draw so extensively from our experience in working with the PPS, it is important to give a brief description of this particular educational system. Chapter 10 considers the rationale and evidence for generalizing from this Pittsburgh experience to other system contexts.

The policy board for this educational system is a nine-member school board. Each board member is elected to represent a particular area in the school district, with four-year terms staggered so that no more than three members are up for election in any given year. The board has considerable power, which includes setting the annual budget, approving all expenditures (including personnel decisions), defining curriculum, and hiring and firing the superintendent.

The superintendent is the chief administrative officer, and over the past 20 years, this office changed hands eight times. The district has tended to hire from within, but there have been three exceptions, all notable: Calvin Gross, who went on to become superintendent of New York City schools; Sidney Marland, who left to become the U.S. commissioner of education; and Richard Wallace, superintendent since the fall of 1980, who previously had extensive experience in educational research, both in a regional laboratory and in a university research and development center.

When we began this new work with the district in 1978, it did not have any formal in-house research capability. There was a director of testing, who was in charge of administering an extensive standardized testing program, but his job was limited to overseeing the administration of tests and the reporting of test results. (In 1982, the district reorganized this office, added over time three additional professionals, and changed its orientation to include a strong research emphasis.)

The absence of a research office that characterized the district in 1978 had not always been the case. Under Superintendent Marland, Malcolm Provus, developer of the discrepancy model of evaluation (Provus, 1971) had been brought in to build a research capability, and he did indeed. But when he moved on to a university position in 1970, that research office disintegrated rapidly, falling victim to reductions in budget and a failure to see the value of the office on the part of district managers and board members. (The rise and fall of research offices in educational systems is a fascinating subject, about which much more needs to be known. Resnick and Schumacher (1980) have produced a good example of what can be learned from such history.)

The statistical profile of the district is dominated by the general population decline, and by the changing characteristics of northeastern urban America. As examples, from 1970 to 1984, student enrollment in the district dropped from 73,000 to 42,000, and the percentage of black students increased from under 40 to over 50. During that same period, the number of schools was reduced from 108 to 88.

Approximately 3,000 teachers are organized by the American Federation of Teachers, and their enlightened leadership has been very concerned about, and very cooperative with, efforts to improve the quality of education in the district. For example, case 9 and the Pittsburgh Federation of Teachers' support for the teacher center illustrates this important point.

Generalizability

Thousands of educational researchers work for thousands of educational systems. Researchers differ. Institutional settings differ. We do not pretend that we are typical researchers working for a typical educational system, nor are we hypothetical. We are actual researchers who have been working for an actual school district. What we have tried to sort out in what follows are the lessons from this experience that are generalizable to other researchers working in other educational contexts. The sorting was guided by the relevant literatures and by our combined experiences of 50 years as educators. In chapter 10 we deal directly with this generalizability issue.

Of course, each reader will have to judge how well our suggestions for conducting DOER fit his/her situation. As Holley (1983) points out so well, each school system research unit is unique. "As the personalities and interests of the directors have differed, so have the units themselves." Also, "a successful unit must be responsive to its environment. As the school systems vary, so do the units" (p. 49). What we have tried to focus upon here are ways of improving DOER that take these differences into account.

The Case History Approach

The idea of using case histories to communicate understandings about social phenomena is not new. In the study of law, this general approach can be traced back to the early work of Professor Christopher Langdel at the Harvard Law School before the turn of this century (Redlich, 1914). Examples of similar, early uses of this approach can be found in the fields of medicine (Flexner, 1910), sociology (Sumner and Keller, 1927), psychology (Overstreet, 1927), and the physical sciences (Conant, 1950). Although the structure and substance of case histories vary widely across the disciplines, they all have the general goal of describing a case (whether a case is an individual, a process, an issue, an institution, a social group, etc.) in enough detail to allow the reader to recapture something of the experience of the actual participants.

The purpose of the case histories of DOER is to share with the reader detailed descriptions of several research experiences that we had through the collaboration with the Pittsburgh public schools. Each case represents a distinct research activity, different from the others to some extent in terms of the nature of the questions addressed, the methodologies used in the research, the policy context in which the information needs surfaced and in which the results were reported, the level of use of the results, or in some combination of these dimensions. While these cases vary in detail, each case history is designed to shed some light on one or more of the five broad questions related to improving the substance and use of DOER:

1. What are the information needs of policy boards and managers?
2. What research strategies can best meet specific information needs?
3. What factors influence the use of research results in the policy process?
4. How might researchers and managers manipulate these factors to increase the utility of the results of that research?
5. How might institutions currently engaged in training researchers modify their current practices to better prepare new researchers for the demands of educational research?

No single case fully addresses all of these questions, but each adds a piece to a larger mosaic that advances our knowledge about DOER. It is important to note that some cases provide evidence of what did not work well, as well as data on strategies that proved to be useful.

Each case history shares a common structure. The core component is a brief history of the major events of the activity. This includes descriptions of the policy context in which the research originated, how the nature of the research activity was clarified through negotiations between the researchers and district clients, what methodologies were selected to meet the information needs, the evolving policy or program context in which the research took place, examples of what resulted from the research activity (e.g., products, substantive findings, etc.), how results were communicated, and what the clients did with the results. The core component may also include summaries of original reports, documents, etc. as are necessary for the reader to develop a reasonably comprehensive understanding of the research task that is the focus of the case. This core of the case history, in essence, is the data that formed the basis for our conclusions about the critical features of DOER.

By providing a rich description of the events and the context of a particular research activity, we hope to accomplish two objectives. First, we intend to give a sense of the evidence that has been used to formulate our conclusions about DOER. Second, it should also provide readers with enough of an understanding of the case so that they can draw their own conclusions, ones that might well be at odds with those of the authors. One of the benefits of a case history approach is that the "data trail" is detailed enough to invite informed discussion and challenges of the authors' own conclusions.

It has been noted that one aspect of each case is a discussion of the methodologies used to address particular research tasks. In addition, it is important to describe the methodology used to develop the case histories themselves. Unlike the task confronting the traditional historian who tries to reconstruct past events, we had the goal of writing case histories from the outset of this research. Therefore, several procedures were developed and put into place early on in the work that have facilitated the writing of the cases. Central to this goal was the development and maintenance of a detailed archive describing the work with the Pittsburgh public schools. This archive, which was begun in 1978, includes:

1. databases used in each research activity (e.g., interviews, questionnaires, student data, etc.);
2. a chronological file of newspaper articles on local educational policies, controversies, etc.;
3. document files detailing specific program initiatives or policy issues;

4. field notes on the public meetings of the Pittsburgh board of education;
5. personal logs and field notes on the development and maintenance of the collaboration with the district;
6. reports and presentations made to district leadership;
7. papers written during the course of the six-year collaboration that summarize what was being learned about evaluation research at a given point in the work.

A first step in the writing of a specific case history was the review and categorizing of the available data using both the substantive themes of this research and the structure of a case history to organize the analysis. Many of the traditional methods of historiography, such as document review and analysis techniques, and care in collecting corroborating evidence, were employed in the integration of data, the analyses, and the actual writing of the case histories (e.g., Commager, 1965; Nevins, 1962; Kent, 1967).

Of all the problems confronting the traditional historian, perhaps the most critical and least assailable is the absence of key data on crucial issues. Barring the discovery of some new archive, there is little chance that an historian interested in the origins of the original Roman/Dacian conflicts, for example, will be able to advance our current knowledge about this subject with new research. In the writing of these case histories we were confronted with the opposite situation. In almost all cases, the issue was one of selection. What data should be reported, in what detail? Where gaps have existed in our database, in most instances, key actors were still available and were interviewed for additional information.

Beyond the problem of selection, we have been confronted with a problem that is attendant to any research that is based partly on data derived from a participant/observer methodology. Our archive includes field notes about our own experiences as decision-oriented researchers. The researcher using this kind of data must always be wary of reporter and selection bias. Three procedures have been used to address this issue. First, perceptions of an individual researcher about an event or issue were regularly tested against those of colleagues knowledgeable about the area through regular project meetings. Second, reports, databases and conclusions developed during the course of evaluation activities were systematically shared with our clients in the district for challenge and criticism. Third, these detailed case histories themselves, as well as numerous papers written along the way during the past five years, have been shared with the larger research and educational administration communities for peer inspection and criticism. Such public access is a further motivation for the chronicler in assuring that the data are comprehensive and accurately represented.

II GENERALIZATIONS ABOUT DECISION-ORIENTED EDUCATIONAL RESEARCH

3 CLIENT ORIENTATION

One set of generalizations that has emerged from the case histories concerns the importance of taking a client orientation as a way of organizing DOER. In this chapter we will describe what is meant by client orientation and why it is important. This approach will be contrasted with several alterative strategies for organizing this type of research. Evidence will be drawn from the case histories to illustrate the nature and benefits of taking a client orientation. Finally, the chapter concludes with a detailed discussion of the potential pitfalls to be found in such an approach and procedures that can be used to minimize these dangers.

Client Orientation Defined

Client orientation has two essential characteristics. First, a primary client is identified for a piece of research and is involved in the design, analysis, and dissemination of the work. Second, the involvement of the client comes through ongoing dialogue with the researcher. This dialogue, at its best, takes the form of a mutually educational process. The educational process in the early stages involves identifying the information needs of the client and selecting research strategies for obtaining the needed information in a timely fashion. As data are analyzed, the dialogue focuses on developing an understanding of what the information means. This development of meaning in the data is shaped and enriched by the researcher's understanding of the procedures used to gather the information and the client's knowledge of the organizational context in which the information was gathered. Finally, client orientation involves some sharing of responsibility in the dissemination of results.

The notion of client orientation might best be understood by contrasting this approach with alternative ways of organizing DOER. Imagine a continuum along which various approaches can be located. The continuum displays differences in who controls the design, analysis, and dissemination of evaluation research, and the accompanying results. Toward one polarity Scriven's (1973) concept of goal-free evaluation might be located. In this approach the evaluator is all powerful. The objective of the research is to judge merit. In doing so the evaluator is charged with the responsibility for identifying all possible effects of a program. The evaluator is not restricted to the explicit goals of the program's designers in the search for effects. Hence the term "goal-free." The effects are to be illuminated whether intended or unintended. Potentially prejudicial conversations between client(s) and the evaluator are held to a minimum so that the net cast for effects is not restricted to a biased set. The evaluator determines the various research approaches to be used. In Scriven's words, "The goal-free evaluator is a hunter out alone, [going] over the ground very carefully, looking for signs of game, setting speculative snares when in doubt" (Scriven, 1973, p. 327). At the end of the process the evaluator determines what effects the program has had and judges their merit based on a prior assessment of the needs various consumers of the program may have.

Toward the other polarity on this continuum of control lies the stakeholder approach (Bryk, 1983). This approach explicitly tries to address two fundamental concerns about the impact of traditional evaluation models: How can the use of evaluation research be increased? And how can a wider variety of stakeholder groups be brought into active participation in the evaluation process? (Weiss, 1983a). In a paper describing the stakeholder approach, Gold (1981) outlines the essential features of the approach, which include: assessing initial program capability; identifying stakeholders and determining their expectations; reality check matching of stakeholder expectations and program capabilities; modifications of stakeholder expectations; timely, regular feedback to stakeholders of evaluative information as the program is implemented. A key objective in this approach is to avoid control or ownership by "any single set of interests" through the development of a broad set of involved stakeholders in the evaluation process (p. 20).

With the stakeholder approach, the evaluator is attempting at all stages of the research to be responsive to multiple client information needs. This approach calls for the researcher to involve a variety of clients with potentially conflicting expectations in the shaping of a research process. This same process is intended to provide information that is useful to every stakeholder group.

A variety of other models for organizing evaluation research have been developed in the field (e.g., Tyler, 1949; Stake, 1967; Eisner, 1975; Stufflebeam, 1971; Alkin, 1975). Each of these approaches differs along a variety of dimensions including who controls the design and implementation of a piece of evaluation research.

The goal-free and stakeholder approaches can serve to help illuminate the characteristics of a client orientation. Unlike the goal-free approach, a client orientation begins with the assumption that the researcher should work hard at understanding the information needs of a primary client, and the policy and organizational context of these needs. Closeness to, rather than distance from, the primary client is essential to defining the problem, designing the research strategies, and analyzing and disseminating the results. The researcher is not working alone but in partnership with a primary client through a rich, ongoing educational dialogue.

Like the stakeholder approach, a client orientation begins with the conviction that improving the use of evaluation research is of critical importance. Similarly both approaches underscore the importance of dialogue between the client/stakeholder and the evaluator at various stages of the research process as a way of increasing the utility of the information produced by the research. The two approaches diverge, however, in their views of how many different clients should be served in a particular research effort. Our experience has convinced us that attempts to serve multiple clients risk the danger of not serving any client well.

In contrasting the client approach to the goal-free and stakeholder strategies, important conceptual and practical questions must be addressed. To risk oversimplification, the goal-free approach emphasizes the importance of evaluator objectivity and attempts to insure this by keeping the researcher isolated from those with a stake in the program or policy. Taking a client orientation, according to the goal-free approach, runs the risk of evaluator myopia and cooptation. On the other hand a critic taking a stakeholder approach might suggest the very same criticism of client orientation, but for quite different reasons. By focusing on the information needs of one client, a stakeholder-oriented critic might say that this blocks the legitimate involvement of a number of stakeholders in the evaluation process, thus, among other effects, reducing the overall utility of the research.

Before addressing those important concerns, it is necessary to provide more detail about how a client orientation works. Drawing upon the case histories, this approach and some of the benefits that might be derived from this organizing strategy are described in the following section.

Examples of Client Orientation

Two case histories, numbers 4 and 9, will serve to illustrate how client orientation works. The first case involved the design and administration of a district-wide needs assessment, and the other provided documentation of the implementation of an innovative staff development program for high school teachers. While the specifics of these two cases were quite different, there was a certain shared sequence to the client–researcher interactions that occurred in both cases. Work began with the identification of a primary client. Initial conversations focused on understanding the client's information needs. This was followed by discussions of possible research strategies that might be employed. Once data were in hand, the dialogue turned from design issues to those of an analytical nature. In each case these early discussions of data stimulated further research activity. Eventually the dialogue turned to dissemination issues, albeit in quite different forms given different natures of the two research tasks.

Case 4

The needs assessment story really began when we met with what was then the newly appointed superintendent and offered our assistance. During the first meeting, the superintendent indicated a strong interest in conducting a district-wide needs assessment. Several subsequent meetings were held to define the task further. During the follow-up conversations two reasons for the suprintendent's request surfaced. First, having just arrived in Pittsburgh from out of state, the assessment process was to be useful in helping the superintendent to better understand conditions in need of improvement in the district. Second, the superintendent was aware that the district had just been through a tumultuous year. The board of education was bitterly divided in its attempts to develop a state-approved desegregation plan. During the previous spring a plan, barely passed at the local level (5 to 4 vote), had been rejected by the Pennsylvania Human Relations Commission. The Commission subsequently filed suit and a Commonwealth Court decision was not expected for eight to ten months. The respite from the fractious debate that the court delay offered was viewed by the superintendent as an opportunity to build a consensus on the board about priorities for improving the district. It was his hope that such priorities could guide his new administration.

These early conversations with the superintendent directly contributed to the design of the research. The goal of consensus building clearly required an assessment of the perceptions of various constituencies in the district about the critical needs of the system. Stakeholder perceptions would be vital factors in determining the political climate, for example. Detailed surveys and interviews were conducted to gather such perceptions. (Notice the important difference between involving stakeholders as respondents in surveys and as clients of the research.) The goals of identifying conditions in need of improvement in the system and of understanding the nature of such conditions well enough to develop rational responses also required a detailed analysis of longitudinal databases on achievement, school climate, and finance variables.

The client–researcher dialogue continued during the data collection. These conversations focused on defining the kinds of information that needed to be collected, how this collection might be arranged, and where relevant data sources were located. Having the superintendent as the primary client, of course, greatly facilitated the organization of the longitudinal databases. Many data sources were scattered throughout the organization. Each office had a "piece of the data pie." There was considerable reluctance at times to release data. Having the superintendent knowledgeable about the work and the specific information needs greatly improved the researchers' abilities to identify and access data sources.

Similarly, the ongoing dialogue was helpful in developing the survey process designed to gather constituency perceptions. The researcher/client dialogue established the importance of developing and piloting the survey instruments and the identity of key actors who should be involved in this process. As a result, a system-wide task force was organized to both aid in the development of protocols, as well as to help in the pilot testing of survey instruments.

As more data were gathered we began to do preliminary analyses. These early findings were shared with the superintendent, the survey task force, and other key actors in the system. The client, as well as others in the system, were important reactors to early results. These discussions were vital in helping us better understand and interpret the information in hand. For example, the reactors were aware of organizational and historical factors that affected trends in such variables as student retention. Without such knowledge about changes in policies the meaning of particular data trends would have been difficult to determine.

Finally, the client dialogue was important to the planning of dissemination activities once final results were in hand. (A detailed discussion of dissemination issues is provided in chapter 9.) Suffice it to note here that the formating of various reporting activities, the selection of audiences, and the arranging of public forums for information exchange were some of the issues covered during this stage in the conversations.

Case 4 illustrates several benefits of taking a client orientation. The primary client in this case was the superintendent. The dialogue with the superintendent helped the researchers understand the purposes behind his request for the needs assessment. These goals had a direct impact on the design of the assessment. To have gathered longitudinal data without constituency perceptions, or the reverse, would have fallen short of meeting the information needs of the client. It is important to note that the goals of the research are usually not even initially clear to the client. It took several rather detailed discussions about information needs before the goals of the assessment were clearly understood by all.

The assessment further benefited from researcher–client dialogue during every subsequent step. At times the research benefited simply because the contact with and understanding of the work on the part of the superintendent, as a result of the dialogue, facilitated cooperation on the part of the system's bureaucracy. At other points the research benefited from the substantive exchange of knowledge about what was possible (i.e., the limits of a research methodology) or about the meaning of data as they were gathered.

It is important to point out that the assessment process brought the researchers into contact with a wide variety of stakeholders. The task force, for example, played an extremely important role in shaping the surveys. Further, many participants ended up as recipients of the wide variety of results developed through the research. Client orientation does not mean researcher–client isolation from the larger organizational setting. The dialogue served as a gyroscope for the research, keeping the process on some reasonable line of progression. It helped to shape client expectations and researcher/client knowledge about what was found. It facilitated movement in the organization and access to data and prospective audiences. Some of these benefits of client orientation were directly attributable to the fact that the primary client in case 4 was the superintendent. Case 9 is an example of client orientation when the client is not the chief administrative officer but rather a mid-level manager responsible for a particular program in the system.

Case 9

Case 9 illustrates the strategy of documenting the implementation of a local-ly developed educational innovation. (This concept of program documenta-tion is discussed in detail in chapter 7.) In case 9 the focus of documentation was the design and implementation of a teacher center, an innovative staff development program for high school teachers.

As case 9 indicates, the original request for documentation came from the superintendent. There were four reasons for the request. First, staff development of the size and scope envisioned by the program's designers was unprecedented in the district. Second, the program was heavily developmental in nature. That is, the actual training experiences to take place at the center for the most part did not exist prior to the initiation of the work. They were created as the program evolved. Third, the program, even in its earliest design stages, was the subject of considerable national in-terest as evidenced from the support received for the program from national foundations. Fourth, the program was potentially a model for future staff development efforts in the system, at different grade levels.

As the case materials indicate, the documentation of the teacher center program had two goals. The long-range goal was to construct a detailed record of the implementation process so that others, both within the district and nationally, might learn from the center's experience. The second, more immediate goal was to assist the program's managers in the design and development of the program by enriching the planning process with relevant data. Such data would include information on the status of implementation of the various components of the program, and perceptions of participants about how the program might be improved. It is this second context, con-cerned with what was in essence a formative evaluation research respon-sibility, that offers further evidence, now at the program level, about client orientation.

The primary client for the formative research conducted for the teacher center was not a single person but rather the dual leadership of the project. This consisted of the principal of the high school where the center was located and the director of the center's program.

The initial dialogue focused on ways data might be organized to enrich the planning process. The conversations began with a discussion of a pro-posed set of documentation activities prepared by the researchers. The research was modified both at the outset and as the program evolved as the dialogue clarified client information needs. This interaction focused on what data were needed, how these data might be gathered and presented, and what information needs could be anticipated in the future. It is important to note that suggestions in each of these areas came from researchers and clients alike.

One task that resulted from these conversations was to participate on a district committee that designed a needs assessment of secondary teachers in the district in the year prior to the opening of the teacher center. In another, observations were conducted of the meetings of the extensive sub-committee structure set up by the district to develop operational plans for the program. Similarly, observations of the meetings of the core planning group of central administrators were undertaken. In the planning meetings, the researchers identified decisions reached at a given meeting as well as issues that were still outstanding, that is, still in need of attention by the group. These data were fed back into the planning process.

As the program moved toward actual implementation the information needs of the clients focused on assessing the perceptions of various program participants about the status of the implementation process and how the program might be improved. Research activities undertaken to respond to these needs included an extensive series of surveys and interviews of center personnel and teachers going through the program. Some of these activities became quickly routinized because of the structure of the center's program. Thus, working with district personnel, the researchers assessed the perceptions of visiting teachers involved in each of the four eight-week cycles that took place during the first year of center operation. Sometimes through structured open forums, sometimes through group or individual survey instruments, the goals of these assessments were to give the director and the principal an accurate picture of what participants were thinking about the program and how the center might be improved.

The data gathered by these assessments were used by the clients and the core planning group to modify the program's structure and content. For example, if one compared the activities of teachers visiting the center during cycle 1 to those of teachers involved in cycle 4, they would look quite different in terms of the amount of time in the schedule that was teacher directed (i.e., more self-initiated activities in cycle 4). Such modifications were, in part, a direct result of the feedback to center planners gained through various formative evaluation research activities.

The important point to stress here is the central role the client–researcher dialogue had in guiding the research activities. The interaction was characterized by a continuous loop of activity starting with the identification of information needs, followed by data collection, the reporting of results to the clients and the larger planning group. This cycle was repeated throughout the two years encompassed by case 9.

Perhaps the benefit of client orientation most clearly illustrated by case 9 involves the contribution such an approach can make to increasing the utility of DOER. The center's experience illustrates this in two important ways. First, because the researchers, through dialogue, were able to understand and to focus on the information needs of the program's leadership, they were never in danger of not asking questions of interest to management. Second, because the research was directly linked through the clients to the planning process, the data generated were well integrated into the decision-making component of the program. This is not to say the decision process was entirely research driven. Decisions were influenced quite naturally by considerations of resources, district precedent, and the political climate in the organization. It is to say, however, that data clearly enriched the planning process in significant ways. The fact that the research was client oriented clearly was a major reason for the impact it had.

Contrasting Cases 4 and 9 with Cases 1 and 3

Cases 4 and 9 provide examples of how a client orientation can work well to structure decision-oriented research. Cases 1 and 3 suffered from a lack of clearly defined clients, and they illustrate the difficulties that can result from such a failure.

Case 1 began with conversations with the local Urban League. These quickly moved to a three-way interaction, at least in the early stages of the work, among the school superintendent, the Urban League, and the researchers. As the research proceeded we had relatively little contact with either League or district personnel. By the time our analyses were completed, district attention had been turned elsewhere. A number of the research findings were found to be useful by League personnel, especially the education director, as they sought to influence the school system's desegregation effort in ways that would improve the distribution of important instructional resources (e.g., class size and experienced teachers). However, use was not evidenced on the part of district personnel. In the absence of an ongoing client dialogue, there was no one person on the receiving end of the results with an understanding of and a vested interest in the use of the results.

We feel strongly that had a closer working relationship been developed with the school superintendent (for example) our questions could have been shaped in ways that would have made the research more valuable to the district. An interesting hypothetical question concerns whether such a shaping would have changed the study in ways that would have been less meaningful for the Urban League. Indeed, given the somewhat critical nature of our case 1 findings about existing conditions in the district, an ongoing dialogue with both potential clients may have been difficult because the two clients were themselves in potential conflict. As we say, this is speculation on our part as we did not achieve an ongoing client dialogue with either League or district personnel. Nevertheless, the case 1 experience with the school district is certainly illustrative of the need to identify a client and perhaps of the problems one could encounter in trying to serve multiple clients.

Case 3 is similar to case 1 in that we failed to establish a working dialogue with appropriate district personnel to shape the research activities. The superintendent initiated the request for an evaluation as a result of board interest. As the board moved on to other issues, the superintendent's own "front burner" topics changed. The lengthy evaluation exercise proceeded over the next several years with minimum contact with the superintendent. It was conceivable that we could have worked harder at establishing a client dialogue with the program's managers. However, given the initial controversy surrounding the program, and the summative aura that was implicit in the board's request for an "evaluation," the operations personnel were somewhat skeptical of the wisdom of such an activity from the outset. Case 3, then, illustrates the negative impact of failing to identify clearly a primary client. It also illustrates something about the difficulties of establishing good client relationships in complex educational systems. The originator of the research task may be different from the communicator of the task who in turn may be different from the individuals most likely to be most closely involved in the educational phenomenon in question and, thus, the most valuable resources to the research process. While there are no easy responses as to how one defines a primary client in such circumstances, it does suggest that both potential clients and researchers have an important role to play and that the involvement of both (whether the client is the board, superintendent, or program management) is important.

So far in this chapter, we have considered what the characteristics of client orientation are, and what benefits might be accrued by taking this approach to organizing DOER in educational systems. We have contrasted our experiences in cases 4 and 9 with those of cases 1 and 3. We would be remiss in this analysis if the potential pitfalls of the approach were not addressed in more detail. In the following section the drawbacks of taking this approach are discussed along with procedures that can assist the researcher in diminishing these dangers.

Problems With Taking a Client Orientation

Client orientation, like any of the alternative approaches for organizing DOER, presents difficulties uniquely associated with the strategy that must be weighed against the potential benefits. The dangers present are classifiable most broadly into those concerned with issues of a fundamental, ethical nature, and those involving difficulties in operationalizing the concept. The case histories provided valuable experience on both the nature of such problems and procedures that can obviate, or at least diminish their impact.

Ethics of Client Orientation

The fundamental ethical issues involve cooptation and bias on the part of the researcher. Presumably these would occur as a result of close researcher interaction with a primary client as a piece of research was conducted. It is important here to distinguish ethical difficulties associated with research generally, and those particularly inherent in taking a client orientation.

In their discussion of ethical hazards in evaluation, Cronbach and associates (1980) note that "evaluators are much less independent than the typical social scientist" (p. 203). This is so because evaluators "typically take their charge from an official [and] even when they do not, they incur obligations in obtaining access to program sites" (p. 203). Add to this the fact that evaluation research is decision-oriented, rather than discipline-oriented, inquiry. That is, DOER starts out with the deliberate objective of generating information that is of immediate use in some policy or decision context. These general features of client orientation can mean that the researcher might get caught in the "cross fire of political antagonists [at best, and] at worst . . . become the corrupt servant of a partisan" (p. 197).

The potential results of unethical influence by clients can range widely. In gross instances, data are tampered with or findings are withheld. More subtly, the interaction can work either to frame research questions in ways that favor one political interest over another, or that fail to address some important issues.

A researcher using a client orientation shares all the general liabilities of the evaluation community in this area and perhaps one or two more. The client-oriented researcher explicitly starts with a determination to work closely with a primary client. Ideally, the researcher will spend a great deal of time with the client (at least compared to what is customary) during the course of the work to shape the research. The researcher in this instance works hard at trying to understand the information needs of the client and to meet those needs. These characteristics of client orientation presumably could increase the receptivity of the researcher to and the opportunity of the client for shaping the evaluation in inappropriate directions.

There are four procedures that can help to diminish untoward influence by the client. The first three are not unique to client orientation but are essential in any piece of evaluation work. They involve following the methodological tenets of one's discipline, making available for public scrutiny the procedures used to gather data, the evidence used to support results, and the results themselves. If the researcher is able to meet these standards, then the public policy and disciplinary scrutiny that will follow will do much to block unwarranted researcher bias or to correct it where it exists, whether this bias is the result of client influence or some other source.

A fourth procedure we are suggesting may well be most applicable to a client-oriented research approach. This involves not doing summative style evaluation research when the program developer or implementor is the primary client. This is clearly a "no-win" situation. If you find a positive impact, you may lose your credibility with others, and if you find a negative impact, you may lose your job!

We will be discussing in a later chapter the notion that summative evaluations are generally of limited validity and utility in educational systems. The point here is that if a summative evaluation is the requirement, taking a client orientation can heighten the danger of unwarranted client influence. The preferred procedure is to convert the question to a more improvement-oriented, formative one.

We would like to close this discussion of ethical issues associated with educational research and client orientation with two additional comments. The question of having a primary client or not is probably often moot when the issue is one of research that takes place in educational systems. The majority of such research is either explicitly commissioned by some official or office in the organization or is undertaken with an explicit decision-group in mind that would "use" the results of the research. Given the likelihood that a client is probably already on the scene, what we are suggesting is that taking an aggressive client orientation can work to greatly increase the utility of the research. So the choice under such circumstances isn't client orientation or not but rather, whether one can turn what is often a "given" (i.e., the presence of a client) into a process that can enhance the work.

The second comment concerns the nature of the dialogue that can occur between the researcher and the primary client. We have found, at its best, that this dialogue can be mutually educational. If such a dialogue is well established, it offers both the researcher and the client a vehicle for sharing and shaping the views of the other. The conversations can be wide-ranging, across issues related to information needs, program goals, research methodologies, and even ethical concerns when necessary. The frank interaction established through such dialogue contrasts sharply with the frequent reality of isolation of a researcher from the decision maker in many educational systems, and the "principle of isolation" suggested by some in the discipline in the name of insuring evaluation objectivity. Of course, the dialogue does not insure that all ethical concerns will be adequately addressed. However, in combination with the other procedures we have suggested, the valid concerns about unwarranted client influence can be reduced to tolerable levels.

A well-established dialogue can help the researcher to avoid two untenable positions in this work: the advocate and the accountability expert. In the advocate role, the pressure is on the researcher to produce results that the client needs in order to justify a preferred course of action. The accountability expert looks for wrongdoing, incompetence, deviation from school policy, noncompliance, etc. Both positions are to be avoided, and researchers can easily be trapped into such roles if open dialogue with the client is not established.

Operationalizing a Client Orientation

Two difficulties of an operational nature are most likely to be encountered when taking a client orientation. One area concerns the initial establishment and then maintenance of an adequate client–researcher dialogue. The second concerns the difficulty of living up to the responsiveness promise of client orientation once a good dialogue is established.

The problems associated with establishing and maintaining an adequate dialogue with one's client are broadly classifiable as issues related to accessibility and the clarification of information needs. The lives of managers of educational systems are busy indeed. The typical manager's schedule affords little time for interaction with researchers or for review of evaluation data (Sproull and Larkey, 1979). This problem of access is further exacerbated by the organizational distance that often exists between evaluation researchers in an educational system and their likely clients (Lyon et al., 1978).

As we worked hard over the years trying to establish good dialogue with primary clients for various cases, one procedure and one characteristic of the client approach seemed to contribute to overcoming the access problem. Early on in cases 1 and 2, we found it useful to observe on an ongoing basis the public deliberations of the chief policy-making body in the educational system, the board of education. These observations of board discussions, coupled with the building of an archive of all print-media coverage of the system, yielded important outcomes. These data deepened our understanding of the policy context in which client information needs were generated. To the extent that in many of our cases the superintendent was the primary client, this procedure of "board-watching" enabled us to directly observe discussions among board members and the superintendent that ultimately were critical factors in influencing subsequent information requests. Case 2 is a good example of where observing board deliberations contributed directly to the anticipation of information needs, even to the range of specific questions that had to be addressed. The point here is that the general procedure of the evaluator becoming a systematic student of the immediate organizational/ policy context of the primary client can be an effective mechanism for supplementing the needed interaction between the client and the evaluator.

Another way of combating the access problem seems to be inherent in the client approach itself. That is, we have found that since the conversation is focused on the information needs of the client, the client is more likely to devote time and attention to the discussion. Once stated, this smacks of being tautological. Yet too often researchers seeking to provide information to educational systems failed on this very point, basically because the research questions were the products of disciplinary concerns and not client concerns.

The second major area of difficulty in operationalizing a client orientation involves maintaining the promise of responsiveness inherent in the approach. In our early descriptions of the collaboration with the district we were fond of saying that the goal was to replicate the experiences of a district research office. In this we felt we had a key advantage of having some time to reflect on the work and thus learn something about evaluation research in this context. What we found in taking a client orientation is that the demands for research involvement increased dramatically as a result of the effect of working on problems of interest to the client. This was not only a problem in terms of our own research needs to write about our experiences in the district but it was also a problem in terms of simply responding to multiple information needs of a primary client. Barring the unlikely event of unlimited resources, this condition of excessive information requests is likely to be a problem associated with taking a client orientation. There is not any magical solution to this problem, other than a common sense one of working with the client to establish information priorities. One advantage in such negotiations lies in the dialogue we have often referred to in this chapter. Given the presence of an effective dialogue, the client is likely to be in a better position to understand the resource stress that may be caused by additional information requests.

Summary

In this chapter we have discussed the importance of taking a client orientation to organizing research in educational systems. This approach has been compared to alternative approaches in the field of evaluation research. Key characteristics of client orientation include the identification and involvement of a primary client in the design and implemention of a piece of research. Involvement comes most directly through an ongoing dialogue between the client and the researcher. At its best this dialogue is a two-way educational conversation about information needs, appropriate methodologies to meet these needs, the meaning of results, and how results are to be disseminated. An important corollary to the approach is that it can be most readily used when the questions are formative (rather than summative) in nature.

In closing this discussion of client orientation, we would like to reiterate two points. First, client orientation, like every approach to organizing DOER, has its limitations. These have been discussed as have procedures that can be employed to help minimize the difficulties. Second, research that takes place in educational systems is inevitably responding to the information needs of specific clients whether these clients are explicitly identified or not. Taking an aggressive client orientation in this context can turn an organizational "given" into procedures that yield more timely and useful data for the decision-making and policy processes.

4 THE IMPORTANCE OF BEING METHODOLOGICALLY ECLECTIC

Introduction

One generalization that has emerged from the experience of conducting decision-oriented educational research is the importance of educational researchers having a range of methodologies available to them as they seek to generate decision-relevant information. This chapter describes what we have in mind when we ask researchers to be methodologically eclectic. The reasons for doing so will be discussed, as will the serious constraints that work against such a stance. Examples will be drawn from the case histories to flesh out the methodological range envisioned. Finally, we will review the practical implications of this approach for research offices in educational systems and for the preparation of professionals who work in such offices.

Eclecticism Defined

In the broadest sense, eclecticism for the educational researcher means being willing and able to draw upon a wide range of methodologies while trying to produce information useful to policy shapers and managers. This position is structured by three convictions. First, we do not believe that any

41

single method for the investigation of educational phenomena in educational settings is inherently superior in all research contexts. Second, we are convinced by our case history experiences that most decision-oriented research benefits from taking multiple methodological probes of the same phenomenon. Third, clients of DOER will vary in the kinds of information they will find persuasive. Let us examine each of these convictions in greater detail.

In suggesting that no single research method is inherently preferred, the important qualifier here is "in educational settings." These are the contexts in which DOER takes place. Given this fact, the researcher will always be confronted with serious limitations in the application of some methodologies (e.g., experimental and quasi-experimental designs). For that matter, when one adds the fact that most DOER probably will be pursued in contexts of limited resources and pressing time schedules, the ideal application of any research methodology, more often than not, is unrealistic.

Our second element of eclecticism complements the first but also extends it in a certain direction. While accepting that no one method is inherently the "best one," most questions addressed by decision-oriented researchers can be answered more effectively if the same phenomenon is examined from multiple methodological perspectives. This suggestion is similar to that made by others in the field (e.g., Cronbach and associates, 1980, calling for the use of a "bundle of studies [using] different techniques to examine subquestions . . ." [p. 73]). It is our contention that taking such an approach will deepen an understanding of the phenomenon under investigation, and often it will increase the external validity of the research. That is, drawing upon data using a variety of methods can aid in increasing the "validity of inferences that go beyond the data . . . the crux of social action" (Cronbach and associates, 1980, p. 231).

What has been suggested thus far is that the researcher should be open to a variety of methodologies, and should actively seek to employ a range of investigatory tools in most DOER research contexts. This does not mean, however, that all methods are equally valid for all research contexts. We suggest two strategies for researchers and clients to use in deciding what method(s) should be applied in a particular context. The nature of the questions themselves is the single most important element that should influence thinking about methods selection. To give an extreme example, if the client wants to know the mean score of third grade students on a standardized achievement test in mathematics, a biographical description of the average third grader's math experiences would probably miss the target!

A second consideration in making decisions about methods should be the likely audiences for the information. Although chapter 3 emphasized the importance of having the primary client's questions drive the research,

DOER will often be in the position of producing information relevant to a variety of audiences. Each key audience may differ in the type or source of information needed. No single piece of DOER can be expected to produce all information conceivably needed by all potential audiences. However, consideration of such needs, how they vary across groups, and how these in turn might require different research strategies are important in DOER.

Feasibility is another important influence on the selection of methods. Costs and availability of competent human resources are, of course, very important considerations. A discussion of the impact of such factors, however, is presented in a subsequent section of this chapter when those issues can be reviewed in conjunction with specific suggestions for modifying the training of DOER's and for organizing research offices in educational systems.

Rationale for Eclecticism

One important reason for taking a methodologically diverse approach to DOER lies in the nature of questions asked by policy makers and managers in educational systems. These questions encompass a wide range of issues. They can be process-oriented at times; in other contexts, outcome measures are emphasized. The kinds of analyses required to address specific questions vary considerably, as do the likely sources of relevant data. To use question classification schemes found in the research literature (e.g., Dillon, 1984), the questions of clients can involve first-order properties of educational phenomenon (e.g., substance/definition, character/description, function/ application); they can also involve comparisons (e.g., equivalence/differences between P and Q), and contingencies (e.g., if P then Q, or if Q then P).

Even a request to conduct a program evaluation might mean different things to different clients in different contexts. Sometimes it is the question: "Who is the program serving?" Other clients may really want to know: "How does the program work?" They may even want the really hard question answered: "What effect is the program having on students?" These different questions require quite different methods even though they all fall under the general rubric of program evaluation. Further, it is important to note that a given research activity might be addressing multiple questions. All the variations noted can have important methodological implications for a researcher involved with DOER.

Turning to the case history experiences, the wide range in the nature of questions and the multiplicity of questions encompassed by any single case are quite evident. For example, in case 1 the initial question was exploratory in nature. What school characteristics can help to explain achievement differences between predominantly black and predominantly white elementary schools? Addressing this question required research that (1) described existing relationships among variables that influenced instruction and (2) analyzed the patterns of association that these variables had in schools across the district, stratified by racial composition. The information produced focused on school differences across the district. The methodologies used emphasized the production of both descriptive and inferential statistics. The research outcomes emphasized a better understanding of the relationships among several key instructional variables and the distribution of these among the district's elementary schools.

In case 3, the work began as a relatively straightforward piece of program evaluation. Was Project Pass working? The more the researchers interacted with potential clients (this case suffered from not having a primary client), the more diversified the questions became. It quickly became clear that what was initially needed, for the school board at least, was simply a good description of who was in the program, and how the participants were being served. This involved an extensive set of field research activities that included classroom observations, interviews with teachers, and the collection and analysis of a number of program-related documents. These field research activities were supplemented by the collection and analysis of a number of school district data files encompassing student achievement scores, truancy patterns, and the distribution of important district resources such as school social workers.

In case 7 the broad question concerned a needs assessment of a recently implemented grade reorganization for grades six through eight. Like the assessment methods used in case 4, the case 7 research procedures involved an extensive series of surveys and interviews with major district constituencies (i.e., stakeholders) and analyses of existing district databases (e.g., achievement data, personnel distribution, attendance, resource distribution). The information produced included descriptions of particular aspects of the program that seemed to be working well or not (across all schools), descriptions of differences among schools on key variables related to instruction and school climate, a suggested plan for further school improvement based on the assessment data gathered in the district, and the best thinking to be found in relevant educational literature on school change and improvement. The type of information produced varied in detail and substantive focus for different audiences. For example, each middle-school principal received detailed descriptions of the needs assessment results for their own school. A more general report was produced for the district that emphasized program details across the entire set of middle schools.

This brief review of the kinds of questions addressed in several of the cases illustrates the wide range often encountered by a researcher in conducting

DOER. The list is not exhaustive, but it underscores the methodological demands that are likely to surface. When faced with this array of questions, one choice the researcher can make is to try to let the questions drive the methodologies. This is the choice we are recommending here. Alternatively, the researcher can decide to restrict the question by the methodology. This can leave the researcher in the position either of not addressing questions that cannot be examined with one's most preferred methodology or of misapplying methodologies. All too often the methodology drives the research, resulting in negative consequences for clients and researchers alike.

This point can be seen in a book edited by Brandt (1981), in which he invited seven distinguished evaluators to describe how they could respond to a request from the Radnor school board to evaluate their middle school humanities curriculum. Each of them emphasized their preferred methodology. Popham defined behavioral objectives and built tests. Stake looked for stakeholders. Scriven passed judgment and declared the program inept. Eisner applied his connoisseurship and found the program promising. Webster outlined the steps of the CIPP (context, input, process, product) model. Two of the chapters — Bonnet ("Five Phases of Purposeful Inquiry") and Worthen ("Journal Entries of an Eclectic Eavluator") — emphasized the need for extensive interaction with the clients of the evaluation. The latter two came closest to the DOER notion we are recommending.

A second reason for suggesting eclecticism lies in the nature of educational phenomena. Simply put, the educational issues, programs, personnel, and questions that are the focus of DOER are often so complex that it is essential that the researcher probe and examine from multiple methodological angles. It is in this way that the researcher will be in a position of being able to generate information that can "reduce the uncertainty levels" (Cronbach and associates, 1980) of one's clients in an educational system.

What is being suggested here is similar to the notion of triangulation as commonly applied in the context of field research or naturalistic inquiry. Guba and Lincoln (1981) note that triangulation

> . . . depends upon exposing a proposition (for example, the existence of an issue or concern; the validity of some alleged fact; the assertion of an informant) to possibly countervailing facts or assertions . . . with data drawn from other sources or developed using different methodologies (pp. 106–107).

Other writers concerned with the credibility of data from field research take similar positions (Webb, Campbell, Schwartz, and Sechrest, 1966; Sanders, 1981; Denzin, 1971). In our case history experiences, the notion of triangulation is not only a useful way of approaching data collection and verification within a specific field research context; it is also valuable in thinking about the choice of methodologies when beginning a piece of DOER. Triangulation, in this latter case, is taken to mean addressing the same fundamental client questions through different methodological approaches. The end result can be much more credible and useful information for the decision maker. Cases 4, 5, and 7 illustrate this point.

In cases 4 and 7, the district-wide and middle-school needs assessments, the clients wanted an overall description of the problems being experienced and some sense of next steps and possible solutions. In both cases, the research design addressed the clients' information needs through several data collection strategies. These included phone surveys, questionnaires, interviews, and analyses of quantitative databases in the district.

Using various sampling strategies, depending on the size of the particular stakeholder group, the major relevant constituencies in cases 4 and 7 were polled as to their perceptions of the most pressing district problems in need of improvement. The questionnaires asked the respondents to indicate whether a specified condition was a serious problem or not. In general, these ratings were organized by major educational topics (e.g., school climate, instructional leadership, facilities, parent–school relations, etc.). At the completion of each section, respondents were asked to identify and rank order the two most important problems within that topical area. The responses to the ratings were summarized in a variety of ways. Means, standard deviations, and rank orders of questions were reported by topical areas both across constituency groups and by specific groups.

The rating scales on the constituency surveys were extremely useful in providing a reasonably efficient mechanism for developing a broad overview of perspectives on the areas in need of improvement. However, such questions were limited in their ability to provide a sufficient understanding of the nature of a problem (especially if it had developed over time), or of potential solutions to a given problem. Several additional data collection strategies were used to address these issues. For example, in each questionnaire instrument, the respondent was provided with opportunities to extend the conditions asked about in each topical area by including issues not anticipated by the survey writers. More importantly, each questionnaire had specific open-ended questions asking respondents to identify possible solutions to problem areas. The first technique helped to avoid the problem of missing key issues not anticipated by the district task forces used to develop survey instruments. Asking for potential solutions to problems in a respondent's own words had the effect of providing a highly visible mechanism for bringing creative ideas for problem solving to the surface in a given topical area, regardless of where the respondent stood in the organizational hierarchy. (A number of respondents expressed appreciation at having the opportunity for such "out of channels" communication.)

Open-ended responses, of course, are more difficult to process. However, the experiences of cases 4 and 7 suggest that such questions can be invaluable in extending one's thinking about the "key issues" to be addressed in a piece of research. They also can be a powerful source of individually creative ideas (in these cases, potential solutions to identified needs).

Another major research strategy used to supplement the surveys of constituencies involved the detailed analysis of other data that could be found within the district. Both in cases 4 and 7, these analyses included longitudinal studies of such data as student achievement scores, student and teacher absenteeism, and resource allocation patterns.

The analyses of these district databases were undertaken for two reasons. First, such analyses often provided data that were useful in either corroborating or challenging the trends that emerged from the constituency perception data. For example, if parents thought that the dropoff in student achievement during the middle-school years was the number one problem faced by the district (e.g., as was the condition in case 4), was this dropoff reflected in the actual scores of students on standardized achievement tests? This kind of triangulation can increase the accuracy of the information being generated.

The analyses of existing district data had a second important function, namely, to deepen the understanding of a particular problem. This function was particularly important in complex areas where many variables were influencing a given condition. It was also important in problem areas where an undesirable condition may have developed over a long period of time. In such cases, it was essential to combine a longitudinal analysis of relevant data with the "snapshot" that was obtained through the survey of constituencies. The analyses of achievement test data in case 4 illustrate the importance of how the supplemental analyses of such databases contributed to a convergence and deeper understanding of the needs identified through the questionnaire process.

Case 5, concerning the documentation of an innovative school improvement program, also serves to illustrate the importance of employing multiple data collection strategies and methodologies when studying complex educational phenomena. The original goals for the documentation effort involved the writing of an overall description of the evolution of the program, and the production along the way of information useful to the planners for improving the implementation process. With these broad goals in mind, and with a variety of specific questions asked by the primary client group over a three-year period, a number of data collection strategies were employed. Two specific examples serve to illustate the range.

Given the broad goals of documentation, we were confronted with the problem of gathering enough data from all seven sites to provide an overall picture of the program's development. At the same time, we needed data that reflected a deep enough understanding of the day-to-day implementation process to be of practical, immediate use to program planners as they confronted specific decisions about program direction. The research design developed with the client group involved a number of key components.

In order to capture the overall view of the program, the documentation team collected relevant documents and built an archive that was a reasonable record of the "paper trail" of the program. This document archive was supplemented by an extensive series of field observations. Key meetings were sampled across all seven sites. The emphasis here was on observing meetings where multiple sites were either directly involved (e.g., joint principal and/or faculty meetings) or where the focus of the meeting was multiple site in nature. One example of the latter type of meeting was the regular weekly planning meeting of the school improvement team which served as a forum for reviewing program developments across all seven sites. The program of observations was further supplemented by multiple-site questionnaires focused either on developing a generalized view of participant perceptions about the program's progress (and how it might be improved), or on the operation of specific program components. These questionnaires were often the direct result of client questions about a particular program component. Finally, key participants in different sites and at different levels of the program's activity were interviewed during the course of the first three years. These multisite data collection activities allowed the researchers to develop a reasonably comprehensive and accurate picture of the overall development of the program. They also provided specific data useful to the program's planners for making mid-course corrections.

A second major research strategy was employed to supplement the aforementioned activities. This involved using a case study approach (Guba and Lincoln, 1981) in years one and two of the program. In the first year, the case study focus was on one of the seven schools. Through observations and interviews, an attempt was made to develop a more complete picture of the instructional climate of the case study school and how various aspects of the school improvement program were interacting with this climate. In the second year, the case study approach was used to focus on one aspect of the program, the systematic use of data for instructional decision making, across all seven sites. Here, the objective was to richly describe the development of this key program component, the constraints encountered, and how these were resolved, or if not, why not.

The case study school in the first year served the important purpose of adding depth to the breadth of knowledge being gained through program-wide research activities. The two levels of analyses were interactive. The case site data might suggest program difficulties in a given area of operation. Program-wide research techniques were then used to discover how widespread the problem might be. Such a sequence happened during the first year of the program and is described in case 5 involving research on the steering committee process initiated in each school. Briefly stated, the detailed observations in the case study school suggested that this committee problem-solving process was constrained by a number of serious flaws in the model (e.g., poor organization and communication skills on the part of the participants, lack of experience in agenda setting among participants, ambiguous goals, etc.). A program-wide survey was developed to test how the case study school's experience compared to those of other buildings. The survey data confirmed the presence of serious problems in a number of sites. Eventually, the program's leadership designed a summer in-service program to address these needs.

Cases 4, 5, and 7 illustrate the importance, indeed the necessity, of using multiple research methodologies when examining complex educational phenomena. Given additional resources, even more could have been done to address the information needs of our clients in these three example cases. The central point is, however, that like the nature of the questions issue, the nature and complexity of the educational phenomena that are likely to be the focus of DOER necessitates the use of multiple research methods.

The third fundamental reason for a methodologically eclectic stance involves the variation that exists among educational policy makers and managers as to what types of data are most persuasive. The point here is that individual clients are often "predisposed" toward certain kinds of data and are often "put off" by others. Alkin and associates (1979) call this "preferred forms of information" in their discussion of evaluation use. This variation among clients in preferred information can have direct implications for one's choice of methodologies in a given research context. It presents both problems and positive challenges to researchers involved with DOER.

Take the hypothetical instance of a client who is predisposed to "knowing" the world of his/her educational system through "hands on," rich, descriptive data. Assume the client requests an analysis of the effects of a recently designed innovation from the system's newly hired educational researcher, who is trained in developing causal models based on large, computerized, quantitative databases. This situation could stimulate the expansion of the researcher's methodological expertise. Alternatively, it could be a challenge and problem to both client and researcher if, in this hypothetical case, the best data to answer the client's questions lie outside what can be reasonably expected from researcher's preferred type of research method. Ideally, in this hypothetical situation the kind of educational dialogue that can occur between a client and a researcher, which we described in chapter 3, can be the forum in which both come to a consensus on preferred methods that best fit the specific information needs.

Case 2 provides an interesting, "nonideal" example of how data/methods preferences on the part of potential clients can influence the direction of the research methods used. This case is a nonideal example because there was not the opportunity for the kind of dialogue preferred between the client and the researcher.

In case 2, the board of education was involved in an extensive debate about proposed desegregation plans. One element in the discussion concerned the insistence by some board members that a K–8 organization (the organizational pattern prevalent in a number of the existing neighborhood schools) was a more effective structure. One relatively efficient way of shedding some light on this issue would have been to review the relevant existing educational research literature on this question. It was clear from our observations of board discussions, however, that if data were to be part of the discussion, the value of locally derived data was considerably higher than information drawn from the general research literature. This predilection toward information on their own system necessitated the analysis of local district data to, in effect, "replicate" findings already well known in the larger research literature.

Similar experiences occurred in a number of the cases. For example, in case 4, there was clear evidence that many board members placed a lot of weight on the perceptions of specific role groups (as gathered by the surveys). If district needs had simply been identified through analyses of district data bases, the credibility of the needs assessment results would have diminished. The point here, of course, is that information predispositions often serve as another factor that necessitates the use of a variety of methods in a given research context.

The fourth major reason for being methodologically eclectic is grounded in the defined scope of DOER. The reader will recall from chapter 1 that a central theme in this book is that DOER encompasses a wide range of possible research activities. In one sense, there is no limit to the scope of DOER other than that which is defined by the information needs of potential clients. The range envisioned here goes considerably beyond what has been typically thought of as the domain encompassed by the term evaluation.

The argument for a more broadly defined range of possible research endeavors is not based on an abstract, philosophical stance. Rather, it is grounded in the information needs of the policy makers and managers of educational systems. Researchers who restrict their undertakings to program evaluation will miss numerous educational research opportunities that could be responsive to vital system information needs. The case history experiences demonstrate the kinds of opportunities that arise and the range of methodologies needed in order to be responsive.

The broadly defined scope of activities (and therefore methods) encompassed by DOER is, in effect, the necessary other side of the first point made in this discussion concerning the range of client questions. The information questions of policy makers and managers have always been diverse. What has often been lacking is a willingness on the part of "evaluation researchers" to respond to the variety of information needs that can surface in an educational system. Both the presence of the range of questions and a predisposition on the part of researchers to respond to the range are important factors that influence the need and value of being methodologically eclectic.

Constraints to Taking an Eclectic Approach

We have discussed the importance of taking a methodologically eclectic approach to DOER, and we have pointed out several factors that encourage, and even require, such a stance. Why, then, is this approach not found more commonly in the field? There are several answers to this question that amount to powerful constraints operating in educational systems and in the educational research profession itself.

One serious constraint to taking a methodologically eclectic approach is grounded in the way the educational evaluation research profession has evolved. The profession of evaluation research is a relatively recent phenomenon. Indeed, it is so recent that there is considerable debate as to whether it is a profession at all. This issue aside, what is clear is that the field encompasses an array of disciplinary traditions. Cronbach and associates (1980) are quite accurate when they state that:

> Evaluators and those who write about evaluation have come from many backgrounds. What we might call the generalist — ready to attack any problem — was perhaps trained in economics, sociology, systems analysis, psychology, or statistics. There are also substantive specialists, familiar with past interventions and with related research on delinquency or mental health or higher education.
>
> Each field has had its own tradition in evaluation, its own criteria of proper procedure, and its own respected sources (Nelson, 1977). As a result, each field provided narrow preparation. Economists and systems analysts were accustomed to large compilations of data, but they had little background in instrumentation and data collection. Psychologists knew a great deal about observing and questioning individuals, but they lacked experience with institutions. Those trained in the laboratory were ill prepared to deal with the fluid field setting, where even the

meaning of a measuring instrument can change from one side to another. . . . [and] Rare is the individual who has been acquainted with investigative traditions other than his own discipline or field of practice (pp. 49–50).

This condition in the profession not only hinders communication but it directly influences the willingness and ability of researchers in specific research contexts to take a methodologically eclectic approach. While disciplinary backgrounds don't rigidly align with variation in methodological predispositions for knowing the world, there is a strong relationship. People coming out of an experimental psychology tradition are inclined to employ experimental methods in an educational research context. Perhaps more importantly, as Cronbach suggests, training in one discipline/methodology tends to preclude much experience with other disciplines/methods.

There are some indirect indications that this is beginning to change. If one looks at the longstanding debate over the application of quantitative versus qualitative research methodologies, there seems to be a trend toward understanding that these approaches can be valuable, complementary tools in most research contexts. Cronbach (1982) writes of the importance of "qualitative backup for quantitative comparisons" (p. 301). Patton (1980) writes that the "debate and competition between [quantitative and qualitative] paradigms is being replaced by a new paradigm — a paradigm of choices [recognizing that] different methods are appropriate for different situations" (p. 20). Reichardt and Cook (1979) have stated there is "no need to choose a research method on the basis of a traditional paradigmatic stance . . . and there is every reason (at least in logic) to use them together" (p. 27). And Campbell (1979), in the context of a discussion of the use of case studies, declares that "quantitative knowing has to trust and build on the qualitative, including ordinary perception . . . [and] methodologists must achieve an applied epistemology which integrated both" (p. 66).

These trends toward a greater appreciation of the unique and complementary contributions that can be made by qualitative and quantitative methods are to be applauded. Similarly, recent development of more cross-disciplinary associations, with professionals addressing common research questions from different disciplinary perspectives is also to be encouraged. Nevertheless, these trends essentially remain more as promises for the future, rather than descriptions of the current scene. In the current scene, the unidisciplinary background that often characterizes educational researchers directly inhibits the use of multiple research methods to address the questions of clients.

What may help to further diminish the qualitative versus quantitative debate is the need to be client-oriented on this work. For example, client-oriented quantitative types soon see the limitations of the quantitative approach when critical aspects of the current problem are not currently (are not inherently) quantifiable. A quantitative type who prefers quantification to client orientation will not last long in DOER. We hope we might shorten that evolutionary process!

Another major constraint to eclecticism lies in the practical domain of the resource limitations confronted by most educational systems. In the ideal world, a client's questions might be addressed by a team of researchers representing multiple educational perspectives, research methods, and disciplinary backgrounds. In such an ideal context, a number of studies might be employed that would be complementary and/or challenging in nature to the others in the set. The information produced would have both breadth and depth. Internal as well as external validity concerns would be addressed. Of course, the reality of educational systems falls far short of this ideal. The training of the personnel available, the time frame for the research, and a host of other factors serve to constrain the realization of the ideal. The client and researcher are confronted with serious decisions, not only about what to research but also about how to go about it. While there are no easy answers to this dilemma, in the following sections we will describe several strategies that can be considered in addressing these practical constraints, as well as those posed earlier based on the organization of the profession.

Diminishing the Constraints

Clearly one important response to the disciplinary divisions associated with the profession lies in developing multidisciplinary programs for people preparing to enter the field. The central goals of such programs would be to ground the research student in a specific disciplinary knowledge base while at the same time systematically exposing them to alternative disciplinary perspectives and methods of examining educational phenomena. At the very least, what we are calling for is exposure to alternative methodologies for use in the examination of educational phenomena typically encompassed within the domain of one's own discipline. Even better is the detailed study of a range of educational phenomena using a variety of methodological tools as part of one's disciplinary studies, where the range includes phenomena not typically the focus of one's area. This would entail, for example, an educational psychologist using quantitative and qualitative methods not just to examine measurement issues at the individual level but also to investigate organizational and political issues that influence the instructional outcomes for individuals.

Ideally, what we would like to see is that same educational psychologist having some exposure to the ways a sociologist or historian might analyze educational phenomena that the educational psychologist would naturally investigate. Also elucidating for this psychologist would be to have the sociologist or historian address subjects typically the focus of their own disciplines. While it is beyond the scope of this chapter to define the details of such a training program, other writers who have considered the issue provide some noteworthy ideas. For example, Cronbach and associates (1980) offer the following:

> Our ideal program for educating professional evaluators of social programs would have four major components: (1) disciplinary preparation — at the doctoral level — in a social science; (2) participation in dozens of interdisciplinary seminar sessions that examine evaluations; (3) an apprenticeship to practicing evaluators; and (4) an internship in an agency where policy is formulated (p. 341).

While the authors freely admit the difficulties in achieving such a training program, the central features are nevertheless well spoken, and they represent valuable goals indeed. A more detailed discussion of what experts in the field say about the preparation issue can be found in Anderson and Ball (1978, pp. 165–190). Interestingly, these authors report a strong bias toward training in descriptive and inferential statistics, and statistical analysis, although a variety of methods receive some mention.

One training issue that rarely surfaces in discussions of how to improve decision-oriented educational research is the need to train policy and decision makers in the research process. Given the importance of research-client dialogue, we believe that the preparation of administrators/managers for their role in information generation and use processes is vitally important in the reduction of methodological constraints, and for the improvement of the utility of educational research, generally. The goals here must be modest. However, some attention to the use of data in decision making, to the characteristics of question-methods interactions, and to the value of multiple perspectives/methods being applied to the same contexts are examples of valuable topics that are typically not found in training programs for educational administrators. The point here is not to turn managers into research methodologists, but rather to prepare them to interact critically with researchers and their products for the betterment of all. Recognizing this need, Alkin, Jacobson, Burry, Ruskus, White, and Kent (in press) have written a book that explores this important issue.

Turning to the constraints of a practical nature, we have several suggestions that can possibly make a significant contribution. One real constraint to the employment of multiple methodologies in a given context lies in the lack of available personnel to apply relevant research strategies. Assuming the presence of researchers knowledgeable about a variety of methods (no small assumption!), the design of ongoing, flexible databases can make a real contribution toward reducing the work involved in a given research context.

The computerized databases described in chapter 6 and case 8, and the archives discussed in cases 5 and 9 are examples of databases that can put a DOER in a better position to apply a variety of methodological perspectives to a new research task. In the instance of the computerized databases, the researcher is in a position to apply a variety of analytic techniques to new questions, possibly without having to gear up for major new data collection activities. The documentation archive (including the field observations, reports, documents, etc.), represents a largely phenomenological database that may be quite relevant to new starts. Such archives facilitate the application of qualitative methodologies to new research contexts, as well as the reapplication (or more accurately redissemination for reuse) of already existing knowledge in new contexts. The notion of redissemination for reuse is discussed in greater detail in chapter 9. Building databases for multiple applications is one practical way of reducing the personnel burden of our mandate to be methodologically eclectic.

In the absence of relevant internal expertise that reflects multiple methodological perspectives, the educational system is seriously constrained in its ability to take an eclectic approach to its research agenda. This problem can be confronted by contracting for additional expertise. School districts, for example, while not having unlimited resources, do have the capability of requesting proposals (RFP's) enlisting outside expertise to address specific research questions for the system. A "no-cost" alternative to the RFP notion is being explored in the Pittsburgh district. Interest in decision-relevant information has grown to the point that it has outstripped the district's available research resources (its emergent research office and our own contributions). Recently, the district's research office has begun to offer research opportunities to available and interested faculty at local universities and colleges. In essence, the director of the research office establishes a set of research questions relevant to a specific research context. These questions are circulated to a growing list of interested others. The incentive for involvement on the part of external research colleagues is essentially one of benign self-interest. The opportunity to pursue questions of personal interest that overlap with the district's research needs, and the possibility for scholarly publication as a result of work with the district, are the most commonly cited reasons for involvement. Experience thus far, not surprisingly, indicates that there are many problems to be overcome. Nevertheless, some involvement has been stimulated by this strategy. If successful, this approach offers a way to increase a system's ability to be more methodologically diverse in its research program.

As we have already indicated, we do not pretend to suggest that the constraints to being methodologically eclectic are insignificant and easily overcome. However, we are convinced that the benefits of working toward such an approach to DOER are considerable and worth the effort.

5 MONITORING INDICATORS AND TAILORING PRACTICE

Another generalization emerging from our Pittsburgh work is that educational research that takes place within educational systems would profit greatly if the emphasis were shifted from discrete studies of particular programs, which generally fall under the rubric of program evaluation, to a continuous activity of data collection and analysis, which we refer to as monitoring and tailoring. Reform efforts in education have tended to assume that the best way to improve educational practice is to adopt a new program that seems to address a particular problem, implement that innovative program, and then evaluate the program to determine its effectiveness in dealing with the problem. Berman (1980) calls this the technological-experimental paradigm of educational change. (Portions of this chapter were adapted from Cooley, 1984a.)

Our Pittsburgh experience has convinced us that the experimental paradigm is inadequate as a guide for DOER. Formal, summative program evaluations that attempt to estimate the impact of a particular program or policy on student outcomes tend to produce results that often should not be used because of their invalidity, or cannot be used because valid impact studies, if they can be done at all, take too long to be timely. Worse than that, such studies represent a substantial opportunity cost. That is, they require so much time and effort that other, potentially more useful approaches are not employed.

An alternative to the experimental paradigm, one not widely used in education but which has considerable promise, is the cybernetic paradigm. It involves developing and monitoring a variety of performance indicators. Then whenever an indicator moves into an unacceptable range, an attempt is made to determine just where that condition is most severe. Focused corrective action is then taken which we call tailoring practice. Although monitoring and tailoring resembles the cybernetic model used in controlling physical systems (as in the thermostat), there are some very important differences when applying it in an educational system, as Sproull and Zubrow (1981) point out.

In applying the cybernetic paradigm to educational systems, it must be recognized that compared to physical systems, the available indicators are more fallible; also it is usually less clear what an unacceptable range is, and it is not as obvious what the corrective action must be when an indicator moves into an unacceptable range. It certainly sounds hopeless. However, the monitoring and tailoring approach can be designed in ways that take these shortcomings into account and can serve a very useful function within an educational system.

Our district-wide needs assessment in case 4 is useful to illustrate the main features of a monitoring and tailoring approach. One purpose of monitoring indicators is to help districts establish priorities for improving the system. In that assessment, we worked up a variety of district-wide data that indicated the state of the educational system in the district.

The indicators included observed variables, such as student attendance, very simply derived variables, such as student–teacher ratio, or more complex, indirectly measured latent variables, such as socioeconomic status. The original unit of observation may have been students, classrooms or schools, and the level of aggregation used depended upon the point to be made. What is common to indicators is that they are a function of a construct that describes some aspect of educational phenomena that people care about. More on constructs in a moment.

Extensive dialogue with the superintendent and board members regarding these indicators led to the establishment of the priority areas for improving the educational program in the district. The dialogue concerned the degree to which the indicators seemed to be in an unacceptable range, as well as which indicators were getting at more fundamental problems which in turn might be affecting the performance of other indicators.

So one function of indicators in a monitoring and tailoring system is to contribute to district-wide priority setting. Examining a variety of indicators (in the form of district-wide aggregates) makes such priority discussions more productive. Since the objective is to improve the performance of the system, district-level aggregates are important for a dialogue about what aspects are in greatest need of improvement and, over time, for indicating whether progress is being made.

The other useful way to examine a performance indicator is to look at how it is distributed. Noticing where unusually low performance is occurring on a priority indicator provides a basis for guiding the action system that is supposed to improve that performance. The unit of analysis for examining distributions, whether it is students, classrooms, or schools, must be consistent with the unit that is the focus of the action system. Let's examine this important point a little more carefully.

As part of the district-wide needs assessment, we analyzed all the achievement data from the district that we could find — in terms of five-year trends, contrasts across grades, and differences among the various subject areas. The results of these analyses suggested that a major problem within achievement was primary grades reading. For example, district level aggregates indicated (on a criterion-referenced basis) that approximately 25 percent of the students were leaving third grade with reading comprehension skills inadequate to deal with the fourth grade curriculum. If those skills were not learned in the primary grades, subsequent remedial efforts became more and more costly and seemed less and less effective.

Further looks at the data (this time at the classroom level) revealed some second and third grade classrooms in which little or no reading growth was occurring in the course of the year for students placed in those teachers' classrooms. (Note that in this particular example the indicator is not end-of-year achievement level but achievement growth; the units being monitored are classrooms, not individual students or schools; low growth was a trend for a given teacher's students, not a one-time event; and initial student abilities were also taken into account in comparing growth.)

Now the question is, What is to be done when the growth in reading ability of students assigned to a particular teacher is discovered to be low year after year? Tailoring requires a deployable resource, an action system, that can respond to such indications. In its response, the action system must recognize that the indicator is fallible. A procedure is needed for confirming the indication. In this particular case, the person that responds to the indicator might be an instructional supervisor, trained in clinical supervision and capable of visiting that classroom, initially to confirm (or disconfirm) the indication that reading instruction is not going well in that classroom. If a problem is then confirmed, diagnosis of the situation is needed coupled with corrective action, generally employing intensive clinical supervision.

As another example, if district-level aggregates indicate that student absence has moved into an undesirable range, and if the action system available for correcting truancy consists of social workers working with individual students and their families, then the extreme cases in the distribution of student-level truancy rates would be the focus of that action system. If other levels of aggregation revealed a classroom or school with particularly low attendance, further investigation might reveal the need for another kind of action system that can work with particular teachers or schools to create a more attractive learning environment.

One assumption central to the monitoring and tailoring approach is that important, significant improvements can be made in the educational system through fine-tuning the system. Some might call it a form of incrementalism (Lindblom, 1972). Recognizing that, it also must be emphasized that there indeed may be fundamental changes that must be made in the system in order to adjust to fundamental chnges that occur in society. But it does seem rational to make sure that current programs and policies are working as well as possible before trying some dramatic departure from current practice. We are not saying that schools should not innovate. There comes a time when the saber-tooth curriculum has to go. But when a problem is detected in a school district, the tendency is to launch a district-wide solution, generally involving a new program, rather than determine just where (i.e., in which schools or classrooms) things are not working well and tailor their practice to improve performance. The district-wide innovation can frequently disrupt those schools or classrooms in which things had been working smoothly and seldom corrects situations where they were not. Without focused assistance, some principals or teachers will not implement the new solution any better than the previous practice. Too little has been done to get the programs that are in place working well. (What is impressive in the followthrough data, for example, is the vast variability in effectiveness among sites implementing the same instructional model, not differences between models. See, for example, Cooley and Lohnes [1976].) A monitoring and tailoring system can help a district decide how to focus its available energies for staff development and remedial attention. Now let us take a little closer look at two of the major components of such a system, the indicators and the action systems.

Major Ingredients of a Monitoring and Tailoring System

Indicators

It helps to think about possible indicators in terms of major constructs. One set of constructs relates to the efficacy of the system as it prepares students for adulthood. Here it is important to have indicators of such constructs as entering student abilities and interests, their educational programs and progress in them, and achievement and other personal outcomes that are indicative of their expected futures. This set represents the familiar system constructs of inputs, processes, and outcomes. Cooley and Lohnes (1976) have suggested one way of organizing such data.

Another set of constructs is needed to describe the quality of the present experience. Schooling is a large part of everyone's life. It is important to seek indicators of the richness of the present experience as well as satisfy the clamor for indicators of how well the students are being prepared for adulthood. For example, Epstein's (1981) measure of the quality of school life is a useful indicator of school climate.

A third set of constructs is necessary to satisfy the need to consider whether the system is fair. Questions concerning the equality of educational opportunity dominate policy discussions, and indicators that reflect such inequities in the system can make those debates more productive. Disaggregations of these indicators can also reveal where more resources may be needed to correct currently unjust distributions.

Dialogue regarding inequities in an educational system is admittedly not a straightforward affair (e.g., Green, 1971). But arguments in terms of the appropriateness of different indicators make those discussions less abstract. Also, concern soon shifts from noticing the inevitable differences in student outcomes and justifiable differences in resource allocations, to unjust inequities in opportunity to learn. In the last section of this chapter we deal with this domain in greater detail.

Having indicators from all three domains (efficacy, quality, and equality) also facilitates discussions about "balancing" the different demands on the schools (e.g., quality of the present experience versus preparation for the future, demand for excellence versus the need for equity, liberal education versus training marketable skills).

For all constructs, it is important to develop multiple indicators and be able to display them at multiple levels (i.e., student, classroom, school, and district levels). Because this requires considerable information processing, an essential ingredient is to build a computer-based information system that allows the development and display of the necessary indicators. Today such computer systems are quite feasible.

One problem in using indicators is that it is frequently possible to corrupt them. That is, indicators are corruptible if it is possible to affect the indicator without affecting the underlying phenomena that the indicator is attempting to reflect. For example, if suspensions are being monitored as one indicator of school climate, and if having many of them reflects poorly on the principal, it's very easy to see how principals could modify their behavior with respect to issuing suspensions (or reporting them!) and still have the same level of chaos in that building. The corruptibility of indicators is one reason why it is important to have multiple indicators of the same construct and to refine them continuously. This is an important task of the evaluation researcher in such a system. It should be pointed out that indicators will be corrupted more readily if rewards or punishments are associated with extreme values on that indicator, than if the indicator is used for guiding corrective feedback.

A lot can be learned about the construction and use of indicators in education from the research on social indicators that emerged as an active area among social scientists in the mid-1960s. That work was stimulated by two secretaries of Health, Education and Welfare, John Gardner and Wilbur Cohen, who felt that social indicators could provide a better basis for federal social policy (Land and Spilerman, 1975). Krathwohl (1975) organized an Educational Testing Service (ETS) invitational conference on this theme in 1975. There now are entire books and journals devoted to social indicators research. MacRae (1985) provides an excellent summary of the use of policy indicators, including their contribution to the public debate on such complex issues as equity and social integration. In education, the book by Johnstone (1981) is particularly relevant.

It must be noted, however, that there has been considerable debate about the utility of the social indicators movement. We sense that it has two major weaknesses as far as education is concerned. One is the emphasis in that literature upon federal level aggregates. Noticing that a national indicator has moved into an alarming range encourages the launching of federal solutions to an isolated problem. That can easily produce programs that end up being counterproductive, because of the counterintuitive ways in which large, complex systems react to change (Meyers, 1981, p. 20). Everyone has their favorite example of an unintended negative side effect from a well-intentioned innovation.

The other weakness in the social indicators movement is the tendency to justify indicators as a way of estimating the impact of social programs and policies. To do that, of course, requires rather well-specified causal models. Economists have been at this for a long time, and it seems pretty clear they are not there yet. It is important to work on developing models that can describe, even predict, how indicators change over time, how they interrelate, even how they seem to be influencing one another. But adequately specified causal models may be a long way off, even at the district level. Meanwhile, indicators can play an important role in the type of monitoring and tailoring system we are advocating for school districts. Now a few more words about action systems.

Action Systems

If system improvement is to follow from monitoring, the information system must be "connected" to an action system. It is very important *how* this is done because it is usually not clear why a student, or classroom, or school is in an undesirable range on some valued indicator. Indicators are a function of many factors in the system. Indicators can only tell you where to look for possible problems. For that reason, the action system that is called into play must be first and foremost a diagnostic system. Corrective action is generally not clear from the indicators because our causal models for explaining their rise and fall are still not adequately specified.

The monitoring and tailoring approach requires the availability of services that can be deployed to correct the most serious cases that are found within a district. At the student level, those who deal with extreme cases on such indicators as attendance, suspensions, and achievement growth would be social workers, counselors, and remedial tutors. Specialists trained in clinical supervision would work with principals and teachers who are low on classroom-level growth indicators, and a school improvement team would work in schools that are extreme on building level indicators.

Notice we are not calling for new staff to perform these functions. What the information system does is show how existing personnel might focus their energies. It also helps to justify that focusing. Guided by an unexamined sense of equality, those capable of this type of corrective action tend to be spread so thin they cannot possibly be effective.

So the necessary action systems are financially feasible because they represent a way of focusing the efforts of existing personnel. Of course it is one thing to be feasible, and quite another to be effective. But even here we are optimistic. One basis for the optimism is the documentation of a school improvement effort (case 5). Focusing upon seven elementary schools that had a history of low student achievement, the director of that program and his school improvement team are demonstrating how monitored student progress data, accompanied by focused, team supervision, are capable of improving the quality of instruction going on in those buildings.

Another basis for the optimism is all the good work going on in our field for the past decade on effective teaching and schooling. For example, by carefully examining the behavior of unusually competent teachers, Leinhardt (1983) has found that these teachers buy considerable amounts of instructional time through the use of well-rehearsed, easily operationalized routines. The effective schools research has been summarized in a special issue of *Educational Researcher* (Bickel, 1983). This literature is beginning to describe ways in which schools can be organized to improve educational outcomes. Such results contribute to the knowledge base needed for guiding the type of focused, clinical action required in monitoring and tailoring. But our Pittsburgh experience is also making it clear that Purkey and Smith (1983) are correct when they point out that while school improvement is certainly possible, it's not always easy.

Also, we are optimistic because of the way the indicators in the district have been turned around. Of course, the improvement we are seeing in student achievement and attendance, for example, is not necessarily the result of monitoring and tailoring. What is clear is that there is new energy in the district. Its sources include a superintendent who is willing and able to provide the kind of educational leadership he expects of others in the district, and a school board that has recognized the importance of what he is trying to accomplish. What monitoring and tailoring can do is indicate potentially fruitful ways in which that energy can be focused, and provide a basis for new hope as indicators begin to improve.

There is a question that quite properly arises as one begins to build a computer-based monitoring system: Is it humane? Part of the answer to that question is a series of other questions. For example:

- Is it humane to expose children year after year to a teacher who is apparently unable to improve the reading performance of children in his or her charge?
- Is it humane to have a child absent 160 days in a school year without so much as a home visit because the social worker's energies are being diverted by a principal to the task of preparing the justification for long-term suspensions?
- Is it humane for a school district to solve the problem of an unsatisfactory principal's performance by an annual game of musical chairs among principals in the hopes that eventually a principal will end up in a school in which the parents don't complain?

The other part of the answer is to note that the monitoring and tailoring system must be designed in a way that recognizes the fallibility of the indicators and the inadequacies of our causal models in determining why an indicator has moved into an undesirable range. It is *not* designed, for example, to issue pink slips to teachers whose students turn in an unsatisfactory standardized achievement performance.

We did not set out to develop a monitoring and tailoring system for the district. We set out to provide evaluation services. We began by doing program evaluation studies, trying to find the impact of particular programs. We moved from that to a district-wide needs assessment. It was in the context of that activity that we became impressed with the vast variance in any indicator we looked at — variance among students, among classrooms, among schools. Measures of central tendency for the district can be a cause for alarm, but noticing how the indicator distributes and where the outliers are can be the first step in an effective improvement strategy. Just exposing weaknesses will not produce the desired change.

Reducing Inequities in Educational Opportunity

People who perform DOER need to be willing and able to discuss issues about the goals of education. This is important in the dialogue that must take place between researcher and client. It is particularly critical in the monitoring and tailoring approach to the improvement of educational systems. Fine-tuning that is simply a directionless tinkering is to be avoided. The best way to avoid that is to have a clear sense of what education should be trying to accomplish in our society, and attempt to develop a shared sense of eduational aims between client and researcher.

This section illustrates the importance of that need. Here we examine the nature and extent of inequities in opportunity that occur in education, identify a philosophy of education which can guide one's thinking about this critically important issue, review the general approaches that have been used in dealing with this problem, and suggest monitoring and tailoring procedures that can be implemented within educational systems that could reduce inequities in educational opportunity.

First, it seems useful to distinguish among the different kinds of inequities in education that have troubled educators, politicians, and the general public over the years. This is important because a lot of the arguments, policies, and programs that have been used in the name of equality have confused three kinds of equalities: equal outcomes, equal inputs, and equal opportunities. We shall deal with each one in turn.

Some equalitarians are concerned about equal outcomes. They point to things like differences in achievement test results as indicative of inequities that exist in education. However, most people agree that achieving equality of outcomes at the student level is neither possible nor desirable. That is, we certainly can't expect all children to read equally well, or do mathematics equally well, any more than we can expect all children to do anything equally well. Some have argued that even if it were possible, it would be neither just nor socially beneficial to have this occur (Rawls, 1971; Green, 1980).

Although no one seems to be calling for equal outcomes among students, many are concerned about equal outcomes among groups. That is, when people look at differences that occur among races, ethnic groups, or between sexes, the question is whether or not those differences are symptomatic of inequities in educational opportunity. This, of course, has been hotly debated and intensely researched, getting into possible genetic differences among the compared groups, the nature–nurture controversy, and the extent to which it is possible for schools to compensate for differences in home environment.

Others are concerned about inequities that exist in educational inputs. This was at the heart of the Coleman, Campbell, Hobson, McPartland, Mood, Weinfeld, and York (1966) report, which attempted to determine whether minority students were being educated in schools that were somehow inferior to those serving the white students. Attempts at equalizing costs per pupil across districts within a state, or among buildings within a district, or making sure that resources such as counselors, social workers, etc., are distributed within the district proportional to students to be served, are all examples of trying to distribute educational resources so that there are equal inputs. Equal resource inputs do not yield equal achievement outcomes, given children of unequal initial abilities.

Other equalitarians want to be sure that all students can realize their potential, and so we find practices where performance is monitored and adjusted for differences in IQ or other measures of aptitude. Here differences in raw outcomes aren't the issue, but rather departures from expected outcomes. That is, if children in one school are not doing as well on achievement tests as they might be expected to do, given their performance on an aptitude test, there is assumed to be an inadequacy in the educational services being provided in that school. Whether or not a child, or a classroom, or a school is performing up to expectation is an attractive notion. The problem is we have no way of measuring potential. All estimates of aptitude are biased by advantages that have occurred prior to that assessment of potential. Admittedly, some measures are more subject to prior environmental influence than others, but nevertheless the problem remains. It is not possible to monitor whether or not potential is being realized because potential cannot be determined independent of prior environmental advantage.

However, it is certainly true that some children arrive at school better prepared to learn what schools teach. It has also been established and reestablished (ad nauseam) that this advantage is related to a variety of differences in home environments that are correlated with socioeconomic status. It is also very likely that individual differences in genetic endowment make it easier for some children to learn what schools teach. What is not known, and what is probably unknowable, is the relative contribution of the hundreds of factors that influence the differences in the scholastic aptitudes between any two children or any two groups of children.

For example, if Johnny scored higher than Billy on a reading readiness test as they entered first grade, it is not possible to know the degree to which that observed difference was due to differences in parental reading habits, use of oral language in the home, differences in kinds of games available, differences in kindergarten or "preschool" experiences, and differences in genetic endowment. What is well established is that, given these differences in reading readiness, it will probably be easier to teach Johnny to read than it will be Billy. An equity question is how much more effort should be devoted to teaching Billy than Johnny. If the same amount of effort is used, then Johnny will probably become the better reader. Providing Billy with more intensive reading instruction until he reads as well as Johnny may not be possible if Johnny is genetically better equipped to learn reading, and it is not possible to establish whether that is the case. That is why it is difficult to justify equal outcomes as the goal. It is also difficult to justify providing Johnny with better reading instruction than Billy. This, however, tends to occur in our society because economic advantage increases the likelihood that both favorable home and school conditions will coexist. That is, higher income increases the likelihood that parental education will have been higher, which increases the likelihood that practices that increase reading readiness will be present in the home. Higher income also tends to insure more favorable school environments, either through being more able to purchase homes in areas being served by better schools, being more able to pay for private education when the available public school is deemed unsatisfactory, or being more able to exert political influence in determining local school policies and practices.

In the results of the sustaining effects study of compensatory education (Carter, 1984), the authors conclude that it appears not to be possible for schools to compensate for the unequal starts children get from their unequal families. This apparent lack of success for compensatory education have led some people to one or more of the following conclusions:

1. Differences between groups are inherent and cannot be eliminated.
2. Differences among homes are too great and too potent for schools to overcome.
3. Even if it were possible for schools to make a difference, they don't now and are impossible to reform.

Educators should not be disillusioned by the apparent lack of success that we have had in attempting to reduce inequities. It seems important to work at clarifying what is both possible and desirable with respect to this just concern.

Let us turn now to the question of equal educational opportunity: what it is, how it's justified, and what indicators might be used to notice inequities that do exist. As the argument develops, it is apparent that the focus becomes one of identifying and correcting rather specific and obvious cases of inequities in opportunity. Difficult as that is, it is far easier to agree on the need to correct specific inequities than to define, defend, and implement some general, idealized notion of equal opportunity.

The kind of opportunity that is of concern in education is the opportunity to learn within a school environment. Inequities in opportunity to learn can be detected in distributions of measures that are deliberately constructed for that purpose. Such measures can involve both inputs and outputs, but are arranged in ways that clearly reveal differences in opportunity to learn. But before going into the specifics of how one might go about detecting and correcting inequities, let us briefly examine the justification for such an effort. An excellent discussion of this issue of equal opportunities is provided by van Geel (1976) in his chapter entitled "John Rawls and Educational Policy." There van Geel points out the great difficulty that reformers have had in attempting to realize equal opportunity and indicates that educators seem to have "turned away from heavy reliance on the mechanism of equal opportunity."

Rawls (1971) provides both method and argument for justifying efforts to reduce inequities in educational opportunity. He develops a social philosophy that clearly places equal opportunity as a "primary good," and as van Geel (1976) demonstrates, one can derive a very convincing educational philosophy with equality of educational opportunity as its centerpiece. Rawls accomplishes this with a fascinating and convincing mental experiment in which he asks the reader to assume "the original position," which is to ask people to design a fair set of principles for distributing resources, but under the special condition that they do not know their own talents, abilities, plans, or status in society, and so cannot argue from their own special interests. From this process emerge some principles of justice that are quite convincing, primarily because of the way in which he derives them. From these principles of justice can be derived both a philosophy of education and a set of implications for educational practice.

Most of the effort to date that has attempted to reduce inequities in educational opportunity have been programmatic, large-scale efforts, whether it be at the federal, state, or local level. That is, the tendency has been to design, adopt, implement, and evaluate innovative programs that try to adjust, in the educational sphere, for inequities that occur in the social sphere. So, for example, the federal government has distributed billions of dollars through Title I (and subsequently, Chapter I) of schools heavily impacted with students from low socioeconomic families, in the hope that the extra support that this money might buy could compensate for the disadvantage of intellectual development that tends to be related to socioeconomic status of the family. Similarly, proponents of desegregation are often driven by a notion that if minority students were mixed with white students in the same building, the educational services will be more equal than they would be in segregated facilities.

Solutions to the problem of educational opportunity have been hampered by a tendency in education that has hindered all types of reform efforts, not just reforms designed to reduce inequities in educational opportunity. That tendency is to assume that the way to solve educational problems is to design and develop new innovative programs which address these problems, then get schools to adopt and implement these innovative programs, and then evaluate these programs to demonstrate their effectiveness in dealing with the problem.

The evidence is quite clear that this approach is seldom successful. The monitoring and tailoring alternative involves developing indicators of opportunity to learn, monitoring these indicators, and then tailoring existing programs to reduce outliers on those multiple indicators of educational opportunity. We shall now turn to a description of how monitoring and tailoring might be applied in an effort to reduce inequities in educational opportunity.

First of all, it is important that this problem is dealt with at multiple levels (i.e., student, classroom, and school) and with multiple indicators. The required student information system contains information on student programs and progress. With respect to student-level data, this would include information on student attendance, suspensions, curriculum indicators, and achievement test results. The computer file also indicates the sequence of teachers and school buildings to which each child has been assigned during his or her tenure in the district. These measured variables are then developed into indicators that reflect variation in educational opportunity. Let's look at some examples of such indicators using actual data.

For example, a student who is absent for 90 days out of the 180-day school year has less opportunity to learn than does a student who is present for the entire school year. Although the absent student appears to have had the opportunity to be in school the same number of days, understanding why the student was absent may suggest otherwise.

Within school districts, class size varies considerably. A student in a classroom with 16 children has a better opportunity to learn as does a student in a classroom with 32 children. Such disparity in classroom size occurs in two proximate neighborhood schools because of rigid boundaries for school attendance areas.

A child assigned to a teacher who is frequently absent does not have the same opportunity to learn as the child who is attending a classroom taught by a teacher with regular attendance. Frequent teacher absence (more than once a month) has become a major national problem (*Education Week*, December

14, 1981). A child in a classroom being "taught" by various substitutes for a significant percentage of the days in a school year has not had a good opportunity to learn.

Turning to student achievement information, results from an annual testing program can be used to identify teachers whose students from year-to-year exhibit little or no growth in the development of their academic skills. Surely a child in a classroom with a teacher who has an apparent demonstrated inability to promote student growth does not have the same opportunity to learn as a child in a classroom with a teacher whose students consistently exhibit normal growth in the course of a year.

Another well-known fact about school life is that some school buildings are so out-of-control that precious little learning can take place within that school building. Disruptions, acts of violence, general chaos have become a way of life in such buildings. The rate at which students are suspended from school is an indicator that is related to this underlying phenomenon. A child in a school of 700 students that reported 1,700 suspensions during the last school year does not have the same opportunity to learn as a child in a school with 800 students that last year had 180 suspensions.

These illustrations of actual conditions show that it is possible to develop multiple indicators of educational opportunity which can be monitored in a student information system. But, of course, the computer can only assist in displaying where problems might exist. As we have noted, there are two other requirements for monitoring and tailoring. One is the continuous refinement and revision of such indicators. The corruptibility of indicators is one reason why it's important to have multiple indicators of the underlying phenomena and to refine them continuously.

The other requirement for a monitoring and tailoring system is to have the information system "connected" to an action system. The monitoring and tailoring approach to reducing inequities in educational opportunity requires the availability of district-wide services that can be deployed to correct the most serious inequities in opportunity that are found within the district. At the student level, dealing with outliers on such indicators as attendance, suspensions, and achievement growth would be social workers, counselors, and remedial tutors. Specialists trained in clinical supervision would work with teachers who are outliers on classroom level growth indicators, and a school improvement team would work in schools that are outliers on building level indicators.

Inequalities are inevitable. The task is to identify and correct unequal conditions that are clearly unacceptable. By displaying inequalities, it is possible to notice those that most people would agree are unacceptable. Many political and legal actions have been taken in education because the proponents suspect that the result of the action will reduce the likelihood that inequalities will exist. As indicated earlier, proponents of desegregation are frequently motivated by the notion that the way to reduce differences in schools that serve blacks and whites is to have the same schools serve both races. Opponents of open enrollment in school districts (where parents may enroll their children in schools other than the one designated by their place of residence) are worried that allowing "parents who care" to change the school their child attends takes political pressure off the school thought to be inferior.

Within a school district, some teachers are more effective than others. Similarly, some principals are more effective than others. Everyone knows that. It is also clear that it is easier to "look good" as a teacher or a principal with students from high socioeconomic homes, for example, when comparisons are made on district-wide achievement tests. When achievement performances for two schools are compared — a reasonable question is whether or not the principal and teachers in the low performing school are less effective than in the high performing school. An examination of their practices is the best way to find out.

There are at least three ways of dealing with possible principal and teacher ineffectiveness: (1) dismissing those thought to be ineffective; (2) reassigning principals and teachers to "even out" the distribution of the ineffective; or (3) providing corrective feedback to those exhibiting ineffective practices.

The problem with the first solution is that the indicators of effectiveness are too fallible (and corruptible) to be the basis for such drastic action. Although reassignment of principals and teachers, the second solution, is used frequently, it is not done in order to make sure that ineffectiveness is fairly distributed. On the contrary, principals and teachers who don't "work out" in one school are sent to another in the hope that the change will be "better for all concerned." Such procedures tend to result in the more ineffective migrating to schools where parents are less aware of what's happening in school or less mobilized to do something about it. It also seems fair to ask, If ineffectiveness is identifiable, why not work at correcting it rather than redistributing it? Which brings us to the third option.

Indicators of ineffective practices are accurate enough to provide a basis for knowing where and how to *focus* the district's efforts for staff development, particularly if that clinical process begins with a diagnostic strategy that can indicate more precisely the nature and extent of an identified problem. Acceptable programs of personnel evaluation must begin with a strong program of staff development. Much can be done in reducing inequities in educational opportunity if teacher and principal ineffectiveness can be detected and corrected.

6 COMPUTER-BASED INFORMATION SYSTEMS

One important thing to note about conducting DOER for an operating educational system is that many factors affect the likelihood of whether this kind of work will be successful. Degree of client orientation is an example of such a factor. If a client orientation is not present, the results tend not to be of interest to the potential consumers of the produced information. Another factor is the extent to which those conducting DOER are willing and able to be methodologically eclectic, so that research methods can adapt to the problem as defined rather than defining the problem in ways that can be solved with preferred methodology. The third major factor we have examined thus far reflects the degree to which the DOER system is closely linked to the action system, so that the information produced will more directly influence what happens.

The factor most relevant to this chapter is the critical importance of timeliness in DOER. In an educational system, as policy questions emerge they must be dealt with at the time when they are "hot." For example, school boards usually will not delay their deliberations until a study is completed. As issues come to the floor, they get dealt with whether or not relevant research data are avilable. When systematic data are not available, anecdotes heard by a board member readily become substituted. Similarly, school managers have a continuing need for data to guide their day-to-day decision making, allocation of resources, and priority setting.

In our discussions with people who are responsible for conducting DOER, we frequently heard the complaint that "the policy board acted before they got the results of our study." Such boards are not likely to change their "personality." What can change is the readiness of DOER to be able to respond quickly to the need for information. Quick response is more likely if a computer-based information system is developed that contains the basic data often needed for such inquiry.

An analysis of the information requirements of school district policy makers and school managers clearly indicates that the same data are needed over and over again, with variations as to how the data are analyzed or what combinations of data are relevant to a particular kind of decision (Burstein, 1984). As the early cases clearly illustrate (e.g., cases 1 and 3), a great deal of energy was expended in pulling together into one place the combination of data needed to shed light on those issues. This was in contrast to cases 2 and 4, in which we were able to respond quickly because of the databases we established in cases 1 and 3. In an extensive bureaucracy such as a school district, different data are "owned" by different offices, be it personnel, compensatory education, transportation, or attendance accounting. These databases can be quite jealously protected by their various owners since that ownership contributes to their status and power in the enterprise. Recognizing the importance of timeliness, the recurring need for the same data to shed light on different problems, and the critical need to bring data from different sources together in one place, educational systems need to establish automated information systems (AIS).

People began discussing the potential use of computers to assist in the mangement of educational systems as soon as computers began to be available in the late '50s and early '60s. (See, for example, Goodlad, O'Toole, and Tyler [1966].) Since that time, all large school systems and even many of the smaller districts have developed computer support for central administative functions. Sometimes these central systems include data on individual students, but these tend to be restricted to data that are needed for central administrative tasks, such as computing average daily membership for state subsidies or home socioeconomic status for federal compensatory education distributions.

Central systems tend to serve central functions, and they almost never get to the part about how to help principals and teachers improve the effectiveness, pleasantness, and fairness of their educational environments. The demands of the central environment tend to overwhelm both the hardware and software development resources of the central computer system.

There also have been many efforts to develop school-based computer managed instruction systems (e.g., Cooley and Glaser, 1969). In the '60s when such systems were tried, the costs were just too prohibitive to justify the effort, both in terms of the costs of the hardware and the costs of developing and maintaining such systems. Baker (1978) provides an excellent summary of these earlier efforts.

Several things have happened since 1983 that are encouraging a reconsideration of school-based automated information systems. The most obvious, of course, is the emergence of the powerful, relatively inexpensive microcomputer. Being able to purchase for less than $5,000 the computer power that would have cost hundreds of thousands of dollars in the '60s is clearly a major factor in the renewed enthusiasm for developing school-based AIS.

Another important development is the availability of software for establishing database management systems. The new applications software such as Knowledge Manager (Micro Data Base Systems, 1984) make it quite easy to develop automated information systems for schools and do it in ways that make modification relatively easy, and ad hoc inquiries possible (that is, not all possible retrieval requests need to be anticipated by the developers of the system).

Another development that makes school-based computer systems feasible today is the desk-top scanner, which facilitates a variety of data entry tasks, including automatic scoring of student tests and reading attendance forms. The relatively inexpensive, accurate, programmable scanner eliminates the big expense of hand-entering data.

Finally, the development of the inexpensive modem and the associated telecommunications software makes it possible to export summaries of school data to the central computer as well as import to the school computer any data on that school which are centrally available. Similarly, as students transfer from school to school, so can their computer-based records. This concept of distributive processing, which has been emerging in the '80s, is contributing greatly to the reconceptualization of how school district information systems might be designed.

Because such information systems are critically important to DOER, this chapter is devoted to that topic. We consider the goals of an AIS, their functions, the characteristics of effective information systems, specifications for a specific system, and some of the nontechnical issues that surround the design, implementation, and use of AIS. Complementing this chapter, case 8 provides a summary of our experiences in working with the Pittsburgh district in moving toward a viable AIS.

The Goals of an Automated Information System

As is usually the case, the consideration of the functions and characteristics of information systems should be preceded by a consideration of the goals for such a system. In general, the goals for an AIS in education are much the same as the goals for the educational system in the first place. A possible difference is that when one takes on the task of defining an automated information system, it is much more important to be precise and explicit regarding goals, if those goals are to guide the development and implementation of such systems.

The general goals that have tended to guide our work are: (1) improving student achievement, (2) enhancing the quality of school life, and (3) providing equal opportunity to learn. To be useful in systems design, these very general goals need to be defined more explicitly. Then, data relevant to the goals need to be specified, collected, and organized in ways that facilitate knowing how well the educational system is progressing toward realizing these goals, as well as guide in their realization. It is also important to recognize that a given data indicator may be relevant to more than one goal. For example, student attendance is a variable that is always part of such a student information system. Sometimes the mere fact that attendance records are required by law insures that variable's presence, but even if it were not required, it is assumed to be related to all three goals. That is, an absent student is engaged in less school learning than is a present student. A student who is unable to attend classes because of difficulties in the home does not have the same opportunity to learn as a student whose home expectations are to be in school. Also, attendance data aggregated at the classroom or school level can indicate rather unpleasant school conditions that are being avoided, and this would be noticed if, for example, a classroom or school had unusually high rates of absenteeism.

Improving the quality of the school experience includes reducing the rigidity with which schools tend to operate. A major problem in breaking up the build-in rigidity of the school and its traditional format of classroom organization is the increased amount of information demanded in more adaptive instructional systems. It is relatively uncomplicated for the traditional teacher to keep track of what happens each day with the 25 students in that classroom. Very little information is required when all children progress through the same instructional materials at about the same rate, varying only in how much they learn from those exposures. When all students are on page 38 in the arithmetic textbook, that single number defines where the class is. When this neat process is broken and individual students are allowed to work at different levels and rates, the teacher has 25 times as much information to monitor for that same class. If students are also allowed to move toward different objectives or toward the same objective through different modes of instruction, the information-processing problem becomes even more severe. Back in 1967, McLuhan and Leonard were arguing:

> School computers can now help keep track of students as they move freely from one activity to another whenever moment by moment or year by year records of students' progress are needed. This will wipe out even the administrative justification for schedules and regular periods, with all their anti-educational effects, and will free teachers to get on with the real business of education (p. 23).

So in the consideration of the goals of an AIS, it is important not just to "automate" the information requirements of the current system but to reconsider the broad aims of the educational system and seek ways to help realize some of the goals that have been more elusive, such as enhancing the quality of the school experience.

Functions of Automated Information Systems

There are many possible functions for an automated information system within a school. Probably, the first and foremost is just plain record keeping. There is a critical need in schools to keep records of who is there, what students are doing, and how well they are doing. These records may be required by federal law, state code, or local board policy, and they are omnipresent. So one function of an automated information system is to satisfy those needs for record keeping, including modifying the files as students come and go.

A second major function is report generation. A serious problem in schools is having information easily distributed to all who might need to know. For example, home information, including emergency phone numbers, that teachers might find useful as they attempt to strengthen school-home relationships, can easily be distributed to all teachers from school-based computer files. Once a school database is up and running, it is amazing how many different applications can be identified in terms of supplying printouts of various kinds to different professionals in the building who have a need to know.

A third function is record retrieval. This is not the routine report generation, but the function of searching for specific records, or sets of records with specific features, that might require special attention. For example, pulling out all the data on a specific student for a parent conference or scanning for students with combinations of failing grades and high absenteeism can easily be done in such automated systems.

A fourth function is data analysis. One turns to the computer for ease of record keeping, report generating, and record retrieval; but the great strength of the computer is its ability to do complex analyses quickly and easily. One of the challenges in developing such information systems today is to try to build into these systems the expertise of a data analyst so that the benefits of such analyses are available to people in the schools. That is, one does not expect principals necessarily to know how to apply multiple contingency analyses to a set of data, but the types of questions which might benefit from such analyses can be anticipated by system developers and the results made available to users.

The fifth function of automated information systems relates to the concepts developed in chapter 5, namely, monitoring data and tailoring practices. Computer scientists call this the process control application of automated information systems, and it is the application of cybernetic models to the improvement of the educational system. The goal of this aspect of the system is to identify ways to tailor the school and its curriculum to the individual needs of the learner, rather than to make the individual learner adjust to the offerings of the typical classroom instruction.

Characteristics of Effective Information Systems

Certainly one characteristic of an effective information system is that it contains data that are reasonably current and accurate. It is with respect to this type of data dependability that central systems tend to fail. That is, if the focus is exclusively upon centralized databases for district-wide planning and accounting functions, and data flow is only from the school to the central computer, there is no reason to believe the central files will be current and accurate if the people in the school are not using the data. So one principle in this work is the need to have the data become part of the operating system in the local school. If the data that eventually are transmitted to the central system are used on a day-to-day basis within schools, it is much more likely that the centrally available data will be current and accurate.

One major problem that has plagued such information systems is how to maintain current and accurate files. The design of such systems must include incentive systems for doing so within the local school. For example, scoring the criterion-referenced tests in a school district can provide such incentives. When the Pittsburgh public schools launched its Monitoring Achievement in Pittsburgh (MAP) program, it was designed as a centrally scored achievement monitoring system. Even with the most heroic of efforts, that central system could only produce two-week turnaround on the test scoring and reporting. Insofar as such tests are designed to guide the day-to-day instructional planning, the fortnightly turnaround is insufficient. With a scanner attached to the local school microcomputer, it is capable of scoring those tests on the day that they are given, with reports going to students, teachers, and principals, as well as automatically updating the school's information system with student performance and pacing data.

Local scoring of tests not only illustrates how to build in incentives for maintaining current files but it also helps to see how they can be more accurate. For example, with scoring taking place and the results being viewed that some day in the school, errors that can creep into such a testing system can be easily found, corrected, and the results rescored. An example of such a clerical error might be a teacher indicating the wrong form of the facing sheet that controls test processing for that homeroom. If a central system scores several thousand such batches (one for each classroom), errors are usually not detectable and the inaccurate data become part of the centrally available file. Of course, when the printouts eventually reach the teacher, the teacher will notice the error and discard the results, but meanwhile they are part of the central system and are unlikely to be purged or corrected.

Another important point here is the way in which locally used data files will reduce the likelihood of the indicators becoming corrupted. That is, if data are collected and used within the local school to help in school planning and improvement, suspicious data (e.g., an overzealous teacher may have administered a test using nonstandard procedures) can be more easily detected and corrected. Data that are used exclusively for a centralized accountability system are far too easily corrupted, and they *will* be corrupted if teachers and principals sense that those data are being used in unfair ways in their own evaluation. So the shift in emphasis from data being used for local school improvement as opposed to central system accountability will result in a central database that is sufficiently dependable for central planning and monitoring. In addition to building in incentives for keeping data files current and accurate, then, it is important that such information systems build out incentives to corrupt the data. The move to distributive processing contributes to the solution of those problems.

Another important feature of AIS is to have built-in checks for noticing out-of-range data. For data that are being hand-entered, this should be part of the data entry procedures. That is, as key strokes occur, any out-of-range character is immediately detected and brought to the attention of the keyboard operator through audio and visual cues. Similarly, data captured in other ways, such as through scanners or files imported from other computers, need to be screened for out-of-range data. Again, the advantages of distributive processing are obvious. Detecting out-of-range data centrally results in a more cumbersome set of procedures for correcting errors. If errors are detected within the school where the correct values can be more easily established, it is relatively easy.

One reason to go to school-based student information systems is to make it possible to examine a broad range of data in an integrated fashion. For example, school principals are often on the receiving end of a wide variety of computer printouts from different sources. They may get attendance reports from the central student accounting system, test results from the state assessment programs and/or the district's standardized test scoring service, listings of students eligible for compensatory education, report card grade summaries, or locally developed criterion-referenced test results. With a school-based student information system, such files can be imported into the school computer so that relationships among these various indicators of student progress can be examined, with inconsistencies noted and followed up. Effective information systems make it possible to examine a wide variety of student data in a correlated manner.

In addition to facilitating the examination of trends across domains of data, effective information systems make it possible to examine data over time. For example, longitudinal data can help to spot a student whose achievement growth seems to have leveled off, or one whose truancy rate has suddenly increased, or one whose grades have begun to decline. This type of "early warning system" can be built into such systems if longitudinal data are available.

Another powerful anlaytic tool is longitudinal data aggregated to the classroom level. For example, a principal who can study relationships between curriculum pacing and student achievement growth for all the classrooms in that school has a better chance of exerting instructional leadership than one who does not have access to that kind of data. An effective information system makes it possible to examine data at the student, classroom, and school levels. Longitudinal trends for the school as a whole are important in assessing how well the school is moving toward its goals.

One possible byproduct of a school-based microcomputer system is an increase in the level of inquiry on the part of the professional staff in the school. When data are easily available and data displays arranged in provocative combinations, serious professionals will tend to "browse" through those displays. Then, when they encounter a surprising result, they will look to see if there are other incidences of that phenomena or will search for factors that may have brought it about. Inquiry can be a guiding force in school change, but the tools for conducting inquiry have to be available. An effective information system, which allows for ad hoc inquiries, is such a tool.

Specifications for a School-Based AIS

What is critical is that the design of the school AIS system have built-in incentives for the school personnel to use the system. The local school AIS must offer the kinds of data that principals need in order to effectively provide classroom-level diagnostic information that is able to guide the supervisory talent available in the schools for staff development. It must provide test-scoring services that teachers are willing and able to use, information to the social workers regarding chronic truancy and attendance patterns, and information directly to the teachers as to the available instructional materials that would be particularly helpful for the students in that classroom given recent test results.

The school-based AIS should have the following features:

1. It has an integrated software package that provides data management facilities and communication capabilities, making it possible to easily download files from the district's central computer which are relevant to the school and send summaries of school-level data back to the district files at the level of detail the district needs for system-wide purposes.
2. It includes a scanner that provides test-scoring services as well as updates the school-based student files with the latest achievement information.
3. It is menu-driven so that school personnel are able to begin to use it easily, and it can generate CRT displays as well as produce printouts that principals can easily share with other professional staff in the building.
4. It has an easily learned set of commands for making inquiries that were not anticipated in the menu options.
5. It has a secure password system so that unauthorized users cannot have access to confidential data that they have no right to see.

There are several commercial systems currently available that perform some of these functions, but none seems to provide the kind of flexibility needed to adapt to local differences in how education is conducted. Given the availability of sophisticated application packages, we think it is highly advantageous to develop and adapt these systems to local differences, such as the types of criterion-referenced tests being used, ways in which student tracking and attendance accounting is conducted, the types of special services available in the buidling for students, etc. It also makes it easier to be adaptive to the curent central computer's file structures and methods of handling data.

Policy, Privacy, and Power Issues

In addition to the technical issues already considered in this chapter, it is critical to mention that there are many nontechnical issues always present in the consideration of automated information systems. Those issues relate to policies surrounding the use of such systems, protection of the data's confidentiality, and the relationship between information and power.

In the design of automated information systems, it is critical to build in procedures for protecting privacy and the confidentiality of data that are in such a system. These are, of course, very serious requirements. One important feature of the new software systems is that they contain provisions for making files secure and available only to those who have authorization to view them, and a secure password system is an essential component of school-based systems.

One feature of a bureaucracy, such as a school district, is the relationship between information and power. One of the reasons people become nervous as school districts build centralized computer-based information systems is that there tends to be a power shift to those technocrats who control the central system. An advantage of the concept of distributed processing which is advocated in this chapter is that it reduces the likelihood of this power shift since it distributes information to those who need it throughout the system. It also reduces the likelihood that any single office or person will be able to use the available information selectively (i.e., use data that support or enhance their position and suppress data that refute or embarrass). By making information more generally available, that danger is significantly reduced.

7 PROGRAM DOCUMENTATION

Introduction

One underlying theme of the preceding chapters concerns the importance of decision-oriented researchers developing alternatives to existing professional practices in order to better meet specific types of information needs of system managers. In our experience, one such alternative that may be profitably pursued involves program documentation. In this chapter we will discuss what is meant by program documentation. We identify kinds of management information needs to which this research strategy is responsive. Evidence from two case histories will illustrate how documentation works. Finally, we will discuss methodological problems associated with this approach. (Portions of this chapter have been adapted from Bickel, 1984.)

Program Documentation Defined

Program documentation in its broadest sense means building a responsive research capability into an innovation process. In our experience this research capability had two primary goals. The first involved developing a detailed description of the design and implementation processes of an educational innovation as they happened. What occurred? What constraints were encountered? How did planners and participants respond to issues that surfaced? What decisions were made and why? How did the program evolve over time? These were the kinds of questions that helped to structure the writing of a "documentary history" of an educational innovation. The purpose of such a history, in the context of DOER, was to build an "institutional memory" into the educational system. Detailed records of previous innovations were an important database that enabled system managers to learn from past experiences in ways that benefited new innovative efforts.

The second goal of program documentation, closely linked to the first, involved providing information about the program to planners and participants as the innovation was being implemented. The formative, improvement-oriented goal associated with documentation produced an evolving, online research process that enabled managers to assess continuously the level and quality of implementation being attained. This formative database aided managers in making systematic course corrections that would improve the reform efforts.

Program documentation, therefore, as a strategy that can be usefully applied for decision-oriented research, has a long-term goal of helping a system become more reflective about its own reform processes; a more immediate short-term goal is to improve innovation processes as they occur. Methods appropriate to reaching these documentation goals are diverse. Certainly research strategies associated with field research generally, and case study research specifically, are important to the writing of the documentary history, as are methods directly associated with historiography. The formative goal, however, implies no necessary methodology, but rather the general strategies we have discussed in relation to DOER (e.g., client orientation, being methodologically eclectic). What we did was contingent upon the specific information needs of a particular program context.

Documentation first emerged in the context of a district-initiated school improvement program (case 5). This use of research resources was further tested and refined in case 9, which involved the development of a teacher center for secondary educators.

Several shared characteristics of the two system initiatives described in case 5 were important factors in influencing management interest in documentation in these contexts. First, both the school improvement program and the teacher center were locally designed initiatives that were unprecedented in the system. In the case of the school improvement program, the district's goal was to apply multiple district resources effectively at the building level to improve instructional processes. What was unique here (from the system's point of view) was the school focus, the commitment to data-driven planning, and the linking across traditional organizational boundaries (e.g., special and regular education, administrative and support services) in ways that permitted a much more focused and coordinated application of district resources. Similarly, the teacher center was also unprecedented, particularly in terms of the scope of the program (i.e., across substantive issues pertaining to content area disciplines, pedagogy, and understanding adolescents), and the length and timing of teacher involvement (eight weeks out of the classroom during the school year). Nothing like these two programs had been tried in the system before.

An important second characteristic shared by these programs was that they were heavily developmental in nature. That is, the programs were not in the position of being merely "transfer" efforts, taking an existing product to a new site (like the installation of a newly purchased reading curriculum). Rather, in both cases, the programs began with little more than a set of broad system objectives, lots of new ideas, and enthusiastic participants. The substance of the programs was developed as the planning and implementation activities proceeded.

A third shared characteristic of the two programs that stimulated management interest in documentation concerned the fact that both efforts clearly had implications beyond the immediate innovation context. The school improvement effort was initiated by the system explicitly as a pilot program. The goal was to start with an initial set of seven elementary schools. Procedures found to be effective in improving instructional processes in these seven were eventually to be disseminated to other schools in the system. The teacher center had broader implications for two reasons. By the first year of implementation, the system was planning a comparable program for elementary teachers. In addition, the center had national implications as evidenced by the amount of nonlocal, private foundation support it received. Further, the timing of its focus on secondary education was propitious indeed, given the national reports that focused on the quality of instruction in high schools released around the time of the center's second year of planning. The district's development of the center was seen as anticipating the problem and being ahead in the development of an effective response.

These three shared characteristics of cases 5 and 9 — the unprecedented nature of the programs, their developmental emphases, and their broader implications for the system — were critical factors in stimulating a management interest to build a research capability into the implementation process. The management was interested in data that could help shape the quality of the programs as they developed. It also wanted a record of their development so that what was learned could be applied in other contexts.

These factors are not idiosyncratic to the two programs involved. On the contrary, it is certainly true that educational organizations often find themselves undertaking initiatives that possess one or more of the aforementioned characteristics shared by these programs. Under such circumstances, the formative and chronicling functions of documentation would be valuable program assets to system managers. In effect, these characteristics can be viewed as a basis for decision rules to assist managers in deciding when documentation should be employed. This use of finite research resources is certainly not equally justifiable in all circumstances. And, where a "new program" is a relatively routine effort, the expenditure of research resources to this degree may not be warranted.

It is important to note that one kind of educational system, school districts, are finding themselves increasingly in the position of implementing "nonroutine," locally developed reform initiatives. There are a variety of reasons for this occurrence, but a major factor has been a diminished federal role in initiating educational change during the last half-decade. Coupled with the fact that many districts are facing tightening budgets, documentation offers the potential benefit of helping managers get the most out of a new initiative by carefully monitoring its progress, by improving the work where data indicate, and by chronicling the effort so that future reform efforts can benefit from past experience.

We have discussed the general conceptual nature of program documentation as we are using the term, and reasons why system managers might find this use of research resources profitable. It is perhaps useful at this point to draw a few examples from one of the case studies on how documentation actually worked. In the summer prior to the opening of the teacher center, the documenter met with the program's management and discussed possible documentation goals and methods for the coming year. The research experiences of the past planning year were drawn upon to help shape priorities in the research plan. Both clients and researchers agreed that a continued tracking of the overall planning process was important to an understanding of the program's development. It was decided that the documenter would continue to observe all relevant planning meetings. Field notes would be taken, structured by three broad questions: What were the key issues confronted by planners? What decisions were reached in relation to these issues? How did the program change as a result of the decisions made? Supplementing the observations of planning meetings was the continued collection and filing (chronologically) of all documents, planning memos, etc., generated by the program.

A second priority for center documentation concerned gathering feedback from various participants. Questions here involved: What had occurred? How could the program be improved? Surveys were developed and administered to participating teachers at the end of each cycle. Further, sample observations of program activities were conducted, as were "exit" interviews of a small number of teachers as a cycle ended.

The third priority established for documentation activities through these discussions concerned the newly developed role of clinical resident teacher (CRT). These teachers were responsible for working with incoming visiting teachers on teaching processes. The CRT role was perhaps the most unprecedented feature of the center's program. Again, a series of surveys, interviews, and field observations were conducted to describe what was occurring and how it could be improved.

In combination, the data collected from the foregoing research activities were integrated into a chronological archive. This database provided an overview of the evolving program, as well as information gathered from more detailed investigations of specific program features considered to be of high priority. A theme that ran through planning for documentation the first year of center operation, and all subsequent years, was the importance of selection and focus. Any documentation effort could only have provided an incomplete picture of all the events surrounding a program's implementation. It was critical that research efforts were focused in ways that were most useful to the program involved. The dialogue that took place between the clients and researchers at the beginning of each year, and during the year's work as needed, was an essential vehicle for focusing documentation research in both cases 5 and 9.

The school improvement program and center documentation plans began with the two goals already noted: (1) producing information as the programs are implemented to help planners make course corrections, and (2) chronicling the innovation process so the system can use past experiences to benefit new initiatives. As the documentation work progressed, it became clear that documentation was serving a variety of functions, some which related directly to the two initial goals just noted, and some which were quite unanticipated. Both the anticipated and unexpected functions are described in the next section.

Functions of Program Documentation

Six categories or types of research functions emerged from the documentation work. The need for these functions was validated over time through numerous discussions with program clients and participants. It should be kept in mind that the functions described are not mutually exclusive; they overlap in important ways. Further, it is worth noting that the importance of each function varied from program to program, and at any given point in time in a particular program's development. Rarely were all of the functions being exercised simultaneously. The patterns of variation reflected the changing needs of the clients as a program moved from early design stages to actual implementation. However, three years of experience across two rather different program contexts gave evidence that these functions were not idiosyncratic in nature. Further, they may be suggestive of tasks worth pursuing by decision-oriented researchers in other educational system contexts.

Improving the Program

Clearly, an important, explicit function of program documentation is the production of information that planners and implementors can use to develop new within-program initiatives or to modify existing ones. This function is what Scriven (1967) has termed formative evaluation. Of course, much of what a documenter does can be thought of as formative evaluation. However, the term here is used to refer to more formal research activities specifically designed to gather data for reshaping program initiatives. This kind of ongoing data collection, analysis, and dissemination was a central goal for documentation in both the school improvement program and teacher center contexts.

In the school improvement program, for example, a number of research activities were initiated over the years, designed to answer questions about a specific component or to develop a broad picture of the implementation status of the program. Very early in the life of the school improvement program, the documenter assisted the team in developing a needs assessment for each of the seven schools. An emphasis was placed on teachers' identifying what they thought were their most critical needs. The team used these data to help shape their initial activities.

Later, as the program developed, perceptions were gathered through various research activities about how particular components were operating and what might be done to improve the program in these areas. For example, detailed observations by the documenter of a faculty steering committee in one of the schools suggested that there were a number of potential difficulties in fully implementing this concept. Surveys and interviews of teachers and administrators were conducted in the other schools to test whether similar problems had emerged. The research focused on how each school committee was functioning, what constraints had been encountered, and what might be done to improve the process. The data produced were used by the school improvement program team to plan summer in-service programs designed to improve the communication and organizational skills of steering committee members.

Similarly, a variety of research activities were used in the context of the teacher center work to generate information to assist planners in making mid-course corrections. For example, district planners worked with the documenter to install a variety of participant feedback mechanisms. One such mechanism gave teachers time to reflect on their experiences at the mid-point of each eight-week cycle. Grouped by discipline area, teachers were asked to discuss the strengths and weaknesses of the program, arrive at a consensus, and present their views in an open forum to center planners. The data produced through these activities had a powerful impact on the direction of the program, with significant differences emerging in the basic program organization as a direct result of this type of feedback.

Serving as a Technical Resource

In one sense, a great deal of documentation activity can be thought of as serving a technical resource function. However, the term here is intended to encompass a particular class of research activities. These fall into several categories. One involves developing basic displays of large databases in ways that are useful to planners. The other involves identifying what is known in the field that might be useful to a particular program's implementation. While technical questions, as the term is used here, can surface at any point in a program's history, they tended to occur more often in early design stages or when a major new initiative was contemplated.

One of the earliest examples of the first type of technical function occurred in the school improvement program when the team was seeking to identify classrooms in most need of supervisory support. With seven sites and over 140 classrooms involved, this was no easy task. The documenter worked with the team to define the kinds of criteria of greatest interest to them, and eventually produced displays of the amount of achievement growth that was realized in each classroom. Classrooms were identified where little or no growth had occurred for a number of years. No one believed that such an analysis would provide all the data needed to set supervisory priorities. However, when combined with other data such as the perceptions of principals, this kind of analysis of a large database served as a useful place to begin more intensive diagnostic activities at the classroom level.

Another kind of technical function concerned the issue of linking the programs to the larger field. For example, there were numerous school improvement programs underway across the country (Odden and Dougherty, 1982) when the school improvement program began its development. While the school improvement program had some relatively unique features (e.g., the participant schools did not volunteer to be in the program), there was still reason to believe that the work in Pittsburgh could be informed by that of other improvement projects in the nation. Further, the literature on the implementation of educational innovations was relevant to many of the issues confronting the school improvement program team as they attempted to install new program initiatives. Summaries of relevant literatures were prepared, either at the director's request or at the initiation of the documenter. Similar requests were made by teacher center leadership early in the planning process. This linking function strikes one as being quite important in education, helping to avoid a "redesigning the wheel" syndrome that too often characterizes system innovation processes.

Additional examples of what might be termed technical functions surfaced. These included such activities as assisting program managers in writing proposals for supplementary funding, developing papers that described their work for presentation at professional societies, and designing informational reports that kept district leadership informed about the programs.

Serving as a Source of Reference

Research activities for both programs included numerous observations, surveys, and interviews. They also involved the collection and cataloging of the various written documents issued during the course of the work. In combination, these activities provided a fairly complete archive of the "material life" of the projects and a comprehensive chronicle of the flow of the major events of the work.

The various components of the archive were used in several ways. For example, quick retrieval of a needed document was made easier by a unified database. More importantly, minutes from meetings and field notes from observations provided a record of issues discussed, commitments made, and ideas suggested. A good example of how this kind of record was helpful occurred in the teacher center program.

An essential vehicle for center development was a series of weekly planning meetings of key district personnel chaired by the center's director and principal. These meetings were used as forums for reviewing a wide array of data regarding the development of the center. As a result of these reviews, decisions were made about the directions the program should take in the future. One of the first requests made of the documenter by the center's director was to observe these meetings and record the decisions reached by the core planning group. In addition to "decisions reached," these notes of the documenter have also included "issues still outstanding." These issues highlighted areas that needed the attention of the planners in the perception of the documenter. The unresolved issues were identified either as a result of reviewing notes from the previous discussions of the planning group, or from other data collection activities of the documenter throughout the program. Each planning meeting began with a review of the documentation commentary from the previous meeting. If discrepancies in perceptions existed (among the planners or between the observer's viewpoint and a planner), they were discussed and a consensus was developed.

Displaying for discussion the decisions reached and questions still outstanding gave the planners a useful point of reference. The "decisions" helped to eliminate discrepancies in perceptions. The "issues" commentary contributed toward focusing the agenda for future planning meetings. Also, in both instances, the documenter made an additional contribution through the way he "framed" the decisions or issues to be considered by planners. To the extent that the framing was data-driven, it was an important vehicle for linking research and decision processes.

As is typical in the implementation of complex programs, the rush of events in both the school improvement program and the center had a way of providing its own momentum for the work. An immediate problem or crisis at times obscured earlier program commitments or objectives. Having a database for reference provided useful information for keeping the program on target. Similarly, records such as the commentary on the center's key planning meetings served as a useful point of reference for planners as they addressed a myriad of complex issues during the early years of program implementation. This reference function played by the documenter in cases 5 and 9 was not too dissimilar from Patton's (1980) discussion of the role process historian.

> In the wilderness education program I was a full participant observer and described my role to the groups as "keeper of the community record." The staff of the project explained that they had asked me to join the project because they wanted someone who did not have direct ego involvement in the success or outcomes of the program to observe and describe what went on, both because they were too busy running the program to keep detailed notes about what occurred and because they were too involved with what happened to be able to look at things relatively dispassionately. There was agreement from the beginning that the community record I produced would be accessible to everyone (p. 171).

Serving as a Sounding Board

One important function that emerged from the documentation experience was quite unanticipated. It involved being a sounding board for ideas, conflicts, and even frustrations among program participants. This function emerged in both cases.

The sounding-board function did not come automatically in either program context. There was a trial period that included a variety of questions from participants about the purposes and benefits of documentation. For example, how will conflicting information be handled? Does the admission of a concern or difficulty endanger the participant's status? Are the documenter's ideas useful? Patton (1980) describes this as the "entry period of field work . . . when the observer is getting used to the new setting and the people in that setting are getting used to the observer" (p. 171). Wax (1971) refers to this time of testing as the "first and the most uncomfortable stage of field work" (p. 15).

While a variety of participants used the documenter as a sounding board, this type of interaction most often occurred with the school improvement team and the teacher center's director and principal. For example, in each program formal and informal debriefing sessions were held with the documenter. In the school improvement program these sessions tended to be regularly scheduled team meetings where an open-ended review of the program and discussions of problem areas and possible solutions occurred. Team members commented on the value of having an "outside observer/participant" present at these meetings in helping them to focus on relevant program issues and to maintain a problem-solving approach to those issues. With the center, this function emerged most often in informal conversations, particularly where a new program initiative or idea to solve a problem was discussed.

There were a number of factors that underscored the utility of the sounding-board function. One important factor stems directly from the way mid-level administrative positions tend to be structured in educational systems. Frequently, individuals in these positions work in relative isolation from their immediate peers and from their superiors.

The director's position in the school improvement program exemplified this phenomenon of administrative isolation. The director's immediate superiors had responsibility for the operation of a significant proportion of the educational programs in the district. No matter how willing and talented the persons in these positions were, it was impossible for them to have direct daily contact with program operations. The director did not have a co-director as a peer on the project to whom he could logically turn to in order to try out new ideas and strategies. Of course, the director might (and did) involve the supervisory team and participating principals in such discussions, but this approach had limitations. Too frank a discussion of alternatives that subsequently might not be implemented could have raised confusion and anxiety on the project. Under such circumstances, the program documenter acted as a useful sounding board for new ideas and initiatives. With confidentiality as a ground rule, all possibilities might be explored without the danger of ripple effects in the implementation process.

The teacher center experience differed from that of the school improvement program in that the phenomenon of administrative isolation was lessened considerably by the ongoing series of high level planning meetings. These kept the center's director and principal in close touch with the district's administrative hierarchy. However, other factors still seemed to support the utility of the sounding-board function.

First, with the goal of formative evaluation, the documenter was likely to be involved in continuous data collection activities across various levels and sites of a program's implementation process. (This held true for both cases.) Thus, the perspective of the researcher presumably was broader than that which might be expected from a participant intimately involved at one level or in one site. Second, the researcher's perspective also was informed by systematically collected data. All of this is not to suggest that the perspective of the on-site researcher was the only one to be valued. On the contrary, it consistently was the experience of this work that the researcher was only one of numerous sources of information. However, the documenter was a particularly useful source to managers, to the extent that the information provided was data-based and had some breadth to its perspective.

One other factor supported the sounding-board function in both programs. This concerned the fact that both directors were new in the roles; indeed the roles themselves were new. This probably increased the desire, in the words of one director, to "bounce ideas in a safe, objective context before taking them to the world."

Increasing Program Cohesiveness

Another unanticipated effect of documentation was that what might be called the cohesiveness of the program benefited from the amount of information that was shared among a program's participants as a result of research activities. The formative evaluation exercises conducted in both programs generally resulted in verbal and written summaries that were shared among planners and participants. This is similar to Patton's (1980) "community record." The dissemination of this information had several beneficial effects.

For one, participants had a broader perspective on the program. Individuals functioning in one dimension of these complex programs gained a sense of how other components were fairing. For example, when results of research analyzing the school improvement steering committee process were disseminated, a number of participants commented that they were relieved to know that their committee wasn't the only one experiencing difficulty. The shared information had the effect of helping participants focus on more generalized implementation issues rather than developments that were, or had been presumed to be, idiosyncratic to a particular site.

Information produced through documentation also tended to increase cohesiveness at times by raising the level of participant understanding of modifications made in the program as mid-course corrections. Such program adjustments were made more palatable because the rationale for them, in part, was based upon publicly available data.

An additional benefit resulting from the sharing of research information was to the research process itself. Data often were shared in open forums where participants could react to the information and challenge or extend specific findings. This was an important mechanism for checking the accuracy of the data and minimizing research bias.

Improving a District's Knowledge Base

One explicit function of documentation that emerged wasn't in relation to the individual programs, but rather to the larger educational system. Having a detailed description of the design and implementation processes associated with the school improvement program and teacher center programs provided a valuable database for the system's leadership to draw upon as they developed future initiatives. This database permitted management to learn from past experiences in ways that benefited new reform efforts. Documentation research, in effect, assisted the system in building a reflective organizational history that was readily drawn upon in subsequent policy and program development efforts.

The reader will recall that this function was intentionally designed into the school improvement program documentation role. Conceived of as a pilot program, one major goal of this program was to develop procedures for increasing student achievement in the seven schools that also could be disseminated to other schools in the district. An example of where this occurred involved the innovative use of supervisory time by the team. A new model for focused, team supervision evolved during the first year of the program (Bickel and Artz, 1984). Documentation data on why the model evolved, its benefits, and what constraints were confronted in implementing it were used by management in developing plans to disseminate certain features of this approach to other schools in the system.

Additional examples of how a documentation database was used in system planning occurred during the third year of school improvement operation. Schools were added to the program. What was learned from the documentation of the experiences of the first three years formed an important part of the database drawn upon by planners in shaping the new school improvement activities.

The teacher center documentation archive served a similar function as the system began to explore the feasibility of implementing a program at the elementary school level. The documenter was asked to participate in early developmental discussions for the elementary center, in part, for the explicit purpose of using knowledge gained through the secondary center's experience to aid elementary planners.

Regardless of the specific function involved, one way of thinking about how documentation was useful in cases 5 and 9 is to understand that the information produced helped shape the working knowledge among participants as the implementation process unfolded. Every program development process begins with a knowledge set about the project among its various participants (Kennedy, 1982). This knowledge set encompasses a wide range of concepts, beliefs, and data concerning the goals of the project, the reasons for involvement, the needs to be faced, the tasks ahead, the resources required to accomplish the program's objectives, and the status of the program at any given point in time. The knowledge set, more often than not, is really a collection of sets with significant variation among participants along dimensions of importance to the development and implementation processes.

The working knowledge of the managers and participants of a program represents the informal "database" that is continually drawn upon during the implementation process as initiatives are developed, activities are engaged in, and decisions are made. These decisions, activities, and initiatives can occur quite apart from considerations about whether the working knowledge is accurate or even collectively shared. The various kinds of information produced through documentation activities can help to shape the working knowledge in ways that benefit the development of programs by raising the amount and quality of knowledge that is shared.

Documentation Methods

Specific research strategies will vary, of course, by the program context, and by the information needs of managers and participants. However, several comments on likely methods for documentation can be made.

The general methodology best suited to the goals of documentation in cases 5 and 9 was what some have termed naturalistic inquiry (Guba and Lincoln, 1981) and others, field research (Bouchard, 1976; Bronfenbrenner, 1976; Leinhardt, 1978; Redfield, 1973; Schatzman and Strauss, 1973). Since these terms can mean different things to different researchers, depending upon their disciplinary perspective, it seems appropriate that the most salient characteristics of these broad methodological domains be described. They are:

1. Data are collected primarily in the field, although other forms of data collection can be used to supplement and verify information gathered in natural settings.
2. The data that are collected concern the field, no matter what the procedure. That is, information is gathered about naturally occurring rather than contrived situations.
3. The instruments and procedures used in data collection and analysis are open-ended enough to provide fertile ground for the generation of hypotheses. They can be both quantitative and qualitative in nature, depending upon the specific question at hand.
4. The field under study is viewed as continuous with and linked to other fields. These linkages are as important to investigate as the elements of the original field (cf. Bronfenbrenner, 1976).
5. A sensitivity to and appreciation of the characteristics of the field under study are required. That is, the researcher must practice what Eisner (1975) refers to as educational connoisseurship and criticism — the arts of perception and disclosure as applied to educational settings.
6. What is encountered in field research may be outside the realm of the researcher's own experience. Thus, the researcher must frequently use "his/her head" (Meehl, 1957) rather than relying primarily on available explanatory concepts or theories.

Field research represents the broadest methodological category in which to place documentation activities. Three additional methodological concepts — the case study, formative evaluation, and participant observation — help to define further the methodological nature of the documenter's role.

The Case Study

Sanders (1981) describes 11 characteristics he associates with case study inquiry. The first five of these would be common to most types of disciplined inquiry. These involve having reasonable access to all important data sources, leaving a data trail to facilitate peer review, building in confirmation steps enabling reported data to be thoroughly scrutinized, using triangulation procedures, and taking care to not extend conclusions beyond what are supported by the data. The characteristics Sanders particularly associates with case study research include the emphasis on inductive reasoning, multiple data bases, rich descriptions, their heuristic function, and the need to be flexible in developing plans and choosing methods. These characteristics of case study research were important guidelines for structuring the documentation research in cases 5 and 9.

Formative Research

Following Scriven's original distinctions, Anderson, Ball, Murphy, and associates (1975) define formative evaluation as "essentially concerned with helping the developers of programs or products through the use of empirical research methodology" (p. 175). Straightforward examples of formative research from the cases include: end-of-cycle interviews and surveys of teacher center participants, and extensive end-of-year surveys of school improvement participants. In each case, a primary intent of the researcher was to collect data systematically from participants on how program operations could be improved.

Participant Observation

Both case study and formative evaluation research methodologies tend to draw upon a wide spectrum of data collection strategies. Many of the tools of historiography, sociology, and anthropology are relevant to this kind of inquiry. Perhaps the single most dominant data collection strategy that was used in the documentation of the school improvement program and teacher center innovations was that of participant observation. McCall and Simmons (1969) described this type of data collection occurring when:

> The fieldworker directly observes the setting but also participates in the sense that he has durable social relations in the setting. He may or may not play an active part in events, or he may interview participants in events which may be considered part of the process of observation (p. 9).

The ongoing involvement of the documenter in the school improvement team's planning meeting was an example of the employment of this methodology where there was an active involvement in the process. Similarly, the recording of decisions reached and outstanding issues for center planning meetings exemplified the participant observation approach.

The foregoing discussions locate documentation in terms of more traditional research methodologies. Another way to describe this work is to refer to field notes taken by the documenter early in the life of the school improvement program at a principals' meeting where it was the principals' first opportunity to hear a description of the research. The documenter stressed several points in the presentation. The primary goals were to produce information about improving schools that would be useful to the program and to the district. In order to do this, the documenter would spend time in their schools and with the consultant team, observing, talking to, interviewing, and surveying participants. Findings would be shared with participants for reflection, verification, and challenge. Sometimes the products would be formal, written reports, but most likely they would consist of informal discussions and conversations. The hope was that the value of the information generated for the program would offset any inconvenience caused by these activities.

Problems in Doing Program Documentation

Several methodological issues are particularly noteworthy as potential problems for the researcher involved in program documentation. In general, the difficulties are quite familiar ones to anyone who has been involved in field research. However, some of these familiar issues may well be exacerbated somewhat when field research methods are employed in a research context that is explicitly decision-oriented.

Observer–Site Interactions

Documentation research in cases 5 and 9 relied heavily on participant–observer data collection strategies. A recurring difficulty encountered in this research concerned the problem of sorting out, in one's observations, what would have occurred without a documenter being present and what occurred as a result of, or heavily influenced by, this presence. Both types of data were important, but understanding which was which influenced the interpretation of a particular event or action. For example, in case 5 one principal had a meeting with a faculty and presented the results of a district-wide testing program. This came in the context of a general push within the school improvement program for principals to exert more instructional leadership in their buildings. Several circumstances surrounding the scheduling of this meeting were unusual. The faculty had no forewarning as to its scheduling or content; the documenter received a special invitation to attend. These occurrences suggested that a primary purpose of the meeting, in the principal's mind, was to demonstrate that leadership was being exercised in that building. The point here is that often things are not what they seem, and in some instances this is true because there is an observer there to see them.

The only answers to the difficulty described above lie in one's general rules of evidence for making inferences, namely, that one must gather as much corroborating data as possible; one must be skeptical, seeking a variety of viewpoints before interpreting an event. These suggestions lie generally in the realm of what Elliot Eisner (1975) has called the exercise of educational connoisseurship and criticism in evaluation research. Furthermore, one must always be interacting with the observed phenomenon, the client, and the participants. Continuous communication loops (mostly verbal) are critical. Every presentation is tentative, every report is a draft, and the subjects and audiences of the work should have ample opportunity to provide feedback.

Balancing the Participant-Observer Roles

An issue that is inherent in the role of participant-observer concerns the question of whether one should directly intervene in an event as it is being observed. This question was, at times, a personally difficult one for the documenter. Taking case 5 as an example, there were steering committee meetings where the process seemed to go awry, and where the interjection of an idea or procedure may have significantly changed the process. With much self-doubt, experience in the school improvement program suggested that nonaction in an immediate situation was generally the best course. Similar situations arose from time to time in the teacher center work.

Nonaction was the better approach for two reasons. First, documentation, by its nature, was committed to trying to influence implementation processes. This commitment was fulfilled through the generation of accurate, useful information for the primary clients. Staying on the sidelines during a particular event did not preclude eventually influencing the future course of the program in ways that would solve the type of problem presented in an immediate situation. Second, a readiness to intervene can have a negative impact on the ability to continue to document. One such instance actually occurred in case 5 when the program's director and one of the principals were involved in a heated debate about the mastery level that should

be set in the principal's school. The documenter interjected data he thought
were relevant to the discussion. Indeed, the data were relevant, but its interjection had the effect of making the documenter appear as if he were taking
sides in the immediate discussion. Subsequent conversations with participants suggested it would have been wiser to wait and share the relevant data
in a less highly charged atmosphere. The point here is that immediate intervention potentially can undercut relationships with clients, or other participants, and certainly risks confusing the documenter's role in a project.

Ethics in Field Research

Any field researcher may end up knowing a lot more than can, or perhaps
more importantly, should be reported. Common sense and experience are
one's primary guides here. For example, one participant in the school improvement program on a particularly frustrating afternoon confessed total
discouragement with the program. This person was in a key position, and, if
the discouragement lasted, it would have had a serious influence on the
progress of the work. Since no ground rule of confidentiality had been established for this particular conversation, the documenter had to decide
what to do with the information. In this case, the discouragement seemed to
be a temporary phenomenon, not rooted in the structure or administration
of the project, and thus the documenter decided that the conversation
should remain private. This perception turned out to be accurate, but the in-
cident could easily have ended with a different outcome. An important skill
in field research concerns the development of what might be termed "situ-
ational savvy" that helps one to decide when to put the pencil down.

Another facet to the issue of when to turn off the recording switch concerns the importance of trading immediate use of information for a deeper
understanding of a problem area. School improvement faculty conversations with the documenter about conditions in their own buildings were
cases in point. Agreeing to confidentiality up front in some instances allowed the documenter to have much greater access to faculty attitudes.
The point came, of course, when a specific issue was serious enough that
the information somehow had to be shared. In such instances, two useful
strategies were to encourage informants to surface the issue themselves or,
at other times, to attempt to focus the attention of program leadership on
an issue without revealing specific sources for the concern. The hope was
that if the managers were able to gather their own evidence, action would
be taken.

Politicalization of the Research Program

The research process runs some risk of becoming politicized when there are competing organizational interests involved in an innovation process. This is so almost to the extent the data produced by documentation are valuable. It is useful to discuss this potential problem in the context of case 9 because the planning process for the center was district-wide, involving sizable amounts of human and material resources. Further, as the center program was implemented, it drew upon numerous resources across traditional organizational divisions in the system. Presumably both of these conditions increased the stake various system offices had in the program and thus risked the politicalization of the developmental process and, in all likelihood, the research activities attached to it. The fact that this did not occur to any great extent in case 9 is of interest, and the possible reasons why it did not may suggest strategies that can be employed in other research contexts.

Five reasons seem to have been important in avoiding the politicizing of center research. First, the information that was produced was shared promptly and freely through the weekly meetings of the core planning group. Second, the research function lay outside the domain of any one district office involved in implementation activities. Third, most if not all of the planners had some prior experience with the researchers, and as a result a certain amount of shared knowledge and trust was present about the functions that could be legitimately fulfilled by the research component. Fourth, like the school improvement program experience, the center's program was breaking new ground in the district. In such circumstances, formative information needs tended to outstrip anxieties about what specific data might hold for a particular position. Finally, it was clear that information produced through specific research activities would be only part of the database used in the making of any specific decision. Organizational histories, resource realities, would all play a part in planning outcomes.

Relationship between Documentation and Summative Evaluation

The theme of taking an improvement orientation to DOER has been noted a number of times in this book. Certainly a major feature of documentation as described here is an improvement orientation. Case 5 provided evidence that underscored the value of improvement orientation and the difficulty that could be encountered in trying to combine formative and summative research. Summative evaluation and documentation were implicitly linked in the original school improvement action plan. The ambiguity created through this linkage was a serious and continuing problem during the early months of the program. In many areas, the possibility that documentation data might become evaluation input complicated the interaction with participants. There was a danger that it would cut off communication or, at least, restrict it to "safe" topics.

The problem was avoided at the outset of case 9. The research plan developed by the district and the researchers explicitly outlined distinctive documentation and impact research plans and located the responsibility for their implementation in separate offices.

Another important reason to separate documentation and summative evaluation functions is that the two tasks, as typically envisioned by policy makers, are quite different, having different goals and often different data collection strategies. Having said that the two functions should be separated where possible, it is also recognized that some overlap probably will always occur, whether real (i.e., eventually some of the documentation data will turn up as fair grist for a summative evaluation mill), or imagined (i.e., participants see a potential overlap whether a design requires it or not).

Documenter Bias

A critical problem in this type of research concerns observer–participant bias. The very essence of documentation research involves becoming closely immersed in a program's operation. This is a strength of documentation in that it greatly enhances the opportunity to collect data on the life of the program. It is a danger to the extent that the researcher loses perspective by such close contact.

The bias issue in this context has two important elements to it. One, discussed most directly in chapter 3 in relation to client orientation, involves unwarranted client influence on the researcher. The precautions noted in chapter 3 also pertain to the documentation context. Making one's methods, evidence, and findings publicly available can be most helpful in diminishing unwarranted client–researcher manipulations.

A second aspect of the observer bias issue that is probably exacerbated in the documentation context concerns the unasked question. The question the researcher doesn't think to ask because he/she may be too close to the phenomenon under investigation. Here the issue is less one of unethical influence than one of insight parochialism. One's questions can become overly dominated by the "realities" of the particular program context. Guarding against this kind of parochialism is particularly difficult because it occurs by omission. Perhaps the most important tactic a documenter can take to minimize this source of bias is to maintain contact with the larger fields of research and educational innovation. Through computer networks that now link educational system research offices, professional associations like the American Educational Research Association, the Evaluation Network, and the Evaluation Research Society, system documenters can share perceptions and broaden their bases for developing research questions in their own program contexts.

Case 9 provides an example of how contact with the "larger field" can be helpful in shaping documentation activities. The center had a distinguished board of visitors consisting of eminent educators and researchers from across the country. Each year the board would conduct a site visit and critique various aspects of the program. Inevitably these visits raised some issues that were not previously considered by the program's managers or the documentation research team. Whether the issue was increasing the research emphasis on the role of principals in supporting center efforts in the home school, or shifting the balance of research methods from observations and surveys to more intensive structured interviews, interactions with the board stand out as important and sometimes disconcerting experiences. They had the effect of broadening program horizons and challenging emerging research findings. This kind of contact, through various mechanisms, can be most helpful in documentation research.

The aforementioned methodological concerns clearly are not unique to program documentation. They are associated with traditional concerns about doing sound research in the field. The specific suggestions given for avoiding or minimizing the inherent dangers can be viewed as augmenting in some instances, and complementing in other cases, methodological cautions already mentioned in earlier chapters.

Summary

In this chapter we have discussed the implications of designing a research capability into an innovation process. Referring to this approach as program documentation, we have described its essential features and the functions it fulfilled in two case histories. Finally, we have reviewed general methods and several methodological issues associated with field research generally that are important to consider when doing program documentation.

The use of research resources for documentation seems to respond to very important information needs of system managers. Documentation can directly contribute to a manager's ability to increase the likelihood that an innovation will reach its full potential. It does this by (1) providing data along the way that can aid in improving the program as it is implemented, and (2) significantly increasing organizational memory in ways that allow managers to learn more readily from past experiences in order to benefit future innovative efforts. School districts seem to have become particularly active in designing locally developed reform efforts. Such circumstances are opportune for program documentation to produce useful benefits for an educational system.

8 UNDERSTANDING ACHIEVEMENT TEST RESULTS

Given all the controversy surrounding standardized testing, it seems necessary to devote a separate chapter to what is known about the major factors that explain test score variation. Considerable confusion continues to surround the interpretation of test results. Throughout the testing controversy taking place in the media, in the courtrooms, and in legislative bodies, schools continue to give standardized tests, and educators and laymen continue to make a variety of valid and invalid inferences regarding what may have caused the resulting variation in the test scores. Whether it is the variation among students within a classroom, among classroom means within a school, among school means within a school district, among district means within a state, or most recently, among state means that everyone has his/her preferred explanation for the differences that occur. This chapter describes an approach to explaining achievement test results that we have found useful in our Pittsburgh experience.

It is possible to explain the variance in standardized test scores by starting with a very simple causal model. A student's current test score will be a function of two major factors: (1) the student's abilities at some prior time and (2) the amount of relevant learning activity in which the student was engaged between that prior time and the current test. The relevance of the learning activity depends upon whether the test sampled the particular skills or subject matter the given student was taught between the prior measure and the current measure, and whether the learning tasks were at an appropriate difficulty level for the student's current abilities.

Let us consider the evidence for this simple model. The degree to which the current performance depends upon prior performance is well established. How well students can perform today is very dependent upon how well they could perform last month or last year. This prior performance is the most important factor in determining current performance, and the extent of the relationship depends upon the amount of time elapsed between the two measures and the functional relevance of the particular measure of prior ability to the current performance. Research relevant to this principle has generally found that prior performance explains between 50 and 80 percent of the variance (i.e., correlations between .70 and .90) in current performance. (See, for example, Cooley and Lohnes [1976] for a summary of that research.)

Turning to the amount of relevant learning activity as an explanation of current test performance, the first consideration is whether or not the activity could have produced the skills or knowledge that were sampled by the standardized test. We call this consideration "curriculum overlap" (Leinhardt and Seewald, 1981; Leinhardt, 1983).

Curriculum overlap refers to the degree to which the test is sampling the same domain that the instruction was designed to teach. It is a measure of how much a test is biased in favor of or against a given child's curricular experiences. In its extreme, the principle is very obvious. One does not give a test in physics to assess the achievement of students who have been studying chemistry even though both are in the domain called science. But this concept is easily confused even when it should be obvious. A classic case was the evaluation of the new physics curriculum developed by the Physical Science Study Committee (PSSC), in which the evaluators contrasted it with traditional physics using a standardized physics test. The test was obviously biased in favor of traditional physics courses so it was not surprising that the new PSSC physics course did not prove its superiority in such an evaluation.

It is also true that there has been a tendency to underestimate the influence of curriculum overlap in less obvious cases, such as reading, for example. Reading materials can differ in subtle ways that still are important in explaining why some children perform better than others on a given standardized test. This may depend upon how similar the workbook exercises were to test items or whether the particular vocabulary in the lessons matched the particular vocabulary in the test. Leinhardt and Seewald (1980) have summarized some of the evidence that has been accumulated on the importance of curriculum overlap in explaining variation in student test performance. Curriculum overlap is second only to prior performance in explaining current performance. It adds as much as 20 percent to the variance explained by prior performance (Cooley and Leinhardt, 1980).

The other consideration in estimating the relevance of the learning activities is whether the learning tasks were appropriate for the child's current ability. Appropriateness is a function of whether the child has been assigned or is choosing learning activities that are too easy (that is, nothing new is learned) or too hard (that is, the lesson requires knowledge or skills that have not yet been learned). We call this a concern for structure because it involves specifying the structure of knowledge or skills to be taught (or at least the designed sequence of the set of lessons used in teaching it) and locating a child with respect to that structure. The kinds of tests that are useful for this location task are what Glaser (1963) called criterion-referenced tests. The function of such a test is to identify where a child is with respect to a curriculum structure. If learning activities are selected on the basis of a good match between curriculum structure and current abilities estimated either formally or informally, then the amount of learning will be enhanced.

It is perhaps useful at this point to take a side excursion into the business of aptitude-treatment interactions (ATI). It has become generally recognized that this search has been rather futile (e.g., Bond and Glaser [1979] review of Cronbach and Snow [1977]). That is, no one seems to be willing to claim that a strong, consistent interaction has been found that is worthy of consideration in making instructional decisions. In a review of this research, Gustafsson (1980) concluded that we probably will never find measures of "aptitudes" that determine instructional branching decisions. But we certainly can find a measure of individual difference that determine what a child is taught, and that good teachers use every day. The relevant individual difference is the child's current ability in the skills and knowledge being taught. If one considers a performance on a criterion-referenced test an aptitude, then in the search for "subtle aptitudes" that should determine instructional decisions, such as learning styles or field dependence, we have missed the big aptitude that must be considered in varying instruction, the child's current abilities relative to what is being taught.

This concern for structure is illustrated by the manner in which Fisher, Filby, Marliave, Cahen, Dishaw, Moore, and Berliner (1978) defined ALT (academic learning time). They did not simply measure how much time a child engaged in learning, but rather how much time a child engaged in learning activities in which the child experienced a high rate of success. Structure is also what Taylor (1977) had in mind when he suggested we go beyond ATI to a consideration of his index of learning difficulty (ILD). The ILD is a measure of the amount of difficulty one will encounter in learning from a communication.

The evidence for the importance of structure is not as strong as for prior abilities and curriculum overlap. Often the evidence is only indirect, as in Bloom's (1976) studies of mastery learning. Also, formal procedures for establishing an appropriate difficulty level have not had the expected effect because some teachers use formal methods poorly and other teachers use informal methods well. Although there may not exist a clear, convincing meta-analysis of the importance of structure, it seems hard to resist the notion that if children are spending time on lessons that they do *not* have the prerequisite skills to master, they will not learn as much as they would if they *had* the prerequisite skills.

Now given this rather simple but hopefully convincing model for explaining the variance in standardized test scores, let us consider some of the things one might do to increase performance on such tests and see whether any of them seem sensible. For a given set of students at a given time, entering ability cannot be manipulated. Of course, the easiest way for a teacher or a school to look good on student outcomes is to select on entering abilities. However, in the context of considering how to improve standardized test performance, that is not a relevant manipulation. It does, though, illustrate the common major fallacy involved in comparing school means, i.e., inferring that schools with higher means are somehow doing a better job of educating their students, when in fact they are simply serving students with higher entering abilities. Recognizing the importance of prior abilities is also important in tempering the often immodest expectations associated with new educational programs (particularly the expectation of finding significant effects in standardized test scores following modest adjustments in the program).

To increase test performance for a given set of students, the amount of relevant learning activity must be increased. As has been indicated, there are two ways in which learning activities can be relevant to explaining performance on a standardized test. The first has to do with curriculum overlap. Manipulating curriculum overlap goes on all the time, largely as the result of the accountability movement, and it has people running around in circles, as illustrated by these three anecdotes.

A school district in a state that had adopted the Iowa Test of Basic Skills as a state-wide assessment battery decided to mount a major effort to bring their curricula "closer in line with" the knowledge and skills tested in that battery. It was felt that this would result in higher test scores, and thus the district would look better when the state published the results of that testing program.

Another school district discovered that criterion-referenced testing is currently hot in this accountability movement. They interpreted this to mean that the test must reflect the content of the curricula, so they purchased the services of a firm that sells "banks" of test items. This kind of system allows the district "to tailor the test to their curriculum" and then report results to the public in terms of the percentage of items correct.

A large state decided to develop its own test battery for assessing the quality of education in that state. Unfortunately, test development began at a time when it was possible to consider other goals for education besides the development of basic skills. By the time the state's department of education had the assessment program up and running, it collided with the basic skills movement, which challenged whether schools had any business interfering with students' self-concepts or their tolerance for other students different from themselves.

What we are witnessing are some schools switching curricula rather than fighting the tests, others switching tests rather than fighting the curricula, others fighting the tests rather than switching curricula, and still others fighting the curricula to save their tests. It is essential that we find a way out of this arbitrary, curricular behavior.

Recognizing the importance of curriculum overlap in explaining student performance on an achievement test forces a consideration of the fundamental question, What is important to learn? That is, to get out of the arbitrariness of changing tests to be more consistent with curriculum or curriculum to be more consistent with tests, it is essential to come to grips with what is important to teach in the first place. Curriculum theory and instructional science can contribute to this consideration, e.g., by making explicit the structure of what is to be taught, by studying how experts differ from novices, and by establishing the transfer value, both vertical and extraschool, of what is to be taught (Cooley and Lohnes, 1976, ch. 3).

Another strategy people are using to increase the amount of learning activity relevant to a particular standardized test is to allocate more time to those activities. This, of course, is one of the big problems with standardized testing programs that are used in accountability efforts. They encourage teachers and schools to emphasize what is measured in their testing program through manipulation of allocated time, without thinking about the relative value of what is being tested versus other school outcomes that are not being tested. Arbitrary allocation of more time to subject matter being tested, without a more general consideration of what is important to teach, is impossible to justify.

So if it is not sensible to manipulate arbitrarily the specifics within subject matter so as to increase curriculum overlap or to arbitrarily shift the relative emphasis among curricula by manipulating the time allocated to different subjects, what does seem sensible? Classroom process research (e.g., Cooley and Leinhardt, 1980; Leinhardt, Zigmond, and Cooley, 1981), has studied ways that teachers might increase the amount of learning activity for a given time allocation for a given curriculum for a given set of students. That research has focused upon three general constructs. One is motivators (the motivating features of the classroom), another is structure (procedures for adjusting the difficulty level of the lessons), and the third is quality of instruction (teacher mediation between pupil and lesson). Figure 8-1 illustrates this more complete model. Let's examine what this implies.

Ebert (1980) has derived from the literature five general principles that aid in assessment of the motivating quality of a learning environment. They are:

1.   The teacher plays a major role in developing and maintaining children's motivation.
2.   To increase motivation, one should address the student's interest and/or relate new skills to previously learned skills and to possible future uses of such skills.

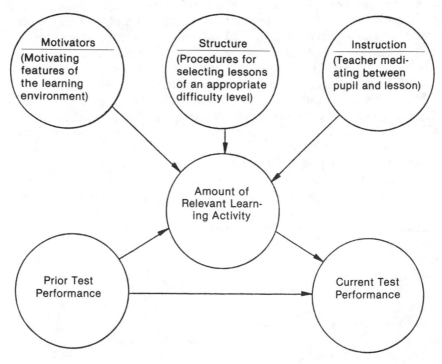

Figure 8-1.   A Simple Model for Understanding Achievement Test Variance

3. Children who had had previous difficulty in school learning may need the aid of an extrinsic reward system to increase their motivation.
4. Motivation increases if the student is given tasks having an optimal level of difficulty. In contrast, motivation decreases if the student encounters frustration or boredom as a result of assignments respectively above or below his/her ability level.
5. Successful learning experiences are needed to create and maintain student motivation (Ebert, 1980, p. 18).

The third motivating principle, the effectiveness of extrinsic reward systems, has been studied extensively and is well established. The fourth and fifth principles show that attention to structure is also an important motivating influence. What is particularly interesting in this list is the importance of student interest. This is another area of individual differences that artful teachers use every day but, as Banks, McQuater, and Hubbard (1978) point out in their review of achievement orientation, surprisingly little empirical research has considered student interest as the basis for selecting lesson content.

The major way in which educators have facilitated the matching of student ability and lesson difficulty (for centuries!) is through grouping students by ability. Having classrooms consist of students who are similar in ability makes it much easier to identify lessons appropriate for that group of students. As other societal goals for education become a reality, teachers were confronted with the task of solving this structure problem within more heterogeneous classrooms. We are finding that lots of teachers need help in figuring out how to do this better.

No model for explaining test performance would be complete without incorporating how much teacher-led instruction is going on. It seems clear that "teacher-proof" lessons are an impossible dream (or nightmare, depending upon your perspective). Teachers can improve the motivating quality of their classroom, they can make sure students are working on lessons they have the skills to master, but they also have to mediate between pupil and lesson in ways that are generally considered instruction. They have to provide models for behaviors, cues for correct responses, corrective feedback, mnemonic techniques, problem-solving strategies, and whatever else it takes to help a child master the components of a lesson. Teachers tend not to realize how little instruction a student receives. For example, in a study of 11 LD (learning disabled) classrooms (Leinhardt, Zigmond, and Cooley, 1980), with only 12 students in each room and with four hours a day allocated to reading, students averaged only 16 minutes a day of teacher-led instruction, and less than two minutes of that involved actual instructional events (defined above).

The causal models that are needed to guide classroom research get more complicated than figure 8-1, in part because measurement problems also have to be considered. However, keeping in mind the probable causal relationships among these six simple constructs helps to keep one's thinking clear when talking about the possible implications of test score results, when helping a school district plan the evaluation of a program, and when trying to help educators think about the results of their test programs and what they might do (or avoid doing) to improve student achievement.

It might be useful to illustrate how we use this model in the context of district-based evaluation. The following are brief summaries of some case histories to illustrate these points.

Case 2

The client (in this case, the school board) was concerned with the relative merits of two grade organization plans currently operating in the district: a K–8 elementary school followed by a four-year high school, and a K–5 elementary school followed by a three-year middle school and four-year high school.

The board was divided on moving to a district-wide middle-school plan, and those opposed pointed out that eighth graders in the K–8 schools were scoring higher on standardized achievement tests than were the eighth graders in the middle school. Their inference was that the K–8 schools were doing a better job of educating these students based on their standardized score results. We showed how the apparent differences disappeared when prior abilities were taken into account.

Case 6

The client (in this case, a director of instruction) was trying to decide among three reading programs currently being used in a Title I program and wanted our help in conducting an evaluation that would allow him to select the most effective of the three programs. He had in mind the usual quasi-experimental contrast using the district's standardized achievement test as the dependent variable. After discussing the (figure 8-1) model, he came to realize that such a three-way race didn't make a lot of sense. The decision was to examine the three programs and determine whether they differed in how they helped teachers adapt the instruction in terms of difficulty level, and also have the supervisory staff work with the teachers on improving the motivating quality of the program since we had also noticed that one of their big problems in this upper grades Title I program was student absen-teeism, suspensions, etc.

Summer Program

The client wanted us to evaluate the effectiveness of some summer take-home materials designed to reduce the high summer loss in achievement among lower socioeconomic status (SES) children. They wanted us to contrast achievement scores for children who had returned the materials in the fall with children who had not. In discussing how this might be done, we discovered that of the 12,000 children that had been given these materials in the spring, only 200 of them had actually returned the materials in the fall. We encouraged them to redirect their attention to a consideration of how it was decided which students got what lessons (i.e., how was the structure problem solved?) and to consider how they might increase both the likelihood that the student would find the materials in-teresting and that the parents would also participate, perhaps by establishing a system of extrinsic rewards for lesson completion.

As was indicated in chapter 3, the most important aspect of DOER is the dialogue between researcher and client. It is an educational process — in both directions. New empirical work may not be necessary, just better thinking and better planning. Although clients often begin a discussion by indicating that they want to compare *outcomes* of different programs or policy options, it is important to point out to them that it is usually not possible to mount a valid, informative, relevant, and timely impact study in the context of district-based evaluation. It seems important, however, that classroom research continue to improve and validate causal models for explaining highly valued school out-comes, and that we get school people to use more valid models as they think about possible ways of improving their educational program. As we work with a school district to identify what might be useful things for district-based research offices to do, we are identifying a number of important functions that are relevant to policy making and program improvement. But we are also quite convinced from this experience that a little "queesy-experiment" of a program's impact is not one of them. See, for example, Cooley (1978) for an elaboration of this important point.

Socioeconomic Status and Achievement

One of the heavily used variables in educational research is socioeconomic status (SES). Within school districts SES became particularly important in the early days of federal compensatory education funding because funds were distributed to schools on the basis of economic need. School districts had to collect data that were descriptive of the families of their students. The most widely used SES indicators were the child's eligibility for free lunch and whether or not the family received aid for dependent children (AFDC).

District researchers soon noticed that such indicators correlated very highly with standardized achievement test results, particularly when such analyses were done at the school level. For example, in a district with many elementary schools, rank ordering the schools in terms of the proportion of children in each building eligible for free lunch produced about the same ordering as using the proportion scoring below the bottom quartile on national achievement norms (within the district correlation among schools usually falling between .80 and .90). Thus school districts suddenly had a very powerful predictor of the achievement level to be expected in each school. Because SES and its relationship to achievement causes so much confusion in district evaluation work, it seems important to review some of the things we have learned about this key variable.

First it is important to recognize how different levels of aggregation influence the strength of the relationship. For example, using nationally representative samples of students, family income correlates about .30 with achievement tests at the student level. Aggregating to the school level, the correlation is between .50 and .60 among school means nationally. If, however, the analysis is done within large urban school districts, the school level relationship is between .80 and .90, as was indicated above.

The high correlation between SES and achievement at the building level is partly due to something that statisticians call the grouping effect. This occurs when membership in the group (e.g., school) is related to either one or both of the variables being correlated. For example, the socioeconomic homogeneity of neighborhood schools produces a relationship between SES and school building, and that relationship produces the larger correlation between SES and achievement at the school level than exists at the student level. Table 8–1 summarizes these various SES–achievement relationships.

The way in which SES is measured also influences the strength of the relationship. As the indicators move from measures that reflect family income to those more likely to influence directly the educational environment of the home (e.g., mother's education, number of books in the home, homework help), the relationship increases.

The fact that the strength of the relationship increases as the SES measures more closely reflect those home processes that can influence student achievement is important in interpreting why the relationship exists. Understanding the why of the relationship is important in considering the rationale for a particular application of that relationship.

Table 8-1. Socioeconomic Background and Achievement

Level	Population Sampled	SES Indicators	Correlation
Student	National	Income	.2 to .4
Student	National	Home environment	.5
School	Large urban district	Income	.8 to .9
School	National	Income	.5 to .6
District	Within state	Income	.2 to .6
State	National	Income	.6

One legitimate application of SES measures is in the search for explanations of why achievement in some schools is lower than in others. Having said that, we must quickly point out that a search for explanations is quite different than a search for excuses. In the grade organization case (case 2), for example, it was important to take SES into account because otherwise the achievement differences among the schools would have been attributed to the known grade organization differences among the schools. If one admits that it is easier to produce higher achievement results in a school where there is strong support for high achievement in the home, then home differences must be taken into account when trying to estimate the possible influences of other ways in which the schools may differ.

Using SES in helping to sort out the relative effectiveness of different educational treatments is not the same as using SES as an excuse for not trying to raise the achievement level in a particular school. It is quite different to say that K-8 elementary schools do not appear to be superior after you take SES into account than to say, the students in this school did not do well on that achievement test, but what do you expect, given the tough neighborhood that school serves. Low achievement is not inevitable in low SES schools (Edmonds, 1979; Bickel, 1983). It is just easier to produce higher achievement results in higher SES schools.

This latter point is important in considering another possible use of SES. Some states and school districts use SES measures in deciding where extra effort may be needed to raise achievement. School achievement levels are compared to those that would be expected (predicted), given the school's SES. If achievement is lower than expected, then special attention is given to that school to see what might be done to raise achievement. If a school's achievement is low, but SES is also low, the implication is "not to worry!" (i.e., What can you expect from such kids?). We do not believe that it is justifiable to use SES-based expectations in determining where educational opportunity may need to be improved. For example, in a targeted school improvement effort where a special task force is created to help improve student achievement in schools, the question of where to focus this effort would seem to be answered by where achievement is lowest, not where achievement is lower than would be expected, given SES. The justification for such extra effort derives from the need to equalize educational opportunity, and the most serious inequities are those that result from differences in home environment.

Our general recommendation with respect to the use of SES is to use it when seeking causal explanations of school factors that influence student achievement, otherwise you might be attributing unusual success to factors that just happen to be related to SES. The other recommendation is *not* to use SES as a statistical control variable when looking for low-achieving situations that are to be improved through extra effort, assuming that the extra effort is a scarce resource and should be distributed on the basis of reducing inequities in educational opportunity.

Another use of SES is to have low SES be the basis for distributing special compensatory services to schools. This may sound like a contradiction to the previous point, but it really is not. It is quite different (and in terms of reducing inequalities in opportunity, quite justifiable) to use SES as a basis for extra resource allocation, than to use it as a way of adjusting achievement differences and assign extra resources where achievement is lower than one might expect, given the SES of the school. It is more difficult to produce good achievement in a low SES school, so the extra effort needed to do that job is justified. In fact, it can be argued that it is more justifiable to distribute extra resources on the basis of low SES than on the basis of low achievement. Let's say that extra effort is given to a low SES school, and through that extra effort achievement is raised to the point that it is now comparable to that of higher SES schools. If achievement were the basis for distributing that extra effort, then it would be taken away from the school where it was needed (to offset differences in opportunity created by home differences) and given to a school with higher SES but lower achievement. It seems safe to assume that when the extra effort is withdrawn, the low SES school would revert to lower achievement. It does not seem rational to establish an incentive system wherein raising the achievement level in a building results in the removal of the extra support that helped make it happen.

9 UTILIZATION AND THE ROLE OF THE DISSEMINATION PROCESS

Introduction

A fundamental goal of decision-oriented educational research is to generate information that is useful to participants in the policy and management processes of educational systems. In this chapter we discuss the broad area of educational research utilization and one particular issue, the role of the dissemination process as it influences utilization. This chapter is divided into four major sections. In the first we review some of the current thinking in the field of educational evaluation regarding what constitutes use. How does one recognize it when it occurs? What is the range of potential "uses" possible and probable for DOER? In the second section, we continue to draw from the literature to identify various perspectives on factors that seem to increase or lower the probability of utilization. The third section focuses on one element in the research process, the dissemination of results, and discusses in detail our experiences and what we have learned about the relationship between dissemination and utilization. The chapter closes with a brief discussion of a relatively novel concept, namely, redissemination and its role in a system's utilization of research information.

Portions of this chapter have been adapted from Bickel & Cooley, 1985.

What is the Nature of Use?

What at first glance might seem to be an easily answered, if not trivial, question is upon closer examination a surprisingly complex issue to analyze. Indeed, the question has been addressed from numerous perspectives including those of policy analysts, political scientists, sociologists, historians, social and organizational psychologists, and educational researchers. The purpose of this chapter must be a modest one: to identify some basic, reasonable markers to employ in a discussion of how research results are used in educational systems. For this purpose we rely heavily on current thoughts among educational researchers. An important caveat here is to note that the literature reviewed most often has program evaluation in mind when reporting results. However, many of the use concepts that have emerged in this context are directly relevant to the arena of DOER.

One of the first issues that must be addressed when trying to define use concerns the view one holds of how organizations arrive at policy or managerial decisions. As we have noted in chapter 1, writers such as Patton (1978) and Weiss (1981) take exception with what they call the traditional view of the decision process that has been employed by some researchers trying to track use. Weiss (1981) indicates that the traditional view overemphasizes a formal, linear decision model. In that model a study is released, recommendations are made based on the research findings, and a decision is implemented that reflects the results of the research. Weiss and others argue that this view of how use occurs misses the mark for several reasons. For the purposes of our discussion here, a primary reason why the traditional view of use is inadequate is because it depicts a relatively inaccurate picture of how organizational decision making works. In contrast, Weiss describes organizational decision making as often giving evidence of what she terms "decision accretion" (1980).

> It [decision accretion] stems from a recognition that many organizational outputs are not decisions by any identifiable group of decision makers. Rather a lot of different people in a lot of different offices go about their work taking small steps without consideration of the total issue or the long-term consequences. Through a series of seemingly small and uncoordinated actions, things happen . . . over a period of time these many steps crystallize into a change in direction (Weiss, 1980).

If one accepts the view that decision and policy generation processes are often diffuse, with "decisions" percolating up or down an organizational structure, then one implication for a search for "use" is that the searcher must necessarily throw a broad net throughout the organization.

A corollary to the idea that a search for use must extend beyond the formalized policy and decision processes in an organization, is the notion that the range of types of use one looks for must be broadened. Rich (1977), Weiss (1981), Leviton and Hughes (1981), and others have distinguished between at least two major types, instrumental and conceptual use. We should note that Leviton and Hughes add a third category, persuasive use. We discuss this category in case 4, but for our broad overview purposes here, we treat this type of use as a subset of the larger category of conceptual use.

Instrumental use refers to documentable use where the information is explicitly employed in the making of a decision, or in solving a problem. This type fits nicely with the traditional model of decision making. The presence of instrumental use would mean that, for example, an identifiable decision maker was observed to have made an explicit decision that was the direct result of or directly influenced by the presence of research results and/or recommendations.

Conceptual use "refers to uses that influence a policy maker's thinking about an issue" (Rich, 1981). With conceptual use there may or may not be an explicit decision or action to be made. What is critical is that the perception or analysis of a problem or issue is influenced by prior research information. Kennedy (1984) provides important evidence regarding how conceptual use influences decisions.

Weiss (1981) points out that there is a danger in attempting to make too arbitrary a distinction between instrumental and conceptual use. She suggests that the best approach is to see "the use of evaluation research as a continuum," having elements of both types in the middle of the continuum (p. 23). Weiss suggests that most evaluation use occurs in this middle ground where "research evidence is taken into account but does not drive the decision — cases where users filter research evidence through their knowledge, judgment, and interests, and incorporate much besides research into decision making" (p. 23). Our case history experiences provide ample evidence of the cogency of Weiss' middle-ground position.

A third consideration in the literature on defining use involves a whole range of contextual factors that can directly affect the type of use one might expect in a given organizational context. For example, Rich (1981) finds different patterns of use emerging over time, with instrumental use most likely to occur in a first wave, "when the information is initially received" (p. 116). A second wave of use seems to occur later on, perhaps "three to six months after the information was initially received" (p. 119). Use in this second wave tends to be of a conceptual type.

Murrell and Brown (1977), Stevenson and McNeill (1979), and others have suggested that the type of use one can expect will probably vary with the kind of evaluation employed and the type of organization involved. As Stevenson (1981) states:

> . . . it may often be uninformative and unreasonable to apply the same utilization criteria to evaluations of major federal programs and local program evaluation activities . . . to the several different kinds of evaluation activity [demonstration, program development, accountability etc.] (p. 39).

Clearly use will also vary by the potential user. In many evaluation contexts there may be multiple potential users, with actual use only occurring with a subset of these.

The preceding discussion only briefly highlights some of the issues related to defining use discussed in the literature. A more complete discussion of this topic can be obtained elsewhere (Ciarlo, 1981; Weiss, 1977; Leviton and Hughes, 1981). What is important here is to employ some of the prevalent concepts in the literature to frame our discussions of use as it occurred in the case histories. To the extent that there is a debate about what constitutes use, our case history experience supports the position of those taking a broader view. In our experience, use occurred at a variety of levels in the organization, varying in degree and types by case, as the result of a variety of contextual and other factors. Specific examples of use are provided in each case history.

Factors That Influence Use

A variety of factors have been identified as being influential in the use of evaluation research results. In addressing this issue some writers (e.g., Rossi and Freeman, 1982; Patton, 1978; Cronbach and associates, 1980; Weiss and Bucuvalas, 1980) have emphasized factors associated with the quality and organization of the evaluation process and its outcomes. Others have stressed internal and external characteristics of the organizations in which use is likely to occur (e.g., Stevenson, 1981; Ein-Dor and Segev, 1978; Love, 1983; Rich, 1981; Alkin, Dalliak, and White, 1979). Still others have found the characteristics of and communications among users and researchers to be significant factors that influence use (e.g., O'Reilly, 1981; Holley, 1983). These broad themes have emerged from numerous studies ranging in methodology from large, retrospective surveys of users or researchers or both, to individual studies of a piece of research and how it came to be used or not, as the case may be. For our purposes, we will briefly review three models of the factors that seem to influence use (Weiss and Bucuvalas, 1980; Alkin, Dalliak, and White, 1979; Leviton and Hughes, 1981). The first two were derived from specific studies of use. The third was based upon a broad review of the literature in this area. These three models have been selected because of their overall range and comprehensiveness, their quality, and the fact that they illustrate some of the ways the issue has been investigated and some of the convergence in thinking in the area over the past decade.

Weiss and Bucuvalas (1980) apply a "sociology of knowledge" (Holzner, 1978) perspective to the examination of questions related to the diffusion and application of knowledge. The authors focus on the identification of "dimensions of research that are salient . . . for [potential users] accepting or rejecting results of research" (p. 302). The authors discuss empirical evidence drawn primarily from interviews of 155 "upper level" officials in federal, state, and local social service-related agencies. The officials were asked to review a sample of research reports and rate them on 29 descriptive dimensions. The rankings were used to identify the frames of reference used by officials to evaluate the research reports.

Five major constructs emerged in the Weiss and Bucuvalas study that are associated with the perceived usefulness of research. One concerned the "Research Quality" of the report (p. 303). Items concerned with technical quality, statistical sophistication, objectivity, quantitative data, and internal consistency (among others) clustered to form a factor that seemed to express a value for the scientific merit of a report.

The second factor identified by Weiss and Bucuvalas, "Action Orientation," related to the "practicality of implementing the findings" (p. 304). Items such as the presence of explicit recommendations, the analysis of factors that decision makers can do something about, and results with direct implications for a course of action were associated with this action construct.

A third major construct that Weiss and Bucuvalas describe involves the "Conformity of User Expectations . . . [representing] compatibility with what users know and believe" (p. 304). Items here include support for user's position and consistency with previous knowledge. As the authors put it, the likelihood of users valuing a report increases when the findings are in "agreement with the users' construction of reality" (p. 304).

The fourth major construct concerns "Challenge to the Status Quo." Somewhat surprisingly, the authors report a positive correlation here. That is, "studies that score high on Challenge . . . [were] particularly likely to be taken into account" (p. 307). Among the likely explanations for this finding offered by the authors is the highly plausible one that officials are often in disagreement with the institutional status quo and thus would be receptive to information that could be used to stimulate change. The fact that the Conformity factor was correlated with perceived usefulness and that the

Challenge factor was not related to the Conformity factor tends to support the authors' explanatory hypothesis.

A fifth factor the authors call "Relevance" was developed through analyses on a slightly different database. Here, the sample only involved explicit decision makers. (The other analyses included these plus an additional sample of 50 social scientists and 50 members of research review committees who had done or reviewed research relevant to the types of agencies used to draw the sample of decision makers.) The Relevance factor emphasized the notion of being germane "to the issues your office deals with" (p. 303).

In summing up their research, Weiss and Bucuvalas conclude that decision makers "involve three basic frames of reference [concerned with] the relevance, the trustworthiness [i.e., Research Quality, Relevance, and Conformance factors], and the utility [i.e., Action and Challenge factors]" of the research (p. 311).

Alkin, Dalliak, and White (1979) use retrospective interviews of key decision makers and evaluators in five case studies to develop their scheme of factors influencing use. In terms of our earlier discussion concerning the definition of use, these authors take a broad perspective. The case studies focus on different ESEA Title I or Title IV-C evaluations: Their research emphasizes the importance of looking at the use question over time, being sensitive to the contexts in which the evaluations took place, and paying "systematic attention to the evaluation as process" (p. 32). Initial interviews of key actors were further refined through followup interviews. The authors report making extensive efforts to field-validate their findings by sharing preliminary analyses with participants in the study for accuracy and interpretation checks. The final report of research results includes comments (generally laudatory) from key participants.

Alkin and associates (1979) present what they term is an analytical framework that can help to serve as a "first step toward a theory of evaluation utilization" (p. 259). The eight categories that make up their conceptual framework encompass "a wide range of factors to be considered in the examination of evaluation situations" (p. 259). While the authors readily admit that the eight major categories do not in all cases "translate unambiguously to variables" affecting use, we believe their scheme makes an important contribution to the area.

Alkin and associates (1979) begin their framework with a consideration of *preexisting bounds* that constrain and direct an evaluation exercise. Citing examples such as state requirements (as are often the case with Title I evaluations), budgetary limits, and characteristics of the communities and organizations in which the research take place, the authors suggest that such "givens" can work to set the "possibilities" or curb the evaluation's range of activities.

The *orientation of the users* is the second major category in the Alkin and associates (1979) framework. By orientation, the authors mean the "expectations of users" about the kinds of information an evaluation research exercise is likely to produce. Orientation here is also intended to include "preferred forms of information" (p. 239). A distaste for heavily quantitative data is cited as one example.

A third category concerns what the authors call the *evaluator's approach*. Issues such as the use or not of a formal evaluation model, the degree and nature of user involvement that is encouraged, and the personal and professional rapport established between the evaluator and the user are encompassed by this category.

The fourth category concerns *evaluator credibility*. Here issues involve the degree of congruence between evaluation findings and prior knowledge of the user, the perceived "adequacy of the evaluation procedures, and the user's trust in the evaluator" (p. 245). The authors emphasize that the trust extended by users is often specific to particular knowledge domains and program contexts. They also note that levels of trust might well vary by user within a given evaluation context and may vary over time. Trust is related both to the evaluator's expertise and to the opportunities provided to demonstrate his/her talents. This category clearly relates to the frame of reference developed by Weiss and Bucuvalas (1980) which they call "trustworthiness."

The fifth and sixth categories encompass a range of *organizational* and *extraorganizational* factors. District responsiveness, degree of program autonomy, institutional arrangements associated with the evaluation office, and the presence of other informational sources are cited as important organizational factors that influenced use in the five case studies. Extraorganizational factors included the influence of the larger community and that of other governmental agencies on the utilization of results. In the latter instance, the authors cite an example of direct state intervention with a local school board to encourage the use of evaluation results.

The seventh category concerns *information content* and *reporting*. A variety of issues are noted including the degree of formal/informal reporting, the use of quantitative/qualitative data, and the frequency of communication. The authors note that these variables interacted with specific program contexts. They stress that the substance, format, and dialogue associated with information content and reporting be tailored to a specific user context; no single approach or direction on these variables seemed to be necessarily appropriate for all sites.

The eighth and last category in the utilization framework presented by Alkin and associates (1979) concerns *administrator style*. One issue here involves administrative and organizational skills, the ability to get things done. As the authors state it, "If the administrators lack the resources or skills to pursue a new course of action, then even highly relevant evaluation information will have little impact" (p. 255). Associated with these skills is personal initiative. When skills and initiative are present, the likelihood of use occurring increases.

Alkin and associates (1979) close their discussion by noting the importance of looking for interactions among the various categories they have described. For example, evaluator approach and user orientation interaction could clearly influence use. If an evaluator's approach tended toward high user involvement, user involvement might further shape the research questions. Such shaping, in turn, would impact on the user's expectations of the research. This sort of interaction is clearly one of the potential benefits of taking a client orientation as discussed in chapter 3.

A third scheme of factors that influence use is offered by Leviton and Hughes (1981) in their review of literature in this area. Their review "focuses on evaluations, but [also] draws on the larger body of information about the use of social science" (p. 526). A second major source of literature for these authors is the writings of experienced evaluators and policy makers addressing the utilization question. Over 70 major studies and articles on use are drawn upon in their review.

Leviton and Hughes identify five major clusters of variables that seem to be consistently related to use. The first cluster is related to what the authors call the *relevance* of the evaluation activity. Relevance is further divided into variables related to the specific information needs of program managers or policy makers and the time lines of the research. The authors report important interaction effects between specific variables in this cluster, the types of evaluation research questions addressed, and the kinds of decision-making context involved. For example, time lines seems to be positively related to use when the likely use involved is of a short-term, instrumental nature. Similarly, information about a program's overall effectiveness is important to policy makers' needs but less so to program managers. Managers are most likely to be interested in specific information on the implementation process and the effectiveness of particular program components.

A second cluster of variables is related to the *communication* that takes place between evaluators and potential users. Direct communication of users' information needs is positively correlated with utilization, as are the direct dissemination of results, and the existence of dissemination networks. Some variables with apparently negative impact in this area include the kinds of communication networks typically associated with bureaucracies, and distortions of data that can occur in these contexts when evaluative information is summarized.

A third cluster of variables reported by Leviton and Hughes involves the issue of *information processing* on the part of potential users. The authors see such processing as a necessary precursor to actual use. The variables in this cluster are categorized into three subsets: awareness of relevance, presentation of information, and information-processing style of administrators. Examples of positive variables in these subsets include evaluations designed to meet specific questions, clear presentation of results, and the use of verbal communication, respectively. Conversely, variables associated negatively include lack of clarity in goal specification, presence of jargon, and differences between administrator and academic (researcher) styles.

The fourth major category in this scheme concerns the issue of *credibility*. The authors note that "just as an evaluator uses multiple indicators of an outcome, an administrator has multiple indicators of the faith that can be placed in information" (p. 539). Variables here are distributed into four major subsets concerned with the preconceptions of users, the credibility of the evaluation producer, the quality of the evaluation product, and the relationship of evaluation data to other information. Some specific relationships identified by the authors included positive effects on use when there is information that corroborates the evaluation data, when users have a high opinion of research, when users tend to rely on research over intuition, and when the methodology is not easily assailed. Some of the negative effects identified by the authors are found when there are contradictions between research and other information, when the research data contradict the users' intuition or expectations, when there is suspicion of cooptation, and when there is a perception of low quality.

The fifth and final major cluster of variables identified by Leviton and Hughes concerns *"user involvement and advocacy"* (p. 542). The presence of high interest in and advocacy of evaluation information is positively related to use. In some cases the explanation for these relationships may be due to such factors as that the majority of uses possible in some of the studies reviewed were the sole responsibility of the committed individual, or that the committed individuals' power may have dictated use by others, or that the actions of a committed individual may have increased the likelihood that information would get to other users without distortion and thus with clearer implications for policy direction.

The foregoing discussion provides only a brief survey of some of the variables that have been found to be associated with the utilization of evaluation research information. For more detailed reviews the reader is referred to the three pieces reviewed. For our purposes here, several features are worth noting about the literature in this area.

While it is clear that some very important work has been accomplished, there is still much that remains to be learned about the nature of use, what factors tend to inhibit or facilitate it and why, and what can be done to increase evaluation use, if this is the end in view. Beyond additional knowledge that must be generated on these basic questions, there is a need to understand more fully the relationships that exist among variables already thought to be important in influencing use. An important element in reaching such an understanding of variable relationships involves tracking how these interactions can change with changes in the evaluation contexts. Does it make a difference if the research is mounted by an internal or external agency? Does it matter if the researchers or potential users initiate the evaluation task? And perhaps most importantly from the point of view of the theme of this book, are variable relationships affected differently depending upon whether the research agenda is formative or summative in nature; whether the research process in an integrated or isolated from the policy and decision-making processes of an educational system?

Much work lies ahead if we are to answer such questions more completely. The experiences documented in our case histories provide some evidence regarding the factors that can increase the likelihood of use: taking a formative, client-oriented approach to DOER; integrating the research process into the decision and policy processes of an organization; and being methodologically eclectic. Some of these insights based on the case histories add further support to findings already in the literature. The generally strong support for user–researcher interaction is one such example. Additional examples stress selecting appropriate methods, being sensitive to a variety of contextual variables, and asking relevant questions.

Another example of where the experience summarized in the case histories overlaps in important ways with some of the existing literature involves dissemination of results, and the importance of taking an activist, process-oriented perspective to this issue. This activist view surfaces in a variety of ways. Alkin and associates (1979) write of an "information dialogue" in which researcher and user have an "open-ended, two-way communication in which evaluation information and its implications are explored rather than presented" (p. 254). Cronbach and associates (1980) advise the evaluator "to seek out opportunities to communicate both prior and subsequent to the release of results" (p. 174). They see it as an obligation of the evaluator "to make sure that his/her story gets out" (p. 174). In his active, reactive, adaptive model of evaluation research, Patton (1978) stresses the importance of both evaluators and those in management positions working together to make full use of the data (p. 288). Many other examples could be cited in the literature that support this dynamic view of dissemination. In the remainder of this chapter we will focus on the dissemination process and try to clarify further what such a process might entail for researchers and managers alike, by drawing upon specific examples from several of the case histories.

Dissemination, the Case History Experience

A few important assumptions must be stated before we turn to the case history experiences on dissemination. One important assumption is that while the literature has tended to focus on dissemination as a discreet topic for discussion, we believe that it is integrally related to the other major components of research — namely, design, data collection, and analysis. Understanding that dissemination is part of a continuum is particularly important from our perspective which emphasizes the value of taking a client orientation and systems approach to DOER. The dialogue between client and researcher that was valuable in defining research activities is equally important in the dissemination and use of results. Indeed, they are part of the same cloth.

A second assumption in this discussion is that dissemination does not begin with the production of a "final" written report, nor is it primarily confined to the distribution of such reports. Reports have their place. We will discuss their utility later on in this chapter, but the dissemination process that works, in our experience, is far more complex than just the production of reports. For the purposes of this discussion, dissemination begins when there is something to disseminate. That is, as the earliest analyses turn up the most preliminary of findings, we consider that the process has begun.

Finally, we will take the position that a dynamic approach to dissemination is an important factor in influencing use. But, as we have noted earlier, many additional factors are involved. Each of the approaches to DOER discussed in previous chapters can positively influence use. Additional factors related to the organizational context in which that DOER takes place are also important. So dynamic dissemination is an important, perhaps necessary condition of use, but it is not sufficient.

We have organized this discussion of the case history experience into issues related to process, communication style, content, and audience. The latter two issues are so intertwined that they will be treated as a single topic with two important facets.

Process

Two cases (4, 5) serve to illustrate key aspects of the dissemination process. Case 4, involving a district-wide needs assessment, provides a more traditional context in which to discuss dissemination issues. We say "traditional" because the assessment was a discrete research task, with a definite time line and major product outcomes. In contrast, case 5, involving the documentation of a school improvemet program over a three-year period, serves to illustrate how dissemination occurs when the research process is continuous and integral to the development and implementation of a new program.

The case 4 dissemination process occurred in three stages. The first, informal stage began not very long after (approximately four weeks) the research was started through periodic updates provided by the researchers for the superintendent. The primary purposes of these meetings were to report on the progress of data collection and to solve any accessibility problems that may have arisen. However, the sessions quickly became opportunities to share the results of early data analyses. In this regard these informal conversations served the valuable purposes of maintaining client interest in the research and of sharpening and expanding the questions being addressed by the assessment. The latter occurred because some of the preliminary analyses raised as many questions as they answered. As preliminary results were discussed with the client, additional research plans were formulated in an attempt to clarify ambiguous findings.

The second stage of dissemination began as the research was nearing completion. Now four months into the research, most of the surveys and data analyses had been completed. A massive amount of data had been gathered and summarized, and it was now time to present a formal report to the board of education. Preparation occurred in two stages. First, a preliminary presentation of results was provided to the superintendent, the present of the board, and a key central administration official. The purpose here was twofold. One goal was to test the researchers' ideas for clarity. We were especially concerned that jargon and complex statistical concepts and diagrams were avoided wherever possible, and where they were necessary, care was taken to explain their meaning. The second goal of this preliminary session was to try to anticipate areas of particularly high interest to board members. Since any key finding of the assessment could be developed in great detail, we tried to focus on issues of special interest to insure their adequate attention in the presentation. (As a further strategy to insure key issues were addressed, each board member had been interviewed about their own views of the priority facing the district.)

The preliminary presentation of results lasted well over three hours. As a result of this session numerous modifications were made. These included: making sure each section of the presentation started with a clear statement of policy considerations implied by the data that were to follow where appropriate; de-emphasizing detail and placing a stronger emphasis on broad, thematic statements; increasing the emphasis on the findings coming from the surveys of district constitutencies (as opposed to the other data analyses); and minimizing jargon (e.g., when referring to "mean scores," we would use the word "average").

The preliminary presentation was a sobering experience for the research-ers. As hard as the research team had worked in attempting to organize a clear and powerful presentation of the assessment findings, this experience clearly demonstrated that more work was still needed.

The changes made as a result of this preliminary review were tested in one more dry run with the research team itself. In this "dress rehearsal" a critical emphasis was placed on timing, transition, and clarity of visual aids used (charts, diagrams, statistical tabulations, etc.). Rough transitions were identified, and the slide presentation was improved (e.g., no slide was put up on the screen until the presenter was ready to discuss its contents).

With these preliminary steps taken, the researchers felt they were reasonably ready to go to the board. The assessment results were presented to the nine-member body in a special, all-day, Saturday session. The meeting was held on a nearby, secluded, college campus. Attendance at the meeting was restricted to board members, the superintendent, one board staff member, and the two senior LRDC researchers. No observers or members of the fourth estate were present.

The meeting started with the presentation of research findings. An em-phasis was placed on an open discussion of the results, their meaning, and their possible implications. The presentation of results was followed by more discussion and closing comments from the superintendent. The board was charged with the task of further deliberating the findings and voting on district priorities. For the last part of the day, the board and the superinten-dent discussed next moves without the presence of researchers.

It is worth noting that the cloistered setting for the presentation of the assessment results contrasted sharply with usual board meetings which typically were held at the central offices, with numerous observers/par-ticipants, and with an extremely complicated agenda. There is little doubt that the setting was helpful in providing the board with an opportunity to both hear and understand the assessment results.

The presentation to the board was followed Monday morning with a press release from the superintendent's office. The release announced the intention to develop action plans focused on two major areas, school im-provement and cost effectiveness; "the decision . . . was made by Wallace and members of the board after they had the opportunity to review preliminary results of the district-wide needs assessment" (Pittsburgh Public Schools, January 26, 1981, p. 1).

The third stage of the dissemination process occurred over the next several months. During this time a series of meetings were held with dif-ferent components of the district's staff. For example, a formal presenta-tion of assessment results was made by the researchers to all district administrators and supervisors on February 24, 1981. This was followed by a closed-circuit television discussion of results by the superintendent and the two senior researchers beamed to each school faculty. As a part of this effort, faculties were led by their school administrators in discussions of the results following the television broadcast. This third formal stage of dissemination ended with the holding of a press conference on March 5, 1981, at which time detailed results of the assessment were released formally to the public.

Even though this discussion of the case 4 formal dissemination process will end here, it is worth noting that a secondary phase of dissemination was already well underway by the time of the March press conference. This dissemination occurred through the task forces set up to develop action plans responding to the district's several priorities established by the board as a result of the needs assessment. Similar to Rich's (1981) notion of a second wave of utilization, the results of the assessment were widely disseminated by district staff and formed part of the grist for the planning activities underway.

The dissemination process evidenced in case 5 differed from that of case 4 in one important respect. The school improvement program documentation research was an extended field research activity. In a sense, results were being reported continuously as a result of an elaborate program of site observations as well as discrete, more formal research activities.

The primary process of dissemination used to share findings resulting from the ongoing field observations was the series of weekly planning meetings held by the school improvement team. These meetings typically included a wide-ranging discussion of the past week's activities. They represented in that sense both a data collection opportunity for the documentation team as well as a forum in which to share findings that had surfaced as a result of research. The word "findings" probably represents too formal a notion here. What often were shared were impressions, half-formulated issues, and possible questions in the minds of documenters that had been generated through the program of field observations about some event, issue, or direction in the program.

An example from the first year's documentation experience will serve to illustrate the nature of this informal dissemination process. During that period one research strategy employed by the documentation team involved undertaking a case study of one of the seven participating schools. A great deal of time was spent in observing program-related activities in this building. A key aspect of this case study research concerned monitoring the school's steering committee process. Detailed, informally summarized observations served as a basis of ongoing discussions during the planning meetings among team members and the researchers. Initially these discussions focused on issues specific to this school. Increasingly, however, questions arose about the steering committee concept per se. While there was much in the literature that supported teacher involvement in an innovation to build ownership, little was known about the possibility of the joint teacher-administrator problem-solving approach used in school improvement, (i.e., building-level steering committees) as a vehicle for achieving ownership. One outcome of the first year's case study research was the development of a formal survey of all seven faculties about the steering committee process, its benefits, and constraints. Data from formal research were instrumental in the team's planning a summer in-service program for all committee members.

As the above episode indicates, documentation also involved formal, discrete research programs. Another example of this type of initiative occurred at the close of the second year of operation. The school improvement team was interested in a broad assessment of the extent to which the various components of the program had been implemented and how these might be improved in the future. As part of the research planned, surveys were undertaken of all participating teachers and administrators. Results of these surveys were summarized by school and program component, and across schools by program component.

The dissemination of survey results occurred in three steps. In late June of 1983, preliminary tabulations by school were shared with principals. This was followed at the end of the summer by a detailed review of all the findings with the team. Finally, program-wide and individual school results were presented at faculty meetings held in each of the seven buildings. These presentations included reviews of the data and explanations of the analyses by researchers, dicussions of the implications of the results from the point of view of the school improvement team, and an open discussion of the information by teachers and administrators. The last of these meetings was completed by October 1983, five months after the initiation of the surveys. Once the faculty reviews ended, school-level results were used to varying degrees by steering committees to develop action plans for the coming year.

The foregoing discussion illustrates the processes used in attempting to disseminate results of our research. They were often extensive, taking place over time, involving clients, program participants, and researchers alike. In the following section we will continue to draw upon the case histories to provide more detail about the form dissemination took.

Communication Style

It is useful here to distinguish between the written and spoken word as communication styles for dissemination. Further, it is important to distinguish whether communication is single or multidirectional in nature.

Implicit in what has been written in this chapter thus far is our conviction that the spoken word as a form of communication of results is at least as valuable, and in some instances more valuable, than the written word. In addition, the case history experience suggests that whether the actual communication style is written or verbal, providing opportunity for the exchange of ideas, for dialogue among researchers and potential users, can work toward improving both the dissemination process, and the quality of the findings being shared. The all-day retreat with the board that took place in case 4 serves to illustrate these points.

The reader will recall that the major findings of the district-wide needs assessment were verbally presented by the researchers with lots of opportunity for questioning, discussion, and challenge on the part of board members. Slides and charts were used to illustrate specific points. Executive summaries were also placed in the hands of board members as findings were reviewed.

One important outcome from the discussion was the restructuring of the way the researchers had organized assessment results. The researchers presented results initially organized under five broad priority categories involving student achievement, personnel evaluation, attracting and holding students, enrollment decline, and increasing the effectiveness of individual schools. As a result of the discussion with board members, some of the results contained in the attracting and holding category were further subdivided to display issues related to student discipline as a separate, sixth priority area. There were several reasons for this change. Board members felt that the strength of the data presented on student discipline concerns, especially from teacher and parent surveys, warranted a separate category. Second, it was felt that identifying discipline as a separate priority served to underscore the commitment of the board to address problems in this area, a major concern among teachers in the district. Third, the findings on discipline clearly confirmed personal concerns already shared among several of the board members about the seriousness of this issue. Fourth, the organizational structure of the district itself made it more sensible to treat discipline as a separate issue. For example, some of the other issues subsumed under the attract and hold priority (e.g., those dealing with concerns about the information the public had about district programs, etc.) were likely to be addressed by district offices and personnel in ways that would be quite different than those that would have to be involved in working on discipline problems.

This vignette illustrates the utility of the spoken, interactive approach to dissemination. Both the understanding and the quality of results were improved.

A second point worth noting about the retreat experience involves the role played by the superintendent. In the spirit of chapter 3, the superintendent was the primary client for the assessment. He worked with the researchers from the design stage to the dissemination of results in the client style we describe. However, it was always clear that the potential user community extended to many levels in the system, including the board, the highest policy level. The superintendent was actively engaged in the discussion of results at the retreat. More importantly, he was critical in identifying potential policy and action implications that should be considered by the board and that, later on, would move other members of the organization.

The activist role on the part of the superintendent more than complemented the energetic dissemination position taken by the researchers. This mutual involvement in dissemination was possible because of the ongoing client dialogue that had shaped the prior research. The dissemination of results was a natural extension of the assessment process for both the researchers and the primary client. The critical point here is that dissemination like other elements of DOER is the work of researchers and clients alike.

So far we have stressed an interactive communication style as a means to disseminate research information. This position parallels in some respects the literature on the communication styles of administrators (Sproull and Larkey, 1979). The involvement of the client in dissemination activities similarly parallels some of the findings in the literature on use that stress the importance of user involvement and advocacy of findings (Leviton and Hughes, 1981). We have referred to cases 4 and 5 to draw examples of our use of this style of communication. In contrast, cases 3 and 7 were not characterized by this approach. In these cases, we relied heavily on the issuance of major reports. This reliance was based, in part, on our failure to identify viable primary clients for the research. In any case, the use of reports for dissemination in cases 3 and 7 fell far short of achieving the exposure of results desired.

Our emphasis on interactive communication should not be viewed as a dismissal of the written word as an important communication style. Indeed, many of the discussions we have mentioned were framed around written materials (albeit more of the short telegram/executive summary types). There are many valid reasons why writing down results is an important thing to do. Some of these reasons are directly relevant to the dissemination question. Some are important in establishing the internal and external scientific credibility of a piece of research. Still other reasons concern the importance of written reports to the building of an institutional memory. In the following section we will discuss the role reports play in the dissemination process in relation to the issues of content and audience.

Content and Audience

One caveat is worth mentioning before turning to a discussion of content and audience issues. While we will generally address these issues in terms of written materials, the basic strategies discussed are applicable to the verbal communication of results as well.

Several assumptions and strategies have emerged from the case history experience regarding content and audience issues. One basic assumption is that systems research will often have a wide range of potential users. A corollary to this is that the content of reports should be tailored to the information needs of specific audiences. One way to increase the utility of research results is to identify the various potential user-audiences and to think about what their specific information needs might be and to frame reports that address these needs. Another principle is that while everyone does not need or want every available finding and report, making results generally accessible can contribute to a positive organizational climate. Of course, there can be reasonable exceptions to this latter principle. Cronbach and associates (1980) note the "legitimate concerns for privacy" that can impinge upon the general ideal of "freedom to communicate" findings (p. 6). For example, the issue of personnel evaluation discussed in case 10 is an example of an area where confidentiality issues can override the dictum of making results generally accessible.

Case 4 provides examples of the strategies or principles mentioned above. The needs assessment results were presented over time to multiple audiences. The results presented to the board emphasized broad themes in the data. The written reports were of the executive summary styles. A great deal of detail was available as backup to the summary documents. But it is illustrative of the nature of the role of this audience (policy making), and the questions in front of it (setting broad organizational priorities), that the level of detail actually needed was minimal.

The summaries prepared for the board differed sharply with those prepared for various central administrative offices in terms of the level of detail and range of focus. In most instances, these reports focused on single issues, largely coterminous with specific responsibility areas in the system (e.g., transportation, personnel evaluation, etc.). The content contained both summaries of data and examples of suggestions for possible solutions to problems identified that had been offered by individual survey respondents. One particularly interesting focused report summarized responses made to a specific, open-ended question on the surveys asking what advice the respondent would give to the new superintendent to improve the system. (It is worth noting that, at least from teachers and administrators, the overwhelming theme was to make an effort to have personal contact with school staff and not become wedded to the central offices.)

Another type of report focused on specific role groups in the system. For example, summaries were prepared of teacher and administrator perceptions. These served both as informational feedback mechanisms to those participating in the research, as well as databases that would permit comparative analyses of perceptions of problems in the district as seen by key district role groups.

A summary report that provided an overview of the assessment methodology, the database, and key findings was prepared for general distribution in the district and to the public. This report was probably as close to a "final" report as the assessment got, and it wasn't the last report written; nor was it the typical "massive tome" usually offered by researchers. The total length of this report was 16 pages.

Descriptions of the process and the results were also prepared and shared with the larger research community (Bickel and Cooley, 1981). One very important outcome of this type of reporting was that it provided an external quality check on the methods employed in the research. We are not suggesting that every system researcher should have as his/her major priority publication in the scientific community. However, some sensitivity to and communication about one's work, perhaps through networks of evaluation offices, can be an important resource to a decision-oriented system researcher.

Finally, it is important to note that several complete sets of all reports were provided to the district and to individual school faculties. Individual teachers and administrators could pursue the entire set or any subset of the documents in their professional libraries at their own initiative.

Comparable strategies to those used in case 4 guided the preparation and distribution of reports in cases 2, 5, and 8. In the remaining cases, either formal reports were not called for, or as was the case in case 10, the issues were of a highly confidential nature with the potential "user audience" usually restricted to a very narrow set. The one exception to these exceptions was case 3 where we overly relied on the production of major reports to serve all audiences with little positive effect.

Linking Information Systems and Action Systems

The literature on evaluation use and knowledge use tends to focus on the results of a specific program evaluation or set of research studies of particular policy relevance (e.g., the effects of class size on student achievement). There is another important way in which the information products of the

DOER are utilized. This refers to the manager's use of continuous feedback information from information systems, as distinct from the various ways in which the policy-shaping community is influenced by the general results of research studies. However, as we point out in chapters 5 and 6, and illustrate in case 8, the monitoring of the distributions of educational indicators by the managers of educational systems (superintendents, supervisors, principals, teachers, etc.) can be an extremely important way in which information is used.

Here the factors that relate to use are quite different. What is important here is to design an information system that is linked to an action system, so that the latter can be guided by the information system on a continuing basis. In this management context, use will occur if the research office works with responsible agencies within the system to develop indicators that can guide the priority setting for that action system. For example, the use of student-level attendance data, distributed so that the most serious truants are easily identified, could be quite useful to the social workers assigned to the task of working with and assisting the most serious truancy cases in the district. Similarly, classroom-level reading growth indicators could assist reading supervisors charged with helping those teachers who seem to be in greatest need of assistance in developing their ability to teach reading. What's important in achieving utility of such information is that it be organized in ways in which the serious outliers are easily identified and the unit of analysis for identifying such outliers is the unit that the available action systems normally deal with: student is the unit for counselors, tutors, social workers; classroom is the unit for principals, supervisors, staff developers; school is the unit for school improvement teams, assistant superintendents, security guards.

Redissemination for Reuse

The last issue we would like to address is one that typically is not mentioned in the literature, but can be a potentially important concept. This concerns the "reuse" of data, information, and knowledge generated in prior research to inform future policy, decision, and program development. What is critical is that educational systems develop a capability and a database that can be the basis for increasing institutional memory. The call for building a redissemination for reuse capability (or perhaps more importantly a role imperative for system researchers) is motivated by two convictions: (1) educational systems can benefit from learning from past experience (e.g., when innovation A is replicated at a different level in the system); and (2) too often such prior knowledge is either uncollected or not readily retrievable.

Of course, one way that past learning becomes available for future use is through internalization. Kennedy (1982) writes of the working knowledge of policy makers and system managers. One important way to improve dissemination is to encourage researchers to work hard at integrating the information they are producing into the working knowledge of key system actors.

To the extent that internalization occurs, prior disseminated knowledge would be "accessible" for reuse as the occasion demands. However, several human and organizational constraints inhibit appropriate recall. One obvious point is that findings that are fresh in the memory when first disseminated can become distorted or forgotten over time. Second, findings generated in relation to one component or program in a large system may not be easily communicated, either in the short term or in the long term, to other components in the organization. Such intraorganizational barriers are well recognized as problems in the dissemination process; these barriers would be of equal importance when considering redissemination issues.

Cases 5 and 9 provide specific illustrations at the program level of how redissemination can work to benefit new system initiatives. In each of these cases a system initiative was closely documented. This documentation had several purposes, one of which was the building of a detailed archive that described the implementation process of these programs. This archive in each instance was used to inform future planning processes when the district undertook new program initiatives that were related to the programs developed earlier. In case 5 this use of prior knowledge occurred when the school improvement program in its fourth year began working in a second wave of schools. In case 9, the redissemination of information occurred when the district decided to develop an elementary model school that included, as a key component, a teacher center for elementary teachers. What had been learned and documented about the secondary teacher center begun three years earlier helped to inform elementary planners as they designed their new initiative.

Cases 5 and 9 illustrate quite clearly the utility of redissemination for reuse, here in the context of documentation research. It is important to note that while documentation information was, in part, explicitly designed to address the institutional memory issue, the process of reuse, we believe, also applies to other types of institutional research outcomes. For example, in case 4 we drew upon some of the findings concerning the lack of coordination among remedial education programs in the district that were first reported in case 3. What we are calling for is a more explicit commitment on the part of those involved with DOER to be sensitive to the notion of redissemination. This role imperative might be expressed as follows. When an information need begins to arise, perhaps the first question is not what new research is needed, but rather, what do we already know from past work that can shed some light on the new questions? Once stated, the point is perhaps obvious. However, what is not obvious is that this approach is a common one either among researchers or potential clients. What is required, first of all, is a commitment, and then a need to organize and preserve data in ways that make redissemination for reuse easy. Finally, there is a need to link those conducting DOER to the larger system in meaningful ways across natural (and "unnatural") bureaucratic boundaries so that communication exchange is made easier.

Obviously all new questions are not merely old ones in disguise. However, many are, and still others are close enough to previously addressed issues to benefit from prior knowledge.

Summary

In this chapter we have reviewed some of the current literature on use of evaluation and research information. Alternative ways of defining use have been discussed. We have adopted the broader definition of use, recognizing that utilization legitimately occurs in many ways and contexts. Variables that seem to influence use have been identified. We have noted both some preliminary convergence in the factors identified in the literature and the need for further research. Finally, we have discussed one aspect of the use issue, that concerned with the dissemination of research outcomes.

Using the case history experience as a base, we have concluded that researchers and clients must play a more activist role in the dissemination processes. Further, we have stressed the importance of an interactive communication style (verbal and written), beginning early in the research process. We believe that this can help to shape both the quality of results and their use. In addition, we have emphasized the importance of tailoring the content of dissemination products to specific audiences. Finally, we have encouraged the explicit incorporation into DOER of the notion of redissemination for reuse. We take this position because of the conviction that systems can often benefit from prior knowledge, but that such knowledge often goes uncollected or is not stored in the institutional memory in ways that makes its retrievability and reuse likely.

10 SUMMARY, CONCLUSIONS, AND IMPLICATIONS

Introduction

We began the work described in this book with two broad questions as the focus of our research. How can the quality of evaluation research that takes place in school districts be improved? How can this type of research become more useful to the policy-shaping and management communities? These two distinct but highly related questions were pursued by working with policy shapers and managers in a large urban school system. In our relationships with district personnel, we sought to understand better their information needs, and to develop and test research responses to those needs. As we were fond of saying in the early years of this work, the goal was to replicate some of the conditions experienced by district evaluation researchers, with the important exception (and presumed advantage) that we would have time to reflect on our experiences in ways that would permit us to share what we were learning with others in the policy and research fields.

The goal of replicating an educational system's research office, with time for reflection, seems somewhat naive six years later. As we became increasingly immersed in attempting to meet district information needs, the pace quickened and the notion of having "time for reflection" often seemed a remote academic dream rather than a comfortable reality. In part, the quickening pace was a very important signal that we were doing some things right. The growing demand was hard evidence of the value of the information being generated. However, the pace was also sobering, and it underscored the challenge of trying to be responsive to system information needs.

Questions of initial naivete aside, as the research progressed, we had a growing realization that as broad as our original questions were, we were becoming increasingly uncomfortable with them as a way to describe our work. Partly because of the range of information needs of district personnel, partly because of the historic connotations associated with the word *evaluation,* and partly because of a growing systems orientation in our work, the focus on improving "evaluation research" seemed to be a confining and limiting descriptor of our experiences. What grew out of this unease was the conviction that "decision-oriented educational research" more clearly captured both the range of information needs of system managers and policy shapers, and the spirit of what researchers can do to meet these needs.

In this concluding chapter we will briefly review what we think has been learned about DOER. This will be followed by a discussion of issues related to the generalizability of these findings to other contexts. That is, what is the utility, what are the limitations of what we have experienced in one setting for other settings? The discussion of generalizability is followed by a commentary on what we feel are the implications of this work in several broader areas of public policy and research.

What We Have Learned

Two sets of understandings have emerged from this work. One set involves basic convictions about how research can be conceptualized in educational systems. A second set encompasses a number of specific research strategies that we have found to be particularly helpful in responding to the information needs of system policy shapers and managers. Each of these sets of understandings will be reviewed briefly in this section.

In chapter 1 we wrote of six themes that permeated the book. These conceptual themes represent convictions that emerged during the course of the work about how to conduct research in educational settings. The first conviction involved the importance of taking more of a systems view of the research context. By this we mean that DOER is conceptualized as taking place within an educational system. The "system" (whether it is a school, a school district, a state educational system, or some other bounded entity) consists of interrelated components. Research that hopes to understand the workings of one component of a system (e.g., a newly designed staff development program) will most likely need to comprehend how the entity which is the subject of research relates to other components in the system. This basic systems approach to research contrasts somewhat with what is known about how research is typically approached in such systems. There seems to be a general tendency to mount isolated, time-finite research efforts (e.g., a traditional program evaluation). What can be lost in such efforts is an understanding of evolving context variables and relationships that can be critical in interpreting any subsystem phenomenon, and the ability to develop over time an organizational structure to a research program that can both anticipate as well as respond to information needs.

A second conviction concerns how one thinks about policy and decision processes and how differing conceptualizations of these can influence research. Here we owe much to colleagues in the field (e.g., Alkin et al., 1979; Cronbach and associates, 1980; Weiss, 1980) for their perceptions that decision and policy processes are diffuse and complex, varying significantly across organizational contexts, and within organizations by levels of actors, and by specific programs or issues. Those notions were confirmed by our own experiences. Policies and decisions are being generated all of the time in educational systems. Seldom is the process discrete. Usually numerous individuals contribute, although the closer one gets to day-to-day management contexts, the more bounded decision contexts become. The import of the generally diffuse nature of decision processes for systems research is that it underscores both the importance and complexity of defining potential clients for information. Further, it implies that in most research contexts, there will be multiple potential users beyond one's immediate client(s).

A third conviction involves the value of thoroughly integrating a system's research capability with its decision and policy processes. A way to think about how to define what we mean by integration would be to suggest criteria to be used to decide whether such integration existed in a particular system. One criterion would be whether the research resource had reasonable access to key management and policy-shaping actors in the system. The purposes of access would be, most broadly, for the ongoing communication of information needs and research-generated knowledge relevant to specific needs. More subtly, the access serves as a mechanism for shaping the working knowledge of clients and researchers alike about specific goals, educational values, and the limits, the promise, and the responsibilites of each in the research process. A further sign of integration would be that the information generation capability of an educational system is linked in meaningful ways to action components of the system capable of "applying" the information for operational improvement. Such linkage can happen through direct interaction with those responsible for applications, or through intermediaries (clients) who expressed the original information need and who themselves are capable of mobilizing appropriate action mechanisms in the system. In either case, integration provides an important infrastructure that can support application.

A conviction directly related to the integration theme concerns the role of the educational administrator in the management of the research process. Too often past writing in the evaluation field has emphasized an analysis of what researchers are doing (or not doing) to improve the value of research, without discussing the responsibility of administrators who set the overall boundaries of a system's research capability, and who define the "legitimate" tasks of the researcher. To the research "task-setters," we would suggest that the institutional research capability represented by DOER is a potentially important resource to the organization. And, just as with any valued, finite resource, there is a need to consider priorities carefully in the shaping of the use of the resource, and to manage the resource in ways that produce the greatest benefits. This management responsibility emphasis, when applied to the research process, is expressed most clearly in the presence of the kind of integration into the larger system which we have noted above, and by the wide range of tasks and applications made of the research resource.

Another theme that has permeated this book concerns the development of a shared perspective about basic goals of education among researchers, those that set the general boundaries of their tasks, and clients involved in specific research efforts. The presence of some commonly held values contributes in important ways to the viability and coherence of the research process. Such shared values can become the basic infrastructure for organizing priorities and for monitoring progress within a system. In our own experience, shared values such as equalizing educational opportunity helped shape the dialogue both at a human level, and in terms of important substantive goals of the research. Values will reasonably vary among individuals and system contexts. What remains, however, is the important contribution that values held in common among researchers, managers, and clients can make to a system's research process.

A final theme that has permeated the preceding chapters concerns the improvement orientation of the work. This conviction, more than any in this set, was clearly an initial bias of the authors as the work began, one that was confirmed by subsequent experience. The other themes, we can say, evolved fairly from the facts of the cases. In some instances, we came to these understandings the hard way, learning from our mistakes. The press for an improvement orientation, however, was there from the beginning. The reasons for this rested with our view of the field at the time this work began, a view only slightly modified during recent years. As we noted in chapter 1, there has been, and continues to be, a strong emphasis on summative-style program evaluation in the literature, and we think in actual practice (to the extent this has been described). While granting the necessity and importance of such activities in specific circumstances, we decry the dominance of this kind of activity. In our view, placing greater emphasis on improvement-oriented research designed to increase the operational value of existing programs, personnel, processes, etc., can provide significant payoffs for a system. The logic of our position is straightforward. In our experience, there is little in an educational system that cannot be improved upon. Better performance can be pursued (and often has been) by cycles of program innovation, summative evaluation, and a new round of innovation when data seemed to demonstrate that the first reform had not had the intended effects. We submit that a more prudent and ultimately more profitable course in many cases would be to work hard at upgrading the performance of existing programs (if this is the type of context at issue) by generating information that can shape the development and implementation of a reform effort.

The generation of information to improve current operations is an attainable and valuable goal of DOER. There will be instances, of course, where the incrementalist, pragmatic approach to systems improvement that we favor is not applicable. However, there are many instances where the improvement approach is appropriate, and we began this work with a conviction that a shift in practice toward this kind of approach is warranted. The case history experiences have borne out this belief.

A second set of understandings about DOER that have been derived from this work involves research strategies that we have found to be effective in meeting system information needs. The first two of these strategies relate to two basic questions faced by any researcher: How can I best organize the research process? What methods should I use? In our experience, taking a client orientation to the organization of the research process has proven to be a highly useful approach. The potential benefits are many. The research task can be more certainly focused and more easily pursued. The information needs are likely to be better understood. The probability of use can be heightened. The value of the research process can be enhanced, both because of the greater utility of the focused research, and as a result of at least some of the potential users' improved understanding of the research process (and the researcher). This improved understanding can shape the client's expectations about what information can be reasonably produced at what cost.

The benefits we associate with a client orientation are not without important qualifications. The development of a mutually educational dialogue is critical. A recognition that a client orientation does not preclude the presence of multiple potential users of the information being generated is important. Thus, a certain publicness built into the research process, and into the dissemination of results, is an important safeguard against client orientation becoming client (or researcher) domination. These qualifications notwithstanding, a client orientation promises much in the way of insuring that decision-oriented research is just that.

What methods should the researcher use? The answer we derive from our experiences is perhaps obvious, once stated. However, as we have noted from time to time in this book, the obvious often is not what is reflected in common practice. The case history experience demonstrates the need to be flexible, to be methodologically eclectic, as we state it, in one's choice of methods. The selection of research strategies should be contingent upon the nature of the questions (the information needs of clients), available research competence, and resources. What is crucial here is to move away from a tendency among researchers (and, to a lesser extent, system managers) to approach a specific research question with a methodological predisposition. Such predispositions are probably unavoidable, given the way most researchers and managers are trained. However, it is crucial to keep them in their place and to balance any predisposition with some recognition of the value of other methods. As a further extension of this point, we found that almost all the questions we addressed in the case histories benefited from the use of multiple research strategies. The vast gulf some see between quantitative versus qualitative approaches (for example) in the pragmatic world of systems research is just not there. The issues are often so complex that researcher and manager alike are grateful for accurate information, regardless of the methodological source.

Another research strategy that we have found to be effective in meeting system information needs involves the use of monitoring and tailoring for structuring the deployment of a significant percentage of a system's research capability. Monitoring indicators and then tailoring practices in light of the indicators is an application of the cybernetic paradigm. The research office's responsibility is to develop indicators that reflect basic goals of the system and display them in ways that reveal how well the system is moving toward those goals as well as guide the efforts to achieve them.

Another strategy that is necessary if research offices are to be responsive to an operating system in a timely fashion is to establish computer-based data files. The research office can and must anticipate the kinds of questions that are most frequently asked by the clients and the kinds of data required to address those questions. Computer files are also an essential ingredient in monitoring indicators.

A fifth strategy involves the use of research resources to document the design and implementation of system innovations. Program documentation, as we have described it, is one practical manifestation of the theme discussed earlier concerning improvement-oriented research activities. Building a research capability into the design and implementation of locally developed innovations can contribute significantly to the construction of a database that helps improve the implementation process and, ultimately, the effectiveness of the program. In addition, a rich description of prior reform efforts can serve to build a growing, systematic, knowledge base within the system of what works and what does not in specific reform contexts. Furthermore, this basis for "institutional memory" can serve as an important resource to future system reform efforts.

A sixth strategy involves a reconceptualization of the dissemination process and how researchers (and clients) can develop more effective methods in order to increase the probability of use. The case history experience provides ample evidence of the value of thinking about dissemination as starting at the earliest stages of a research project, as preliminary notions about the meaning of data are being formulated. This contrasts sharply with at least some of the writing in the field that tends to associate dissemination with the issuance and distribution of a summary report at the end of a research study. In our experience, reports are valuable and valued, but their worth rests more with providing a public documentary trail of how the research was conducted and a description of the basis for any conclusions offered. Actual dissemination, at least in what has been called the first wave of a research context, seems to work best when there is the opportunity for informal, interactive sessions among clients and researchers. Further, it is clear that much DOER research will most likely have the potential for multiple uses by multiple audiences. Organizing and communicating information in ways that recognize the potential for multiple use is another aspect of how dissemination processes can influence use.

A final specific strategy in this set of understandings is the need for a reasonably well-validated model of the major factors that influence student achievement test scores. An important component of the research task in school district educational systems involves understanding what is happening to student achievement. Since clients often put great emphasis upon standardized achievement test results, sorting out trends and group differences requires (at the very least) an informal causal model for explaining variation in test scores. Chapter 8 summarizes a model that we have found useful in this work.

Comments on Generalizability

In the preceding sections we briefly summarized what we learned about decision-oriented research through our work in one urban school district. These understandings emerged across time as we reflected upon the experiences encompassed by the case histories. It is reasonable to ask whether these understandings are applicable to other settings, to other districts, to other educational systems, or even to other kinds of social systems. In this section, we will discuss first the nature of generalizability as it applies to case study research. We will then turn to a review of the logic and evidence for suggesting our experiences may be useful for clients and researchers in other settings.

We begin this discussion of generalization by locating our work in a larger research tradition. This book summarizes what amounts to a case study research project. In a discussion of the characteristics of the case study, Hoaglin, Light, McPeek, Mosteller, and Stoto (1982) describe it as an "analytic description of an event, a process, an institution, or a program" (pp. 126-127). At one level, the work described in this book is a case study of selected information needs in one school district setting, and how we went about responding to those needs. The 11 case histories represent specific research tasks and, in effect, microresearch contexts in which the larger questions related to decision-oriented research were investigated. The fact that the work took place over a six-year period, encompassing a variety of important organizational changes (i.e., board elections, administrative reorganizations, changes in the superintendency) means that within our macro case study, the 11 histories collectively represent a rich set of experiences to draw upon in our analysis.

The basis for generalization in such case study research contrasts sharply with the traditional use of this term in experimental research. In the latter instance, generalization is contingent upon many factors, but key elements involve the quality of the sample design, the use of comparative control groups, and the reduction of the contextual variables to a limited number in order to understand specific relationships better, or to test hypothesized theoretical or propositional statements. These valuable underpinnings for generalization from experimental research are not "generalizable" to case study research.

In contrast, case study research emphasizes rich descriptions of particular contexts. The researcher, in essence, is attempting to offer enough information about his/her own experiences to provide the reader with a sense of "being there" (Stake, 1981, p. 35). The burden for generalization, in one sense, shifts from the researcher (where it lies in experimental design) to the reader. That is, in the case study narrative (chapters 1-10), and in the case study records (our case histories), the reader should be provided with a basis for understanding the work and the context in which the work took place. This understanding offers a basis for what Stake (1983) has called naturalistic generalizaton. Such knowledge, constructed by you, the reader, is

. . . arrived at by recognizing the similarities of objects and issues in and out of context and by sensing the natural covariations of happenings. To generalize this way is to be both intuitive and empirical . . . (p. 282).

This type of reader-centered knowledge (Stake, 1981) is, in part, the basis for what Guba and Lincoln (1983) refer to as the transferability of information generated through naturalistic research methodologies (including case studies).

While a significant responsibility for "knowledge transfer" is placed upon the reader, the researcher using naturalistic methods also has to meet important standards. Guba and Lincoln (1983) suggest a number of significant criteria for judging the trustworthiness of naturalistic research. Perhaps the most crucial of these concern the issues of credibility and the confirmability of the research. Regarding these two issues, the confidence of the reader can be enhanced if the study provides evidence of the use of procedures such as triangulation, sustained observation, debriefing by one's peers, member checks within the research context, and rich descriptions of the methods used, the context in which the research takes place, and the basis upon which the researchers are drawing their conclusions.

We hope that the chapters in part II of this book, in combination with the 11 case histories, meet these important criteria. This is not to suggest that, given the presence of them, each reader will necessarily draw the same conclusions from the case study. It is precisely in the engagement between reader and case study material that an opportunity for new knowledge exists because each reader will bring to the interaction a somewhat different set of experiences that will be used to shape meaning. What we do expect or intend is that the reader will have a basis for understanding how we arrived at our conclusions, and enough data about the case to develop his/her own constructs of meaning.

Although we have emphasized the importance of reader-contingent constructions of naturalistic generalizations about this work, we would be remiss if we did not offer some of our own initial views of where and how these experiences and/or conclusions seem to connect with other settings and contexts. In making these comments, we draw upon experiences of our own in other settings, and the experiences of others in our case study setting and in other contexts.

One basis for suggesting that some of what we have learned may be relevant to other settings is based upon opportunities to share and to test our understandings with researchers and clients in other educational systems. An example of such testing occurred when one of the authors had the opportunity to visit state-level research and testing offices in Australia.

Elementary and secondary education in Australia is organized at the state and territory level. Thus, all of Australia is served by only eight public school systems. Each system has an office (the name varies, as is true of the states) that conducts educational research. Each of those offices was visited to establish what they were doing, how they were doing it, and what their potential clients thought about the quality and utility of those efforts.

The specifics of those visits are summarized elsewhere (Cooley, 1984b), but the results were very encouraging. The most serious challenges to the strategies we have discussed in this book were related to our emphasis upon client orientation. A major concern was that if the researchers were primarily guided by the information needs of the bureaucrats responsible for managing the state system, serious conflict of interest problems might result. Of course, there is no way of making certain that the within-house research capability isn't simply a tool for justifying a particular state policy. However, some notions emerged from our case study experience that might increase the likelihood that the research office would produce information useful for improving the system, and not simply protect those who are directly responsible for its operation.

One way to reduce the likelihood of that happening would be to insist that the information flow between research office and system managers be more public in nature. It would also seem to be healthier if policy deliberations had more open debate. If policy-relevant information is presented in an open forum, there are opportunities for people to challenge various aspects of the study or the interpretation of the results.

Another way of keeping the system honest would be to make technical reports publicly available. Although technical reports are not effective communication devices between researcher and client, they are important to produce so that interested stakeholders can be reassured that the clients are receiving reasonably competent services from the research office.

A third way of reducing conflict-of-interest problems is to minimize the deployment of research resources for summative evaluations which attempt to prove the value of a particular policy or program. For example, an untenable situation arises if the research office is asked to prove that the latest innovation or policy of the client is producing the desired results. A formative approach, in which the research seeks to suggest or guide more specific ways in which current policies and practices might be improved, are more credible and more relevant to the incremental way in which managers improve systems.

A second basis of generalized support for some of the understandings derived from our case study is grounded in a sense that other researchers in the field are coming to similar conclusions, albeit with different terms and often with different kinds of settings as the contexts for their research. Perhaps the best examples of convergence can be found in the research on use. Although much of this work has been focused explicitly on program evaluation contexts, notions about defining potential users, shaping research activities more clearly toward user information needs, and employing a range of dissemination strategies to increase the probability of use are examples of scholars coming to similar conclusions in different contexts.

Another basis for some optimism about the utility of our understandings is grounded in observations of the district's own new research office. During the last three years of our case study it has successfully employed many of the same kinds of strategies for DOER that we were recommending from our own work. The point here is that while the district's office was obviously still operating in the same system context, it was doing so as a true "insider," in contrast to our own situation. Thus, this experience addressed directly the question of whether some of our understandings about how to approach DOER in this research context were overly dependent upon the fact that we were both a part of, yet not entirely one with, the system in question. While there were differences in our circumstances and those confronted by the new research office, (e.g., the ability to pace the work was less for the research office), it was clear that the district's office was able to use similar approaches to DOER with much success.

The preceding comment about insider–outsider contrasts brings us to one last issue related to the generalizability of case study research. The nature of cases dictates that each setting will have its own configuration of context variables which differentiate it in some ways from other settings. As a reader seeks to construct what might be generalized from one case study to other contexts and settings, the particular characteristics of the case are the places both to note connections and differences. As we reflect upon our experiences, several particular characteristics of our case are perhaps important to reiterate. The research took place over a six-year period, involving at different points numerous educators from every level of the system. The research tasks we were asked to address represented a wide range of information needs, indeed. And we think in some form or another the tasks were fairly typical of information needs that surface in educational systems. We had the special advantage of having ongoing support external to the system from the National Institute of Education for much of the work. In addition, in case 9, the work was also supported by the Ford Foundation. Further, it is fair to say that district leadership, and especially Superintendent Wallace, demonstrated a clear orientation toward the use of data in policy and decision processes. We invite the reader to consider these particulars in our case as he/she seeks to find connections with other settings.

Implications for Education

We believe that we have learned some things about DOER from our Pittsburgh experiences that may apply to other systems and settings. We also believe that this work can make a contribution to debates surrounding three broad policy questions that are of considerable import to the larger field of education: How can educational systems best utilize newly available technology to improve the quality of their operations? In what ways can system managers and researchers be better prepared to work together to solve system information needs? How can public systems become more accountable to their constituencies? In this closing section, we will comment briefly on these policy questions and on how our experiences may relate to them.

Education is clearly in the information business. What is striking is how difficult it seems to be for educators to take advantage of the new information technology. In our view, the area of application that deserves first priority consideration is applying information technology to the task of understanding how the education system works and how it might be improved.

For example, school boards across the country have been trying to move forward in terms of computer applications in education. But the expected miracles in improved student achievement have not occurred from the investments to date, and now hard questions are being raised about what all these computer expenses are achieving, whether the most needy students are receiving the benefits, whether particular strategies are cost effective, etc. It is only when we have sufficiently detailed and accurate student information systems that we will be able to answer these types of questions quickly and easily. So one lesson from our experience is that we see the new information technology as a way of facilitating the introduction of the new instructional technology, both in terms of guiding the use of such scarce resources and in justifying their expansion.

A related important lesson about the new technology is to get information systems into the schools. This emerging trend is quite important in bringing this technology to bear on the instructional problems of schools, and not only in satisfying the needs of central administration information requirements. In fact, it seems quite clear that until data become used in the schools on a day-to-day basis, those summaries of such data that can be important in central district-wide planning functions will not be sufficiently current and accurate to do the job well.

Turning to the preparation of system managers and researchers, one of the clear messages that we derived from our experiences was the importance of researchers being methodologically eclectic in their approach to DOER. This mandate was induced from the facts that: (1) the phenomena that were the subjects of DOER were complex; (2) the information needs were diverse; and (3) the data predispositions of clients were varied. These facts have direct implications for the preparation of researchers interested in becoming "DOER's." While a single researcher cannot be an expert in all methods, some exposure, and perhaps more importantly, an appreciation of alternative methods is vital. Although we haven't made a study of this, it is our impression that existing training programs for researchers are heavily fragmented by traditional disciplinary and methodological camps. We recognize that the notion of multidisciplinary approaches to the preparation of anyone for a given field often is looked down upon in university settings. Nevertheless, it is our position that the nature of the "DOER field" requires such an approach, including serious opportunities for extended internships in field settings.

Although there seem to be few examples of actual training programs for researchers of the type we are recommending, there has been some recognition in the literature of the need to broaden the background of those interested in systems research (e.g., Cronbach and associates, 1980; Anderson and Ball, 1978). What strikes us as having received very little attention is the preparation of system administrators for their role in DOER. One of the special qualities of our case study experiences was the receptivity — indeed commitment — of specific managers to the integration of data into their policy and decision processes. In a few instances, the individuals came to the interaction with some prior background that encouraged the use of data. In most instances, it was something that emerged during the course of researcher–client interactions. Whether a prior background was present or not, what is certain from our case history experiences is that when the client was actively involved and knowledgeable, the benefits to the research process were significant. Integrating into the preparation of administrators some exposure to various methods but, more importantly, to the potential use of managed research resources for improving system operations seems to us to be an important message from our experiences. One critical aspect in our emphasis on the role of administrators is that we recognize in most systems this group will be setting the organizational boundaries and priorities for researchers. Management recognition of the potential of systems research can change the manner in which such resources are applied in ways that differ from current practices and in ways that increase their potential utility to the system.

We would like to close this chapter with a comment on the role of DOER in the very important process of public institution accountability. One aspect of the role concerns the right of the public to know how public dollars are spent, how publicly supported educational systems are functioning, what priorities are being set, and how are they being addressed. A related aspect involves assurances that the system is working to improve its performance in sustained and meaningful ways. DOER can make important contributions in both areas. We are convinced that information generated by DOER can enrich policy and decision processes. We take this position without claiming that systems are totally rational, data-driven organizations. No one who has worked at length in any organization would claim or, we submit, would want to have organizations following such a completely rational model. Nevertheless, information can make an important contribution to the life and health of an educational system. And, in terms of the two accountability issues we have raised, DOER can be a significant public resource. It can be a tool for the policy-shaping and decision-making communities to use in improving system operations, and it can be an important part of the system's public record of the performance levels it reaches.

III THE CASE HISTORIES

CASE HISTORY 1
ELEMENTARY SCHOOL
ACHIEVEMENT STUDY

In the spring of 1978, the Pittsburgh public schools released to the public the most recent results of the standardized achievement tests given to all elementary students in the system. The scores were reported in the local newspapers in terms of the proportion of children in each school that were achieving at or above the national norm. The education office of the Pittsburgh Urban League took the available achievement data and re-ranked the schools by percentage of black students in each school and then compared this ranking based upon percentage of black students to the rankings based upon achievement. It was quite obvious to League personnel that the two sets of rankings produced almost identical lists. Schools with all or many black students were not achieving as well as those with few or no black students. Those achievement results were discussed at the next monthly meeting of the League's education advisory board. One of the authors was a member of this board. The suggestion was made that representatives of the League and LRDC researchers meet to discuss the achievement issue.

This led to a series of meetings during which the League shared the data they possessed on the elementary schools of the district. League members felt that the achievement results reflected inequalities in educational opportunity. They wanted us to examine issues related to whether the children in the predominantly black schools were receiving educational experiences that were inferior to those in the predominantly white schools. Rather early in those discussions, it became apparent to all parties that additional data would be required to examine more fully why achievement varied so dramatically among district schools.

The additional data required were not publicly available. The League went to the district, described the discussions that had taken place, and requested that the superintendent meet with representatives of the League and the LRDC researchers to discuss the possibility of acquiring the needed data. This meeting was held in the fall of 1978. The first meeting with the superintendent led to a series of working sessions between representatives of the League, the research group, and the superintendent's key administrative staff. What emerged from an initial request for additional information was a new, informal, three-way collaboration. (Funding for the work was provided internally by each organization.)

There were three central reasons for the responsiveness of the superintendent to the proposed research effort. First, the Urban League represented an important constituency of the district. At a time when the student population was almost 50 percent black and when the district was under a court mandate to desegregate, a request from the League was not to be taken lightly. Second, the League had historically been very active in district affairs. Typically, these activities (e.g., parent awareness groups, student counseling, community workshops) had been undertaken with the cooperation of the district. As a consequence, although the Urban League had at times been critical of district policy, it also had built up a past history with the district of mutual cooperation. Third, while the superintendent spoke about research as an important administrative tool, the district had little research capability. A rather large research bureau had been a part of the district for years, but it was disbanded as a result of budgetary pressures in the early '70s. This left research and evaluation work as a shared responsibility among line superintendents and the director of the testing. Under these circumstances, the district was able to meet external mandates for evaluation (e.g., Title I) but was not readily able to initiate more exploratory policy-oriented research since the administrative officers were already overburdened with daily management affairs.

The Research Question

The initial client, at least in terms of the initial request for information, was the Urban League. The questions they wanted addressed were: How can the achievement differences between predominately black and predominately white elementary schools be explained? Did these achievement differences reflect differences in the quality of the educational programs in those schools? When the discussions were initiated with the district, the district, in an informal sense, became a second client. The questions remained the same. That is, the presence of two clients did not seem to present a major difficulty because we thought a consensus had developed among the participants regarding the questions to be addressed.

Several meetings were held involving the League's education director, the superintendent and the research group. Two essential kinds of information were exchanged: (1) the nature and accessibility of data; and (2) the technical strategies available for analysis as well as their strengths and limitations. These discussions took place in the context of a continuing refinement of the questions to be addressed. In these discussions, it was determined that the answers could be found through analyses of many kinds of data currently available in various district offices. While these three-way conversations were helpful in defining the early stages of the research, it is important to note that their numbers were limited as was the time period in which they occurred and the range of issues discussed. They did not reach the level of the "mutually educational dialogue" discussed in chapter 3. The early task in the research was to gather all the available data into one large computerized database (see chapter 6). The data, which covered a three-year period from 1975–78, included student level information on achievement, race and sex, and school level files that contained information on teacher experience, class size, grade organization, expenditures, and the number of teacher aides. Once the database was constructed, the research group engaged in a series of analyses designed to produce relevant information on questions important to the two client organizations.

The Main Findings

The data were analyzed using the school as the unit of analysis. To do that we derived school means for the student level information (e.g., standardized achievement test results) and added these to the other information we had collected for each school. Thus we created a file of 72 records, one for each elementary school in the district at that time, and each record included data on over 200 variables.

Over half of those variables were different kinds of achievement results. For example, just one of the achievement tests, say mathematics, yielded 10 school level statistics—the means and standard deviations for each of five grade levels. Because the number of achievement test results were so overwhelming, we decided to derive a school achievement index (SAI) that combined the data across grades and subjects, and which represented the general student achievement level in each school. This SAI indicator then became a central variable in the analyses.

We conducted two major kinds of analyses. One kind analyzed school factors (e.g., average class size) that might explain differences in school achievement, using multiple regression models of student achievement. The other analyses related these school factors to the school's racial mix. Thus we were looking for factors that seemed to be related to a school's general achievement level (SAI), and then checked to see if important determiners of achievement were fairly distributed among schools with different percentages of black students.

There were two factors that stood out as most important in explaining student achievement. One was the average number of years of teaching experience. Schools with a high proportion of inexperienced teachers were not performing as well in student achievement. The other factor was class size, where schools with smaller classes were doing better in achievement. Both of the trends were noted after statistical adjustment for other factors known to influence achievement that the schools could not control, such as the entering ability level of first graders.

Table C1-1 reports the correlations between those two school factors that were influencing achievement, and the percentage of black students in the school and the home socioeconomic status (SES) of the students in the school, as measured by free lunch eligibility.

The correlations indicated that the more experienced teachers tended to be in schools serving fewer blacks ($r = -.4$), and tended even more to be in schools serving a higher SES clientele ($r = -.5$). The relationships with class size were not as strong, with blacks tending to have slightly larger classes.

Another set of findings was also of interest. We found that the use of classroom aides was negatively associated with achievement. In other, smaller studies, and from a review of research on aides, there was growing evidence that this was not just a spurious finding. Case 3 considers this question of paraprofessionals (classroom aides) in more detail.

Table C1-1. Possible Inequities in School Practices (Correlations for 72 schools)

	% Black	SES
Teacher experience	-0.4	0.5
Class size	0.2	-0.1

Reporting of Preliminary Results

Oral presentations took place on two separate occasions. The first was a formal presentation to the superintendent and his executive board which occurred in March 1979. This presentation focused on factors influencing achievement (e.g., class size, teacher experience, and the presence of aides) and on equity issues related to school resources (e.g., distribution of experienced teachers and smaller classes in relation to the race of the students). Policy responses to the results were not included in the presentation. The second presentation was to the Urban League; it consisted of review of the results with the executive officer of the League and the director of his education staff.

The two presentations elicited lively discussions. For example, the district presentation stimulated a discussion among attending administrators about the possible policy implications of the results. Similarly, the Urban League representatives were interested in publicizing some of the results in order to place pressure on the system to change certain of its current policies. (It should be noted that both the discussions with the League and school officials tended to uncover similar policy change alternatives.)

The League representatives were particularly concerned with the negative relationships found between the percentage of black students in a school and the number of experienced teachers, a variable that had been found to be an important positive influence of student achievement at both the national and district levels. The League also found disturbing the evidence that the use of instructional aides in the classroom was possibly not having the desired effect. As a policy advocacy group (as opposed to a decision-making body), the League representatives indicated a desire to press school officials to modify their policies in light of these findings. For example, at a time when the district was considering a number of desegregation plans which would move significant numbers of students and teachers, the League wanted the district to ensure that this process would improve the relationship between the number of black students in a school and the number of experienced teachers. The willingness to advocate this type of policy change reflected a relatively straightforward example of utilization. The fact that the questions asked were of direct concern to League interests had clearly been an important factor in improving the chances of utilization.

The district response to the March presentation was a less certain example of research utilization. The format used to present the results of the research, an overhead slide presentation, had apparently been successful in that district administrators rather quickly involved themselves in the discussion. The substantive results also seemed to be of great interest to the group.

As noted earlier, part of the discussion involved the identification of specific policy changes that could be made as a result of the research.

The direct outcome of the meeting was that the superintendent placed the results on the agenda for further discussion at the next cabinet meeting of district administrators. Upon the completion of this further review, the district would then inform the researchers concerning additional steps to be taken. It should be noted that the researchers had made it clear to the school personnel that all of the results were of a preliminary nature; therefore, further investigation was recommended before any policy changes were considered. Under such circumstances, a reasonable measure of utilization would be the district's indicating those areas in which they wanted further research undertaken. This was considered a legitimate measure of utilization because it indicated the client's desire to maintain an ongoing relationship with the researchers and implied that the client considered the research activity valuable.

Months went by without formal response by the district. During this period, however, the superintendent indicated a continuing interest in the activity through various private communications.

The most obvious explanation for the lack of followup on the part of the district was that the desegregation issue had heated up to a point where all of the district's energies were being concentrated on this issue. The research that had been done was interesting, but it simply was not a top priority item at a time when the district had to produce a system-wide desegregation plan within two months. This view of the process does have merit. The desegregation crisis was real; the interest expressed in the preliminary results seemed genuine.

A second potential explanation of district non-response was that the implications of the preliminary results were thought to be potentially critical of existing district conditions and, therefore, would be embarrassing to the current administration. Again this explanation was logically plausible but no evidence of this kind of reaction was uncovered. Further, the superintendent continued to express informal interest in the research and at later points (cases 2 and 3) supported research involvement in sensitive district concerns.

Several alternative explanations for the lack of response from the district can be identified. It is possible that what were thought to be consensus research questions between the two clients were indeed shared interests, but were also of varying organizational priority. That is, the questions answered were of more central interest to the League than to the district, and consequently the League rather than the district gave evidence of greater utilization. Reflecting upon the utilization literature, one possible conclusion was that we were suffering from the malady of not clearly defining our clients, or perhaps trying to serve too many clients with the same research.

Another possible explanation of the district's nonaction was the timing of the reporting of the research results and the expectations held by the researchers for the March discussions. The presentations were made months after the initial conversations that defined the study, and the results presented were of a preliminary nature. Each of the results required additional work, data collection, and analysis before the researchers could be confident of recommending policy changes. The reason for bringing preliminary findings to the attention of the district rested upon the researchers' conviction that clients should be involved in each phase of the research process.

The researchers hoped that the sharing of early findings would heighten the interest of district administrators and would further involve them in giving direction to the endeavor. The expectation of further involvement may have been somewhat naive given the amount of time that had evolved and the changing circumstances in the district.

Relationships to DOER

The research results were not utilized by the district, at least not in the direct, immediate way expected by the researchers. The following factors apparently contributed to the absence of utilization:

1. the district as potential client had its organizational attention turned elsewhere due to the desegregation crisis;
2. the district was less of a client for the questions researched than the researchers realized;
3. we did not engage anyone in the district in the mutually educational dialogue that we describe in chapter 3;
4. organizations do not use information, people do; it was necessary to define the key person that was to be the primary client and not think of an institution (the district) as a client;
5. developing an educational dialogue with a client is easier said than done, but is essential to try to achieve.

In contrast, the League as client had the involvement of the education director, at least in the early stages of shaping the research. Although we never achieved (indeed in this early case we weren't trying to achieve) an ongoing dialogue with clients through each phase of the research process, the original questions asked by the League remained at the core of the research. The results, therefore, were still of interest. (This was so despite the slow turn-around.) Further, the League had an individual, the education director, in a position to actually care about and use the results.

Several things became clear to the researchers from the lack of response from the district and the interest of the League. First, greater attention to defining the person who was to be the primary client was required. Second, the research to be undertaken must be synchronized closely with the current concerns of the client. That is, the focus of the work should be relevant to immediate policy or management questions. Third, direct discussions with the client may not be the only strategy to use in seeking to refine the direction of the research. Fourth, results, when reported, should be as unambiguous as possible and should not require further refinement if the results are to be relevant to the policy process. A final understanding involved the potential difficulty of trying to serve too many clients in a single piece of research with the result of not serving some or all well.

With these clarifications gleaned in this first experience, one new strategy that was instituted involved the direct monitoring of the district policy process. An observer attended all meetings of the district's board of education that were open to the public. (Public meetings for the district constitute a significant amount of time, approximately 20 hours per month. A graduate assistant usually observed.) In addition, a systematic clipping of the local press coverage of education was instituted. The basic goal of the observation and review strategy was to identify those current policy concerns of the district that could possibly be informed by DOER. It was hoped that this approach could aid the researchers in developing productive research questions of interest to potential clients.

The strategy worked. Direct or implicit information requests would surface in the discussions among board members and senior administrative personnel. Some of the information requests by board members were relatively straightforward and required the simple compilation of such data as student enrollment statistics. However, questions also surfaced that clearly required some significant research activity.

One question of a researchable nature that emerged concerned the impact of grade organization on student achievement. This issue provided the opportunity for the researchers to undertake a new set of policy-relevant analyses. The findings of this work were eventually reported directly to the board of education at the behest of the superintendent. The sequence of events that led up to this second reporting of research results to the district is described in case 2.

CASE HISTORY 2
ACHIEVEMENT IMPLICATIONS
OF GRADE REORGANIZATION

In 1979, grade organization emerged as an important policy issue for the district because of its relationship to the desegregation planning process. At the heart of the plans developed by the school administration to desegregate the system was the commitment to a 5-3-4 grade organization plan. Several different grade organization plans were currently operating in the district. The main two were a K-8 elementary school followed by a four-year high school, and a K-5 elementary school followed by a three-year middle school and a four-year high school. All K-8 elementary schools were to be closed or converted to K-5, with the sixth, seventh, and eighth grades being sent to newly organized and desegregated middle schools.

There was strong disagreement among the nine board members over the desirability of such a change. The five board members who had, in the past, been opposed to desegregation efforts also opposed the dismantling of the K-8 schools. These schools tended to be in predominantly white neighborhoods. Over the summer a public discussion ensued concerning the grade organization issue. This discussion often surfaced at board meetings and was extensively reported in the media. One claim made by the proponents of the K-8 configuration was that these schools were more effective than the middle schools. As evidence, they pointed to higher standardized test scores for the eighth graders in the K–8 schools. The LRDC researchers saw in the grade organization issue an opportunity to generate relevant information for district policy making. Using the data that had been collected during the previous work for the Urban League (case 1), several analyses were conducted (at the researchers' own initiative) concerning the impact of grade organization on student achievement.

As the initial work on grade organization progressed, a separate, parallel series of events occurred within the district that provided the specific opportunity for the researchers to address the board of education. In early September, the district's testing office released to the board and the public the most recent results of its system-wide testing program. A key feature of the report was the significant dropoff (from national norms) found in the sixth through eighth grades. Board members expressed a great deal of concern about this drop in achievement in the upper grades and several called for a study investigating possible causes. "I want to know why those kids are turned off," said one board member at a district meeting (also quoted in the Pittsburgh *Post-Gazette*, September 26, 1979).

In response to this, the superintendent cited the past work conducted with the Urban League and the LRDC research group as an attempt to analyze achievement test results in the district. The superintendent's comments sparked interest among board members in hearing about the district's testing program generally, and more specifically, the recent analyses of achievement. The subject was placed upon the agenda for the next month. The director of the testing office was in charge of the program. Rather early in his planning, the director contacted the LRDC researchers (with the support of the superintendent) to invite them to participate in the October presentation. The researchers agreed and suggested that a part of the presentation focus on the issues of grade organization as well as sixth through eighth grade achievement score decline.

Board members who favored the status quo had noticed that the eighth graders who attended K–8 elementary schools tended to have higher scores on the current standardized achievement test (Metropolitan Achievement Test — MAT) than did eighth graders attending middle schools. They argued that therefore the K–8 schools were a more effective grade organization.

Using the school level files that were established in case 1, we analyzed the achievement data in several different ways. The most important was to examine growth between grade 5 and grade 8. There were no grade organization differences in grade 8 performance when we took into account the ability levels of the entering sixth graders. Thus, during grades 6, 7, and 8, middle-school students increased their achievement scores as much as similar students did in the K–8 schools. A similar result was found for growth during grade 5.

We also showed that the differences in observed eighth grade means between the two types of schools were completely explained by differences in socioeconomic status (SES) of the families being served. The data clearly indicated that the largest single factor that determines differences among school averages on the MAT was the SES of the population served by that school. For example, ranking schools in order of the percentage of the students scoring below grade level resulted in the same ordering as ranking schools according to percentage of students eligible for free lunch. Although an *individual* child's performance cannot be predicted very well from the child's home SES, the small but important influences of the home get magnified in school averages because of the very large socioeconomic differences among schools. Such school differences, of course, result from the socioeconomic similarity of homes within the neighborhoods served by each school.

There was a 30 percent difference in the poverty indicator between K–8 schools and middle schools. That is, less than 50 percent of the children in K–8 schools were eligible for free lunch, and about 80 percent were eligible in the middle schools. Just on that basis alone, one would expect an advantage of one grade level on the MAT between K–8 schools and middle schools. That actual difference was less than that.

As we point out in chapter 8, one has to be very careful in using SES expectations in considering student achievement performance. The point here was that it could not be inferred from grade 8 achievement results that it was the neighborhood K–8 elementary school that was responsible for producing higher achievement results.

However, it was also important to point out that lower test scores are not inevitably linked to lower SES. The SES relationship was important in considering the relative merits of different grade organization schemes. It is clearly more difficult to achieve higher achievement means in low SES schools than in high SES schools. The observed differences in achievement, statistically controlling for prior abilities, suggested that the two kinds of grade organizations were equally effective.

Actually, what we showed was that the two kinds of schools were doing equally poorly. Addressing the concerns of board members about the dropoff in achievement in the upper grades, we showed that it was more pronounced in Pittsburgh than nationally. Thus, we tried to shift board attention from the merits of different grade organizations to more pervasive concerns about improving the quality of instruction in the schools.

The presentation to the board and school administrators occurred on October 31, 1979. The director of the testing office began the meeting with an overview of the district's extensive testing program. This was followed by a presentation by a representative of the research group. This presentation included: (1) a brief review of the earlier evaluation activities; (2) a substantive presentation on the analyses of the effects of grade organization; and (3) some general comments on the decline in achievement scores in the upper grades along with a presentation of the limited results in hand on this issue. The presentation was followed by a lively discussion among board members and school administrators.

Did the research results have more of an impact on the district than in case 1? Evidence suggests that this second attempt had considerably greater impact. First, an explicit outcome of the board's discussion of the results was a mandate that the administration pursue research on the issue of the decline of upper grade achievement scores. Second, the presentation removed from the board debates about desegregation plans the argument that "K–8s do it better." Third, soon after the presentation, the superintendent requested the assistance of the researchers in three additional evaluation activities with the district. They were asked to conduct an evaluation of (1) Project Pass (a major system-wide initiative to improve the achievement of students who have failed, described in case 3); (2) the Summer Skills Maintenance Program (designed to prevent summer learning loss among Title I students); and (3) an all-day kindergarten program that had been recently instituted by the district.

The evidence of utilization was less a measure of direct impact on a particular policy than a recognition on the part of district managers that such research was a potentially valuable addition to the policy process. That they viewed this as so was evidenced by their interest in expanding the work to a variety of new policy areas.

The impact of the case 2 research was greater than in case 1, but what made the difference? Three features of this second effort seemed to be of greatest importance. First, the strategy of observing board meetings had permitted the research group to understand better the nature and substance of the immediate policy issues being confronted by the district. This enabled the researchers to focus more upon what Datta (1981) has called "the few key questions." In effect, the observations of the public board meetings had given the research group valuable additional time with their clients (e.g., the superintendent and the school board). Although the time gained was not in the direct interactional mode described by Patton (1978), it was time not readily available previously through direct contact because of the generally pressing schedule of school officials.

A second feature of this work was that the strategy to observe board meetings enabled the research group to be aware of the current policy process of the district. That is, the questions addressed were *important* to the district, and the results were presented at a time when they were still relevant to the decision-making process. The importance of timing in the reporting of evaluation results has been noted in the work of Hill (1980) and of Datta (1979), particularly in terms of what we call "first wave" research utilization in chapter 9.

Third, the results presented on the key question, grade organization, were not presented in a preliminary fashion. The results of a number of analyses made it clear to the board that no one grade organization gave evidence of superior student achievement when the characteristics of students served by various schools were controlled. The higher scores of eighth grade students in K–8 schools cited by some board opponents to the 5–3–4 grade organization plan of the superintendent were the results of SES bias in the student populations. While the research group did not recommend a particular grade organization, it did contribute information that was directly relevant to the decision-making process.

It is important to note that the organizational context of the second presentation had not changed appreciably. That is, if anything, the pressures on the district had increased since the March presentation, so the heightened interest of district personnel in research results in September was not a measure of a more relaxed climate in the system. The district was still faced with the desegregation issue since the Pennsylvania Human Relations Commission had turned down the latest plan that had been submitted the previous June. In addition, the issue had become greatly politicized because of school board elections to be held in November.

Several other features of the September experience should be noted. The additional time spent with the clients through the observational strategy also improved the research group's understanding of the multiple objectives a client might have for a specific program. For example, the design of a research that was subsequently conducted with the district on the all-day kindergarten program was heavily influenced by a board discussion of that program that occurred in July. In a debate over the advisability of expanding the kindergarten program, five separate program goals emerged from various configurations of board members. Some board members saw the program as an important tool to attract and retain students in a public school system that had been experiencing significant enrollment decline for the past decade. Other board members were concerned over the impact that these kindergartens would have on achievement and desegregation. Still others justified the program as a service to communities where 40 percent of the mothers worked or simply because they were popular in the community. Each of these perspectives represented important aspects of the clients' views of the program. Knowing this enabled the research group to design a potentially more relevant research activity that took into account the multiple concerns of the district.

Finally, the research activities in September were possible because an extensive, flexible data bank had been built up during the case 1 work. The changing nature of a school district's policy process and a research group's goal of contributing information directly relevant to policy issues requires that a great deal of attention be given to data collection strategies. To the extent that any data-gathering activities can be designed in ways that are predictive of future possible research needs, they can contribute measurably to the goal of improving the linkage between DOER and the decision-making processes.

Relationships to DOER

Case 2 illustrates the importance of several key strategies that increase the utility of DOER. Key strategies included being aware of the general policy climate and producing substantive results on time and in concise, understandable fashion. These were contributing factors in improving the link between researchers and decision makers in this case study.

There were some features of the study, however, that differed with certain components of the ideal notion of client orientation as discussed in chapter 3. That notion suggests that the researcher should work closely with the client during each phase of the research process. This case study demonstrates that such an approach can be difficult to attain for at least two reasons. First, system managers face a myriad of problems, pressures, and tasks, each on a rather short time line. The difficulty in getting time with chief school officers, for example, was not simply a function of the fact that the research group involved in the case study was not a part of the district's staff. Rather, the problem of the researcher in gaining access to the decision maker's time stems, in part, from the nature of the role of chief school officers, particularly among urban school systems. Cuban (1976) describes the world of urban school superintendents:

> . . . there was a perpetual crossfire of expectations, requests, and demands from board members, middle-level administrators, principals, teachers, students, and different civic groups. With crises breaking daily and enormous demands placed upon the chief's limited time . . . The superintendent was not unlike a juggler who, in order to keep a dozen objects in the air on a windy day, must constantly move about, keeping his eyes roving; he may be very uncertain that he has the whole dozen but he doesn't dare stop to find out! (p. 167).

Under such circumstances the interactive mode may not be possible. Other strategies must be developed. In this study, observation of board–administrative interaction was found to be useful. The goal of having the client's concerns and orientations define the research program is, itself, a sound objective that can improve the utilization of research results.

The interactive mode also may be somewhat difficult to attain because of a gap in technical knowledge between client and researcher. Given the diversity of the role, it is unlikely that key district decision makers will be thoroughly aware of the changing technical aspects of research. This is not to suggest that the decision maker in this instance should simply defer technical questions to the "experts." But it does mean that if researchers want the input of decision makers on design and methodology issues, the burden probably rests with them to specify clearly the available alternatives, as well as each strategy's strengths and limitations.

The goal of improving the links between researcher and decision maker as a means for improving the utilization of research results is an important objective. This issue is of particular importance to the expanding research efforts of local school districts. At a time when district budgets are under increased scrutiny because of rising costs and declining enrollments, each activity sponsored by the schools must be justified on the basis of its own merits. DOER can make an important contribution to the decision-making process of a school district. It can only do so, however, if the information produced is timely, valid, and relevant to that policy process.

CASE HISTORY 3
EVALUATION OF PROJECT PASS

Background

In February 1979, the Pittsburgh public schools administrative staff proposed a new program that was designed to supplement the desegregation plan prepared by the Magnet School Advisory Committee. Called Project Pass, it was intended to provide a special program for students who had failed a grade. Students who were scheduled for retention were to be removed from regular classrooms for a year and placed in a special class called Pass. Limited to 14 students, Pass classrooms were to be self-contained, with a teacher and an aide in each classroom. Since the Pass classrooms would not necessarily be in the failing student's home school, it was hoped that enrollment in Pass would improve racial balance among schools. The instructional program in Pass classrooms was designed as an intensive, individualized program of remedial education in the basic skills. The students who had failed a grade would be taken "off the track" for a year and would then rejoin their original cohorts if they did well in Pass or, at least, would be promoted to the next grade following their year in Pass.

Because this innovative program was announced as a small part of a very controversial plan for desegregating the Pittsburgh schools, which included

171

extensive busing and grade reorganizations, Project Pass initially was not a major issue. Public reaction to Pass was minor compared to the reaction to the desegregation plan in general.

At the February public hearings on the desegregation plan, Pass was supported by the teachers' union and one or two other speakers. One individual was concerned that Pass would result in pupils being labeled as "dummies" and would create social problems among peers. The media gave Pass very little coverage and focused more on the other features of the desegregation plan. However, that spring, as the board trimmed back on the general desegregation plan, Pass eventually became the only mandatory integration measure, and as such took on much more significance in the political arena.

Beginning in April, leaders of the black community expressed concerns that Pass would result in further segregation and stigmatization since a very large percentage of children who fail are black. In the course of that debate, it was agreed to withhold judgment until the end of that school year and see what the statistics looked like. In June it was learned that of the 1,200 students who qualified for Project Pass, 70 percent were indeed black. This result produced reaction from the black community and from black members of the school board. One newspaper article quoted a board member as saying that he feared that the classes would be used as "a dumping ground for problem kids." Another board member expressed concern that it would pejoratively label youngsters.

At the June board meeting tempers flaired over the issues surrounding Pass. One expressed concern that the district had not adequately explored other methods for dealing with student failure. But the proponents of Pass argued that the program shouldn't be condemned before it was tried, and one board member argued strongly that the program be implemented with an evaluation, so that "its effectiveness could be established." At the June legislative meeting, the board voted to establish Pass but make it voluntary. Pass then shifted from being promoted as a desegregation device, which was part of its initial intent, to being a means of improving student achievement for students who were not keeping up with their classmates. So in September 1979, Project Pass was implemented as a district-wide effort for students who had failed a grade (grades 1 through 9) and was implemented on a voluntary basis.

Then in November 1979, a meeting was called to consider the evaluation of Project Pass. One of the LRDC researchers joined a group of district administrators and two university faculty members to discuss how this might be done. At that meeting, district administrators shared with the group the evaluation design which they had already put in place. Their plan relied heavily on showing the achievement impact of participation in Project Pass, using the district's standardized testing program.

Following that meeting, we composed the following memorandum to administrative staff in which some possible additional approaches to this evaluation task were described. The memorandum reflected the benefit of our having begun to monitor board meetings closely in January 1979.

At the outset, it seems useful to distinguish among three types of information that might be generated by evaluation activities: (1) information useful to the school board for considering whether or not it is sensible to continue the program in subsequent years; (2) information for "on-line" monitoring by the implementors of critical aspects of the program; and (3) information for considering how the general design of Project Pass might be improved, or for considering whether or not the problem of student failure might be more effective and/or efficiently solved with other procedures.

With respect to the school board, there seems to be three types of information that would be useful to generate by the spring of 1980. We expect that the board will want to know answers to the following kinds of questions:

1. Who is the program serving? This would be answered with descriptive information of the children in terms of sex, grade, race, SES, attendance records, disciplinary history, etc.

2. How does the program work? They would certainly be interested in such aspects of the program as how students were selected, parent acceptance of the program, how the classroom operates, what is the curriculum, and most importantly, how does a Project Pass classroom differ from the classroom in which the child failed?

3. What effect is the program having on students? For the immediate needs, this question will have to be answered in terms of attendance and discipline information, and teacher and student opinions. In addition, some student progress information may be available, including progress tests in reading and mathematics. However, the use of standardized tests at midpoint during the year would have been too short to expect a noticeable change.

In terms of monitoring the program during the current school year, it seems important to collect information on attendance in Project Pass classrooms. This monitoring information could also include information on disciplinary actions, teacher/aide attendance, reports from supervisory personnel, reports on parent involvement, and specific statements from teachers as to difficulties they are having with the project. The purpose of this monitoring would be to identify trouble spots early so that problems can be corrected in the course of the school year.

Following completion of this first year of the program, if continuation is recommended based upon the information in hand, it will then be important to answer questions about the effect of the program on student achievement — how students in Project Pass compare with similar students who opted not to take Pass — in terms of subsequent school performance, behavior, and motivation. Another important question is whether or not it is possible to identify the particular features of Project Pass which seem to be the reasons for success (if it is indeed successful). The purpose here would be to figure out how those features might be incorporated into the regular school program so that students don't have to go through the pejorative act of being classified failures and then given the remedial work. That is, can the effective features of Pass be identified and can they be focused upon students who are *heading* toward failure for one reason or another?

With respect to information that might be useful for program improvement, an obvious need is to try to identify general characteristics of those classrooms in which the students seem to benefit greatly from the Project Pass experience and the kinds of classrooms in which they did not. This can be done from the kinds of data collection activities that have been suggested, but would emphasize the search for general principles. This would require some independent looks at the Project Pass classrooms to determine whether or not programs are indeed being implemented along the lines envisioned by program designers. Evaluation research staff at LRDC could be made available for this purpose. We would use a mutually agreed upon observation schedule and procedure. I think this additional information would be important in order to help to understand which features of the program were critically important to its success (e.g., the quality of in-service experiences for each Pass school and how these influenced the program's implementation).

Another aspect of program improvement might be to consider improving selection processes and examine the characteristics of students who seem to benefit most from the program.

A very important aspect of the program would seem to be the decisions that are made at the end of the school year with respect to the "graduates" of Project Pass. That is, which students are to be advanced in grade and which students are to be returned to their peers? To examine this aspect of the program, general and specific criteria for student placement in regular classrooms needs to be developed. Related to this, I would think that a followup next fall of adjustment problems of former Project Pass students would generate some useful information. Another aspect of the program that should be examined is whether or not students who went to a different school to participate in Project Pass and those who remained in their home school differed in performance.

It also would be rather important to compare Project Pass with remedial reading and math programs. This is said not in the sense of a horse race between the two, but rather to critically examine the major features of the two programs and see whether or not they might be combined in ways that are consistent with federal Title I policies. One thing that is emerging from the research literature is the ineffectiveness of the "pull-out" strategy, which is currently dominating Title I programs because of the federal guidelines. It is our understanding from officers at the [U.S.] Office of Education that if a strong case can be made for mounting a program that does not require pull-out practice, and has a sound educational rationale behind it, that such proposals would be well received. If effective instructional practices can be identified in the Pass experience, then practices may well be applicable to Title I students. The Title I funding base would permit expansion in the use of effective practices without putting a heavy financial burden on the district. Of course, it might be quite undesirable to confuse Pass with Title I, but

it seems that the intent of these two programs could be merged into a very successful effort for educating children who are having difficulty learning to read
and cipher.

The evaluation group at LRDC is available to help on the evaluation of Pass.
We have considerable capabilities in the area of classroom observation and data
analysis and could be helpful in all aspects of evaluation design.

Several meetings were subsequently held to discuss the points raised in
that memorandum, and in January it was agreed that LRDC would conduct
an evaluation of Project Pass along the general lines outlined in that memorandum. It was agreed that the intended audiences for this evaluation were
the superintendent and the central administrative staff. We also agreed that
"any dissemination beyond that would require the approval of Superintendent Olson" (Cooley memorandum to Faison, January 10, 1980).

We viewed LRDC's function as assisting board staff in clarification of
evaluation questions, and the collection, organization, and interpretation of
data relevant to those questions regarding the operation of Project Pass,
and policy questions of interest to the board.

What We Did

For the balance of that first year of Pass, the data collection focused on the
more descriptive questions that were being raised about Pass, particularly
who was being served by the program and the general nature of those services. We also conducted teacher interviews and classroom observations to
attempt to generate information that would be useful for program improvement and for describing how the program worked.

The task of describing Project Pass participants proved to be more difficult than we had expected. The district's ability to track individual students
was "in disarray." It proved difficult to find out which students were in
what schools, much less whether they were in Project Pass. It was in the
context of this effort that the critical need to improve student information
systems became crystal clear. Most of our energies this first year were
devoted to data collection tasks which should be part of any school district's
student information system, such as information on enrollment, sex, race,
test scores, absenteeism, prior experience with failure, and so on. It proved
to be a massive effort just to get these descriptive statistics together, yet
such statistics would address several of the major concerns that the board
had regarding this program.

Our first report dealt with a fundamental concern that was expressed by
several board members (as well as members of the community) when the

board considered the establishment of Project Pass. The concern was that a special pull-out program for students who have failed a grade may result in stigmatizing students. Others worried that Pass might become a "dumping ground" for black students. The possible danger of unnecessarily labeling, stigmatizing, and isolating students who had difficulty with normal classroom instruction, or who may have received inferior instruction in their prior schooling, needed to be carefully examined.

In our report, it seemed important to recognize that there were a large number of children who were not learning the academic skills in the primary grades that were essential throughout the remainder of their formal education, and that this was occurring for a variety of reasons. At that time, approximately 70 percent of the children that were experiencing this difficulty were black, so it was not surprising that 70 percent of the students in Pass were found to be black. Many would consider it unfair if the district established a program to serve needy students, and it was determined that 70 percent of the students with those needs are black, yet only 50 percent of the students in the program were black. Advocates of Pass, for example, were not concerned about the large number of black students in the program per se because they saw Pass providing extra help for students who seemed to need it and whose parents apparently wanted them to be in this voluntary program.

Our recommendation was that the district continue Pass for a second school year, but at the same time try to identify new ways of providing for children who may be *heading* for failure. It seemed possible that by finding ways of focusing district resources upon the primary grades, children who are not learning the basic skills could be given the extra help they needed for subsequent success in their schooling. If children did not learn those skills in the primary grades, they experienced difficulty throughout their schooling. If procedures could be established for identifying where these problems tended to occur in the district, then methods found to be effective could be directed toward their solution.

This first report also pointed out that if Project Pass continued, program implementors should examine the strategy to be used for running the program. As initially conceived, Pass was primarily designed to improve the instruction offered students who failed in school. Additionally, preliminary data (e.g., teacher comments) indicated that the program had a positive impact on students who experienced learning problems. However, other data indicated that many of the students assigned to Pass classes had different or additional types of problems, e.g., emotional, behavioral, and/or attendance problems. Thus, it appeared that the Project Pass students presented diverse problems, and this implied that diverse solutions had to be found to solve these problems.

Therefore, a re-examination of the intent of Project Pass, whom it was to serve and how this service was to be offered, was necessary. These issues were framed in terms of a basic policy question: Is Project Pass for children who experience only learning problems, or is it for children with a wide variety of academic, emotional, behavior, and attendance problems? The answer to this question had important implications for the direction and design of Project Pass the following year.

If the program was to serve students who failed solely because of low academic abilities, then Pass should be viewed primarily as an instructional program. As such, it would focus on a target population of students who had poor math and reading skills but who were able to function effectively in a classroom. Students with severe attendance, emotional, behavior, and/or discipline problems would not be placed in the program. Rather, students would be selected on the basis of having learning problems which could realistically be ameliorated by a short-term intervention program.

If the program was to serve a diverse set of students (as was the case the first year), then several new features needed to be incorporated into the existing program. For example, teachers and educational assistants needed more intensive training on how to handle the wide variety of problems they would encounter. Teachers had to be made aware of and strongly encouraged to use all available support services (e.g., social workers, counselors, etc.). Furthermore, a decision to include a variety of students in Pass had implications for the operation of these support services; that is, more effective procedures for dealing with chronic absentees and emotional, family, or drug/alcohol problems were needed. Additionally, policies on suspensions, and the role of social workers and counselors dealing with these problems needed to be reconsidered.

Dissemination of First Year Results

Although our evaluation of Project Pass benefited from the fact that we had begun monitoring and recording school board deliberations, it did not benefit from our subsequent insights into the most effective ways to disseminate our results. We relied heavily on the preparation of written reports. The first report was 60 pages long, and the second was 37 pages. Both were issued in the summer of 1980. We were quite disappointed in the lack of impact those reports had on either board policy or program improvement. Although Pass was continued into the second year, it was not because they followed our recommendation, but because the board never got around to considering whether or not Pass should be continued. The board had a large number of distractions at that time, so it was not surprising. The State Human Relations Commission had rejected their most recent desegregation plan, the board did not renew the superintendent's contract so they had to find and hire a new superintendent by September 1, 1980, and the teachers' union was threatening to strike. So in the fall of 1980, we issued a brief 12-page report. It focused on the highlights of our first year of evaluation.

The summary reviewed the major accomplishments of Pass during its first year of operation, presented our suggestions for immediate program improvement, and summarized the major research findings that seem to have implications for more general policy issues. We did not, however, have any opportunity to make an oral presentation of these results, and so even the 12-page summary tended not to have much impact. There was, however, "verbal enthusiasm" for our first year evaluation results on the part of the central administrative staff, so we are encouraged to continue our evaluation of Project Pass for a second year.

One finding that did seem to make an impression on the school managers was the need for a more effective means for dealing with student absenteeism. We found that for grades 6 through 9, about one-fourth of the Project Pass students were absent more than one-third of the time. Many students were absent more than they were present. There was a modest effort to add a teacher in-service prior to the opening of school in the fall of 1980, to try to prepare these teachers to deal with other problems besides the learning problems which the children exhibited. So there was not much done to try to change the composition of Pass participants, but there was some effort to try to deal with the diverse problems that they exhibited.

Student Absenteeism

As was mentioned, student truancy was a large problem in Pass during the first year of this program. So we decided to take a closer look at that problem. One of the reasons there was so much student failure was the fact that the board, several years before, had passed a resolution to abolish social promotions, so part of the impetus for Project Pass was the fact that people began to notice that a lot of students were failing. About the same time that the district had passed the no-social-promotion policy, it had also negotiated an agreement with the teachers' union that allowed teachers to fail students who were absent from class more than nine days in a quarter.

So in the fall of 1980, we did some special analyses that examined the relationships among student attendance, student achievement test performance, and retention. What we found was that a major predictor of whether a student was going to fail was not low ability, as measured by standardized test scores, but chronic truancy. This was not just for Pass students, but for students in general. The following spring we took a more in-depth look at how chronic truancy was being handled within schools and found that there still was no good connection between Project Pass and the action system that was intended to deal with the chronic truants. In fact, it was discovered that some of the serious truancy cases apparently never even had a home visit from the district social workers (Carter, 1982). So, once again, we recommended that a more formal system be implemented which dealt directly with the chronic truant. If students were failing for that reason and not because they were having particular problems in basic skill development, Pass was not helping a large proportion of its students.

Classroom Aides

A key ingredient in Pass was the placement of paraprofessionals (instructional aides) in each classroom. In some of our other research at LRDC, we had begun to worry about the possible negative effect of using sides, particularly if the teachers used them in the direct instruction of students, or if the classroom management system hadn't been designed in ways that would effectively incorporate a second adult in the room, or if there was not adequate in-service for the aides. So one of the things we did was produce a 50-page report on the "The Instructional Effectiveness of Classrooms Aides" (Schuetz, 1980) in which we pulled together the research that had been done on how to use aides effectively.

The report was clearly too academic in tone. It was a suitable submission for a journal such as *Review of Educational Research*, but was not a useful vehicle for communicating to busy school people. One page, buried deep in the report, summarized the implications of that research. Had we pulled it out and, through personal contact, shared it directly with one or two key people in the district, it might have had some impact, but a big report with 15 pages of references did not. So little was done to improve the ways in which aides were used in Pass classrooms.

The Second Year Study

During the second year of Project Pass, we focused on two major aspects. One was a followup of the first year students to see what academic placements they received in the year following Pass and whether there were any changes in the student population being served by Pass. The other major aspect was to do a special study of the chronic truants in Pass to see what Pass might do to alleviate that problem.

With respect to the academic placement of Pass participants, our findings included such results as:

- Only 8 percent of the elementary school participants in Pass were advanced a grade so that they rejoined their peers.
- In the middle school, 14 percent of the previous participants were still in Pass in spite of board policy that Pass was to be a one-year program. However, a larger percentage of the middle-school participants (17 percent) actually rejoined their original peers.
- In ninth grade Pass, 20 percent of the participants dropped out of school during the year following Pass.
- We found that most students had been in one or more previous efforts at trying to improve their special programs to improve their academic performance. Two-thirds of them had been in Title I, Compensatory Education. Almost a third of the Pass participants had failed two or more times prior to their placement in Pass.

Another analysis we did of the second year data was to establish what proportion of the eligible population was actually participating in Pass. This varied quite a bit by grade level with a low of 12 percent of the fourth grade failures being served by Pass and 55 percent of the sixth graders in the middle schools being served by Pass.

With respect to race, two-thirds of the students in Pass were black. In terms of attendance, the Pass students absence rates were pretty much the same the second year of the program as they were the first year, so the few initiatives to try to improve that situation did not seem to be having any effect. The special investigation into chronic truants revealed a rather heterogeneous group with respect to why they were absent, so there didn't seem to be any one single thing Pass could do different. But what seemed clear was that a very large number could be helped significantly by trying to prevent failure early in the child's academic career.

Dissemination: A Second Phase

As is spelled out in detail in case history 4, during this second year of Pass we undertook a massive district-wide needs assessment for the new superintendent, and had the opportunity to report on this to an all-day retreat of the board in January of that year. It was possible to work into that presentation some things we had learned in the conduct of the Project Pass evaluation. We emphasized the problems that ensued for children who were unable to master the ability to read with understanding during the first three grades and the patterns of failure and remediation that followed from this. We had found, for example, that by middle school over half the children were in one or more remedial programs including Pass with the tendency of moving these remedial efforts all the way to the twelfth grade with little obvious success. We indicated that we could not be sure that a more intensive effort in the primary grade would solve the problem, but it seemed from the data to be worth a good try.

Our direct studies of Project Pass ended with that second year of Pass, but the program continued for a third and fourth year, and it wasn't until the summer of 1983 that serious budget pressures forced the board to consider closing down Pass classrooms because of the extra added expense of small classes and aides. At that point, the district eliminated Pass in the middle schools and high schools, but preserved it in the elementary schools in order to try to reduce the need for extensive remediation in subsequent grades. The superintendent reported that the decision to focus such remedial efforts in the primary grades was in part a function of our studies.

Relationships to DOER

Our studies of Project Pass proved to be a very valuable learning experience for us. For one thing, this effort suffered from the lack of a clearly defined primary client. The board wanted a summative type of evaluation so they could decide whether or not to continue this expensive program. The central administrators wanted to preserve Pass as a desegregation tool. The supervisors directly responsible for Pass wanted assistance in implementing a program that would really help needy students. Meanwhile, what we tended to do was study Pass with no clear primary client. When we worked with program implementors, we were viewed with suspicion as board spies. When we worked with the board, we were considered, by some, to be too close to the program's operations to be "open-minded."

Another shortcoming of our Pass studies was the complete reliance on printed reports as a dissemination mechanism. This was in part a function of the lack of a primary client. No one cared enough about what we were doing to hear the results of the effort. This does not happen when there is a clear client from the beginning, since the client also then has an investment in the effort.

It was also during the Pass "evaluation" that we became most acutely aware of the negative connotations of being known as "the evaluators." From then on we worked hard at being referred to as the LRDC researchers, trying to generate information that someone in the district clearly wanted and needed.

The importance of building a better student information system also came out in this Pass research. That first year of Pass, 80 percent of our energies were devoted to collecting basic student data that could and should be part of any district's computer data files. Chapter 6 and case 8 go into more detail on that important point.

CASE HISTORY 4
A DISTRICT-WIDE
NEEDS ASSESSMENT

Initial Request

The needs assessment story began on September 10, 1980, when we met with the new superintendent, Richard Wallace, and offered our assistance. During our first meeting, he indicated that it would be very important to conduct a district-wide needs assessment that would enable the board to establish priorities for the district. The question was: Would we do it? We said yes. Several subsequent meetings with the superintendent were held to define the general nature, purpose, and procedures to be used for this assessment.

The primary purpose of the assessment was to determine the degree to which the Pittsburgh public schools were meeting the educational needs of the children, and do it in a way which would suggest priorities for improving the educational program in the district. The general objective was to identify conditions that can and should be improved. That is, the focus of the assessment was on identifying problems and solutions that were within the realm of the district's ability to influence and implement. In this way, the results were to be a basis for immediate local action.

183

Approaches Used in the Needs Assessment

Two approaches were used in this assessment. One approach was to survey different stakeholder groups regarding their perceptions of current conditions in the district. The groups sampled included administrators, board members, counselors, custodians, nurses, paraprofessionals, parents, principals and other building administrators, psychologists, school secretaries, security guards, social workers, students, supervisors, teachers, and other Pittsburgh citizens. This approach to needs assessment is what Stufflebeam (1977) calls the democratic view.

The other approach to the assessment involved collecting and analyzing existing school district data in order to establish the current status of the educational needs of the children. Such data included student achievement, failure and dropout rates, attendance, suspensions, and demographic descriptions of the students in each school, as well as data describing the resources available in the school, such as the number of teachers. The resulting database covered the five years prior to the assessment. This made it possible to examine trends over time as well as relationships among the many different variables in any given year. Stufflebeam (1977) calls this the analytic view.

Constituency Surveys

The surveys were designed, conducted, and analyzed on a very tight schedule. The initial plan we had submitted to the superintendent was quite ambitious and had the leisurely time schedule of academics. The superintendent reminded us that he had a three-year contract. He wasn't much interested in a three-year study!

A 30-member task force was appointed by the superintendent to assist in the design of the surveys. Half of the task force were community leaders; the rest were representatives of various district employee groups (e.g., teachers, principals, etc.). The first meeting of the task force was October 28, 1980. At that meeting, following an initial orientation by the superintendent, the large task force broke up into subcommittees charged with the task of identifying the major questions to be addressed to each of the populations being surveyed. By the end of that afternoon, the recorders for each group came away with long lists of topics to be covered in the survey instruments.

During the month of November, LRDC staff (Bickel, Cooley, two research assistants, and a secretary) composed the instruments and tried them out on people from the various target populations. During that month we also designed the sampling frame and the mode of survey (i.e., mail, telephone, or personal interview) for each of the groups. Then on December 2, 1980, the task force met again to review, revise, and approve the instruments and sampling plan.

It was decided to survey all members of small populations (e.g., board members) and random sample the large populations (e.g., 150 of approximately 3,000 teachers comprised a 5 percent random sample). Two of the populations — community leaders and students — were not randomly sampled. Student views were obtained through a board staff member who met with groups of students and was successful in getting them to "rap" about their school experiences. Community leaders known to be interested in the schools were personally interviewed.

The surveys were conducted during the first three weeks of December. Data processing began as soon as the first responses were received. Important to this step was the fact that the question formats were designed for ease of data entry and analysis. Survey questions were of three general types: ratings (on a five-point scale) which tried to establish the perceived seriousness of a problem (e.g., teacher absenteeism); rank orderings of conditions that could and should be improved (e.g., lack of instructional leadership on the part of building administrators); and open-ended questions (e.g., What was the most unsatisfactory part of your job?). The open-ended questions were important "venting" devices, but we also learned a lot from them. (For example, these responses often suggested specific, imaginative solutions to problems that otherwise would not have surfaced in the assessment process.) They were just hard to code! The number of responses for each group is indicated in table C4–1.

Data analysis was conducted between December 19 and January 6. The major analytic tools used were frequency distributions for each question response and cross tabulations across questions. The objective of the analysis was to establish the priorities for district-wide improvement, as viewed by each of these stakeholder groups.

The task force met again on January 6, 1981, this time to review and react to the preliminary tabulations. They discussed what the results meant to them and recommended subsequent analyses that helped to clarify the results in hand. Analysis of the surveys continued until the board met to review them on January 24, 1981.

Analysis of Other Data

As chapter 6 points out, decision-oriented educational research is dependent upon having good data readily available. This was certainly true of this

Table C4–1. Populations Surveyed

Survey Group	Number Responding	Response Rate
Board members (interviewed)	8	89%
Building administrators (mailed)	66	66%
Business/community leaders (interviewed)	18	100%
Central staff (mailed)	40	66%
Counselors (mailed)	19	63%
Households (telephone)		
Public school children	102	51%
Nonpublic school children	99	50%
No children	100	50%
Nurses, social workers, psychologists (mailed)	18	60%
Paraprofessionals (mailed)	14	21%
Students (group interviews)	500	100%
Supervisors (mailed)	26	84%
Support staff (school secretaries, custodians, security) (mailed)	19	45%
Teachers (mailed)	78	52%
Total	1078	

needs assessment. If we had had no data to start with, we never could have delivered on the time line needed by the client.

In our previous work with the district (e.g., cases 1 to 3) we had established a school level file that contained general school characteristics (e.g., enrollment), demographics (e.g., race), school environment (e.g., number of suspensions), and program-related indicators (e.g., class size, teacher experience, number of classroom aides). Most of these school data were available for the previous five years. The student level data consisted mostly of standardized achievement test results, but they did include student participation in special programs, particularly Title I compensatory education.

These data were worked up in ways that showed trends across grades (e.g., percentage participating in remedial programs), trends over time (e.g., enrollment changes, suspension rates), and comparisons among schools (e.g., costs per pupil). Most of the analyses were simply descriptive in nature, but some of them were explanatory (e.g., why per pupil costs were going up much faster than inflation).

Because most of these data were already in our computer files, the analyses began in October and extended into January. We mention all these dates because it is important for would-be DOER's to realize the critical importance of timeliness in this work. It just cannot be done with the sort of relaxed schedule that discipline-oriented research tends to enjoy.

Results

The results (Evaluation Unit, 1981) were organized initially in terms of five broad areas that were found to be the district's most pressing needs. Although some groups ranked them differently than others, there was consensus that the district's most pressing needs were to: (1) improve student achievement in basic skills; (2) implement better procedures for personnel evaluation; (3) attract and hold students; (4) manage the impact of enrollment decline in order to hold down unwanted costs and increase quality where it is needed; and (5) develop a strategy for improving individual schools.

An important aspect of working up these results was the design of a set of overhead transparencies that would convey the most salient points in a "memorable" way. Their use is discussed in the next section of this case. A few of these (20 were actually used in the presentations of results) are shown as figures in this results section to illustrate the general technique.

The more specific survey results and the five-year database were used to define further the nature of each of the major problem areas that had been identified and possible strategies for dealing with them. The student achievement issue illustrates this approach.

Need to Improve Student Achievement

The improvement of student achievement was identified as the number one problem in the district by most survey respondents. This fact was not surprising since previous reports of standardized test results in the district had received much attention. The achievement problem that had been previously highlighted was that students began to fall behind national norms at about the fourth grade. The phrase "fourth grade slump" was commonly heard during board deliberations of achievement issues.

As part of this needs assessment, additional analyses were conducted to determine possible reasons for this decline. A major achievement problem identified in the analyses was that a large number of children left third grade still not reading well enough to use reading in subsequent learning. The test results indicated that approximately 25 percent of the students completed third grade with inadequate reading comprehension skills. It was also noted that this percentage varied considerably among schools. That is, in some schools as many as 50 percent of the children did not comprehend what they read as they entered fourth grade, whereas in other schools, all of the children seemed to be reading well enough to begin fourth grade. Figure C4-1 illustrates the slide that was used to make this point.

In an attempt to improve achievement, the district had developed, prior to the needs assessment, many remedial programs for children who were not learning from normal classroom instruction. These programs included Title I, Project Pass (case 3), special education programs for the mildly handicapped (e.g., learning disabled and educable mentally retarded), and a twelfth grade remedial program. Such programs had become so extensive in the district that in some grade levels, 50 percent of the children were participating in one or more of these remedial efforts. Figure C4-2 is the slide that was used to make this point. As part of the assessment, the operational structure of remedial programs was investigated. The investigation included a "reuse" of some of what was found in case 3 in terms of how various programs related to each other. The results indicated that lack of coordination among the various remedial efforts was a serious problem.

An examination of the achievement levels of the students in these remedial programs suggested that these different programs were serving students with similar achievement problems. Thus, children were labeled and isolated for special treatments in spite of the fact that children with different labels appeared to be having similar academic difficulties and were receiving

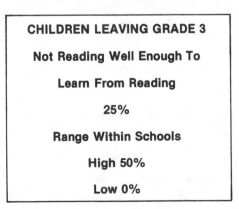

Figure C4-1.   The Major Achievement Finding

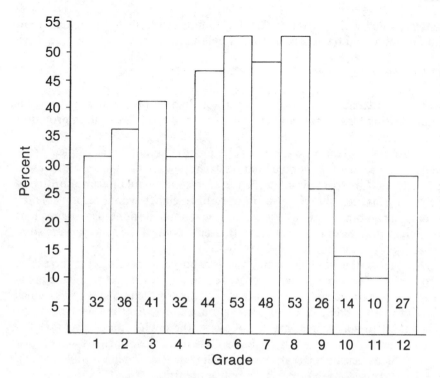

Figure C4-2.   Participation in Remedial Programs

similar treatments under these different labels. (This phenomenon was not unusual to the district [Leinhardt, Bickel, and Pallay, 1982].) Different programs were trying to work on similar problems, often with the same general instructional strategies, but the teachers and supervisors involved were not benefiting from each other's experiences. Different supervisory staff were assigned to the different programs, even in the same building.

Another need was to improve the coordination between what was taught in remedial programs and what was taught in regular classrooms. Teachers, principals, and supervisors all recognized this as a critical task for improving remedial instruction. This assessment suggested the need to integrate the remedial services insofar as possible, reduce the use of stigmatizing labels for these children, and put the focus on the early grades so that students developed the basic skills before they moved into the intermediate grades.

Results from the surveys and from analyses of longitudinal data bases, in combination, gave a much greater sense of both the extent and the exact nature of the achievement problem. Further, the combined assessment strate-

gies provided a richer source for developing solutions for problems than
that which could be derived from a single approach.

Other Needs Identified

In addition to achievement, the other four major problem areas were examined using both survey and existing district data. It is useful to provide a
brief description of the other results at this time.

Personnel evaluation was one of the most consistently mentioned problems by the people who worked in the district. Few seemed happy with present
procedures. Employees wanted their evaluation oriented toward improving
job performance, and felt it was important to clarify who is responsible for
evaluating whom and how those evaluations should be done. The suggestions
for improving personnel evaluation that came out of the surveys were summarized in a slide shown as figure C4-3.

Another serious problem facing the Pittsburgh schools was the increasing
proportion of children going elsewhere for their education. It seemed to many
that this was threatening the health and vitality of the public schools, which
have been and should continue to be a critical ingredient in this democracy.
The major reason people gave for avoiding the public schools was that student discipline was a serious problem. Teachers and principals agreed that
there was a lack of alternatives for dealing with discipline problems, and
teachers stressed a need to enforce policies consistently.

The need to manage enrollment decline also emerged as a priority area. On
a per pupil basis, costs were going up faster than one would expect from inflation. This was primarily because fixed building costs were being spread over
fewer students in each school, and class sizes were getting smaller (figure
C4-4). Although smaller classes can be an important component of a
strategy for improving the quality of classroom instruction, the reduction in
class size was very uneven and was not necessarily occurring where it was

---

Clarify Who's Responsible For Whom

Set Goals Together

Follow-Up With Corrective Feedback

Specify Incentive Systems

Take Strong Action When All Else Fails

Figure C4-3.   Survey Suggestions for Personnel Evaluation

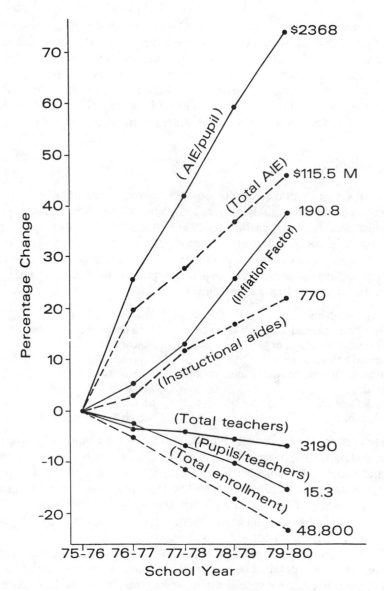

Figure C4-4.   Five-Year Trends (Costs (AIE), Enrollments, Teachers, Aides)

needed. The assessment concluded that the money saved by closing additional schools could be used to increase the quality of the educational program where it is most needed.

The needs assessment also suggested focusing reform effects upon individual schools because most of the identified needs must be attacked at the building level, and because some schools were clearly in greater need of improvement than others. An index of school descriptors was developed that indicated where to begin a focused school improvement effort. It was suggested that a detailed diagnosis of the needs of the identified schools could be the basis for designing improvement strategies in each school (see case 5).

Dissemination

Informal dissemination of results took place through researcher–client interactions as preliminary analyses were completed. More formal dissemination activities occurred between January 13 and March 5, 1981. Two approaches were used: interactive slide show sessions and written reports. The former proved to be especially useful in both getting the message across as well as sharpening the message through helpful interpretive comments offered by the audiences. The schedule was as follows:

Superintendent	January 13
Superintendent and school board president	January 20
The board of education	January 24
Central administration	February 12
Building administrators and supervisors	February 24
Teachers	February 25
Task force	March 3
Press conference	March 5

Each dissemination session involved looking at the results, with overhead slides and handouts, in an interactive mode. This was particularly true of the meeting with the nine-member board for whom a one-day retreat to a nearby college campus was arranged. For the 3,000 teachers, however, we had to settle for a one-hour TV presentation which they viewed in their buildings. This was followed by a discussion of the results among the faculty and building administrators in each school.

The written reports were kept short. We prepared a 2-page abstract, a 16-page summary detailed to the degree of the achievement discussion in this case report, and six special topic papers, running about 10 pages each, on themes of particular interest: achievement, discipline, communications, personnel evaluation, organizational structure, and school improvement. We also prepared a memo for the superintendent which summarized specific "suggestions to the new superintendent" that emerged from the surveys of the various groups.

Examples of Use

The first indication that the assessment was going to be used came in the form of a news release on the Monday following the weekend retreat with the superintendent and board when the preliminary results of the needs assessment were described in detail. Here are important excerpts from that release.

Wallace Announces Plans for School Improvement

Pittsburgh, Pa., January 26, 1981 . . . Superintendent of Schools Richard C. Wallace today announced that he will immediately begin to develop "action plans" for the School district that focus on two major areas, school improvement and cost effective management. . . .

The decision to focus on the two major areas was made jointly by Wallace and members of the board of education after they had the opportunity to review preliminary results of the district wide needs assessment initiated by the superintendent shortly after he took office in the fall. . . .

"This needs assessment information combined with other educational data, such as an analysis of test scores over the past five years, helped us establish the priorities," Wallace said. "Once we develop the action plans, all of us in the district can channel our energies in the same direction and respond to concerns identified by the groups of people the schools serve."

On February 25, 1981, the board passed the resolution that adopted school improvement and cost effective management as the top two priorities for the district. In that resolution, the board agreed to assign resources and concentrate its efforts to resolve problems within these priority areas in relation to (1) student achievement in the basic skills, (2) staff evaluation, (3) student discipline, (4) attracting and holding students, (5) enrollment decline, and (6) increasing the effectiveness of individual schools. The resolution made it clear that the two priority areas and the six specific needs surfaced as major concerns as the result of the district-wide needs assessment. Five of the six priority areas were stated in language identical to that used in the assessment. The addition of discipline as a separate priority was a modification that occurred during the dissemination process as early drafts had included this issue under the priority of attracting and holding students. More is said about how and why this change came about in the discussion in chapter 9 on utilization–dissemination relationships.

As indicated in the January press release, the superintendent set in motion the development of action plans for each priority area. Task forces established for this purpose consisted of representatives of various segments of the district, and each group worked toward a July 15 deadline, at which time detailed action plans were presented to the board as a followup to their February 25 resolution. The board was given two months to review the action plans, and on September 23, 1981, one year from the initiation of the assessment, they were formally adopted.

The presentation by the superintendent to the board of the results of the assessment and the passage by the board of the priority areas identified in the plan is a straightforward example of what Leviton and Hughes (1981) have described as *instrumental* use of research information (see chapter 9). Research was commissioned to identify current conditions in need of improvement in the district. Summary reports were prepared and presentations were made. On the basis of these data, the board resolved to attack the identified problems through the development of specific action plans and through the allocation of district resources to support these plans.

The needs assessment process also provided an example of what Leviton and Hughes (1981) have called *conceptual* use, influencing the way decision makers thought about a problem. This occurred in relation to the studies of achievement.

As noted earlier, achievement reports prepared by the district's testing office had identified a decline in achievement starting at about the fourth grade and gradually increasing through the middle-school years. The term "fourth grade slump" had become a common term used among board members during the past several years to describe the achievement issue in the district. Also, remedial programs in the district had expanded into the middle and upper grades in an attempt at dealing with that "slump."

The needs assessment more closely examined the achievement levels attained by district students in the primary (1–3) grades. District managers were shown that 25 percent of the students were bringing serious reading problems into the fourth grade and that the root of the problem lay with the instruction received in the early years. The net effect of this research was to refocus the attention of district managers upon instruction in the primary grades as a way of solving the decline in test scores in the district that surfaced in the fourth grade.

The needs assessment *process*, as distinguished from the needs assessment results, provided an example of utilization for *persuasive* purposes. Leviton and Hughes (1981) define persuasive use as the use of research data in an attempt to convince others about, or to defend, an existing or changing organizational direction or political position. This type of use occurred at a variety of levels in the district and in a number of ways. The persuasive use in the context of superintendent–board relations is illustrative.

When the new superintendent took office in the fall of 1980, he was confronted with a nine-member, elected board that had a recent history of sharp division and fragmentation. The primary issue of contention among board members involved plans for district-wide desegregation. The termination of the previous superintendent had been the result, in part, of a failure to work out a solid majority on the board for any single desegregation strategy. Fortunately for the newly arriving superintendent, the desegregation issue had temporarily been relegated to the "back burner" for the board. An uneasy and fragile coalition of six board members had passed a plan the previous summer. While litigation challenging the plan was underway, there was a general consensus on the board that everyone should pull together to make the opening of the school year as quiet and reassuring to a nervous public as possible. There also seemed to be a feeling of exhaustion among many board members over the acrimony that had attended so many of the discussions on desegregation. There was a willingness to let the courts (or the elections to come in 1982) stimulate new moves.

Arriving with a knowledge of this context, the new superintendent sensed the time was ripe for some new initiatives in the district. As an "outsider" (the previous three superintendents had come up through the system) he had the advantage of being able to take a fresh look at the issues. He also was not bound by previous relationships and commitments likely to be built up during a career-long rise within a single district. Yet, the problem remained of how to develop some consensus for action among board members that had been so recently divided.

The development of a needs assessment, especially that component of the assessment that surveyed all of the major constituencies of the district, was an important mechanism for building a consensus for action among board members. Issues identified through an assessment process clearly could not be attributed to the special interest of one or the other of the board factions. As such, the assessment provided a "neutral ground," in effect, for building a new consensus among key decision makers in the district.

Similar persuasive uses of the assessment *results* (as opposed to process) occurred in the superintendent's relationships with his own central administrative staff. The point here is simply that the assessment process did indeed fulfill a persuasive use as defined by Leviton and Hughes (1981).

Although examples of instrumental, conceptual, and persuasive utilization have been treated as discrete entities, it is not the intent here (nor is it the intent of Leviton and Hughes) to leave the impression that these are necessarily mutually exclusive categories. For example, the achievement study cited as having conceptual use also turned out to have an instrumental use. Over time, programs, policies, and resources were shifted as a result of the realization that the fourth grade slump can be reduced by improving primary grade instruction. Nevertheless, the three categories are helpful in describing the complex influences decision-oriented research information can have.

Relationships to DOER

Case 4 and its relationship to DOER is noteworthy in several respects. A clearly identified client, the superintendent, was present, actively participating in every stage of the research from initial data collection activities through the analysis and dissemination of findings. The needs assessment procedures illustrate the range of methodologies that were needed to respond to the system information needs. To have not queried constituencies would have drastically reduced board interest in the results and thus diminished the utility of the study for the primary client whose goal was to develop a basis for board consensus. To have surveyed constituencies only and not probe longitudinal databases would have severely limited the district's understanding of the problems that surfaced in the surveys. This case also illustrates the importance of having flexible, computer-based data systems as part of a system research capability. As was pointed out in this case, if the databases used for the longitudinal analyses had not already been constructed as the result of prior work, we would have been hard-pressed to meet the tight schedule mandated by the primary client.

Finally, in some respects this case is our "best case" example of dissemination processes. In contrast to cases 3 and 7, for example, we employed a variety of interaction mechanisms along with writing numerous reports, each targeted for specific audiences and information needs. In combination, these dissemination strategies, starting with the earliest discussions of preliminary findings with one primary client, worked to integrate research information into decision and policy processes.

CASE HISTORY 5
DOCUMENTING THE DEVELOPMENT
OF A SCHOOL IMPROVEMENT
PROGRAM

Introduction

This case describes the documentation of a school improvement program initiated by the Pittsburgh public schools in 1981. The case is of interest for several reasons. As pointed out in chapter 7, the role of documenter represents an unusual and potentially potent use of evaluation resources to assist managers in the development and implementation of new programs. Both the length of this case (three years) and the degree of interaction provided a rich database on the changing information needs of clients and how documentation can respond to such needs. Finally, the program itself was an interesting, early example of what became a national trend, namely, the use of the findings contained in the literature on effective schools (Bickel, 1983) to frame programs for school improvement.

This case history is organized into five main sections. The first provides information on the origins of the school improvement program. This is followed by a discussion of the major initiatives that were developed during the first two years of the program. The third section describes the origins of the role of documenter. A discussion follows of the methodologies used for documentation. The last section provides examples of research results produced through documentation activities and of the uses made of the information.

Background: Origin of the School Improvement Program

In February 1981 the Pittsburgh Board of Education resolved that the district would develop action plans in six priority areas identified through a district-wide needs assessment (case 4). One of these areas, school improvement, reflected the need for the district to design mechanisms to enable administrators and faculties to better solve educational problems at the building level. During the spring and early summer of 1981, the district, along with LRDC researchers, developed a preliminary action plan to address this priority. This plan outlined a broad strategy for "increasing the effectiveness of individual elementary schools, focusing upon their need to increase student achievement in the basic skills" (Pittsburgh Public Schools, 1981, p. 1).

Three databases were used in the initial plan's development:

1. Data collected as part of the needs assessment (e.g., achievement scores, student demographics, personnel perceptions).
2. Reviews of the educational literature concerning questions such as: What was an effective principal? Teacher? Supervisor? What was known about the efficient implementation of educational programs?
3. Information gathered in several district elementary schools through a related LRDC research project focused on special education issues. This project provided valuable insights into organizational conditions in the district that might influence a school improvement initiative, as well as ideas about how an improvement process might be organized and managed (N. Zigmond, personal communication, June 1981).

The early draft of the action plan was then shared for the purpose of comment and revision with a district-wide task force that consisted of principals, teachers, supervisors, and central administrators. The task force submitted a final plan (PPS, 1981) to the board of education. The plan was formally approved in July 1981 as part of a larger set of plans addressing the priorities identified in the needs assessment.

The plan approved by the board in July outlined only the broad parameters of the school improvement program. Themes contained in the document included:

• improving basic skills as the first priority goal;

- using several diagnostic phases in order to identify target schools and needs within those schools;
- developing a collaborative improvement model that utilized strong leadership from the principal, faculty involvement through a building steering committee process, and resources external to the schools (both within and outside the school system).

The plan emphasized that this was a pilot program designed to develop and test school improvement strategies that would improve instruction in participating schools. The long-range goal was to disseminate effective school improvement strategies developed in the program to other schools in the district. The pilot stage of the work extended over a three-year period. The program was under the general supervision of a management group consisting of the superintendent, the deputy associate superintendent for elementary schools, and one of the LRDC researchers; actual program design and operations were the responsibility of a director and a team of supervisors.

School selection was based on the review of a wide variety of school climate, student achievement, and demographic data prepared by the LRDC evaluation unit for district leaders. The management team reached a decision to include seven schools in the program. There was considerable variability on such factors as size and, to a lesser extent, racial mix among the seven sites. While there was also variation in achievement, every school in the set fell well below the district's mean on standardized tests in reading and math, and was considered in need of significant improvement. Some of the school characteristics are summarized in table C5-1.

It should be noted that the schools selected did not volunteer to be in the program. This represented a significant departure from many other school improvement programs in the nation. This characteristic was also at odds with the school change literature which emphasized the self-selection of participants as an important strategy in developing program ownership. On the other hand, the fact that the selected schools were in great need of improvement provided an opportunity to determine whether a focused improvement effort could work. The real challenge was trying to figure out how to turn around any school that had significantly low achievement, whether or not the principal and faculty were willing to volunteer for such an effort.

The next step after school selection was the appointment of the district's consultant team: the project director, two regular education supervisors, and one special education supervisor. In December 1981 a teacher on special assignment with expertise in the teaching of reading was added to the staff. The consultant team was the major design and support group for the school improvement program.

Table C5-1. Profile (1980–81) of Schools Selected for School Improvement

School	School Size	Class Size	No. of[a] Teachers	Pupil-Teacher Ratio	Percent Black	Percent Free Lunch	Special Education			SAI[b]	Rank[c]
							SED	EMR	LD		
A	520	21	36	14.4	100	70	—	1	—	-1.00	52
B	231	22	17	13.6	97	70	—	—	—	-0.62	41
C	334	22	26	12.8	68	70	—	2	1	-1.39	56
D	637	20	46.5	13.7	65	70	1	3	1	-0.80	45
E	321	22	32	10	99	70	—	1	1	-1.41	57
F	308	21	19	16.2	100	90	1	1	1	-1.33	55
G	422	17	30	14.1	69	70	1	1	1	-0.21	35

[a] 1979–80 data.

[b] SAI was a standardized achievement index that used combined reading and math scores on the California Achievement Test (spring 1981). The index was scaled so that the mean was 0.0 for all 57 of the elementary schools in the district.

[c] There was a total of 57 elementary schools in the district at the time of selection.

The project director brought to his work a strong conviction about what constituted an effective school. He was a principal for nine years in a school with an impressive basic skills achievement record prior to his appointment. Based on his experiences as a principal and on his reading of school effectiveness literature (e.g., Venesky and Winfield, 1979; Edmonds, 1979; Weber, 1971; Brookover and Lezotte, 1979), the director's conviction about effective schooling included a commitment to encourage strong instructional leadership, develop sound discipline procedures, and closely monitor student achievement.

The consultant team further developed the goals of the program after the passage of the action plan beginning with a school level needs assessment administered to each participating faculty. By the early fall of 1981, orientation workshops had been held by the team for the principals and faculties of the seven schools. The results of the needs assessments were summarized by LRDC researchers and given to newly established steering committees in each building. Finally, a detailed plan that contained program objectives and suggested implementation strategies was developed by the director (Venson, 1981).

During this startup period, the relatively significant developmental role played by the LRDC researchers in the early design phase evolved into one of technical support to the management and consultant team's planning processes (e.g., data analyses for the school selection process, analyses of the school improvement program needs assessments). An exception to this technical support role was the emergence of the position of documenter, which became an ongoing resource to the development and implementation of the program. The exact origins of this function are discussed at a later point in this case.

The School Improvement Program

The initial plans for the program were rather ambiguous. The details of the program evolved during the course of the first year's activities. This period of development was followed in the second year by a focus on assisting individual schools to fully implement school improvement initiatives. What emerged during the course of the developmental year was a series of program components that were classifiable as either process or programmatic in orientation, and that were focused either at the program level or at the individual school level. A brief description of each major initiative is given below.

Collaborative Planning

Collaborative planning was a principle of school improvement contained in the earliest drafts describing the program. This grew out of a conviction, supported in the school change literature, that collaborative planning was a way to stimulate ownership of an innovation. Building ownership among the principals and faculties, as well as the team, was deemed to be especially crucial to the success of the program, given the nonvoluntary selection of the schools.

Collaborative planning was stimulated in three ways. First, the director scheduled numerous team meetings that served as open forums in which to discuss program needs and future initiatives. Second, regularly scheduled meetings with functions similar to those of the team planning meetings were held with the principals and the team. Finally, faculty steering committees were set up in each school as problem-solving mechanisms.

Achievement Expectations and Monitoring

An important feature of effective schools as described in the literature is that students are expected to learn and, concomitantly, that student progress is monitored closely. Early assessments by the consultant team of the seven schools (e.g., the "reading cards" of each student were reviewed) indicated that in most schools expectation levels varied considerably and that achievement was not being closely tracked.

The team developed an achievement monitoring system consisting of a series of forms and data collection procedures designed to array achievement data so that the principals and the team could readily identify students and classrooms in greatest need. The goal was to work with teachers to develop improved skills for reteaching components of the curriculum not mastered by some students. The establishment and communication of acceptable mastery levels to be expected from each student was an integral part of this system. This type of standard was not present in many of the schools prior to the program's initiatives.

Focused Team Supervision

During the course of the first year the consultant team dramatically revised the role of instructional supervisor, partly as a result of documentation activities (described below). The revisions constrasted sharply with the way supervisors were typically used in the district.

The traditional model of supervision had several key characteristics. Supervisors tended to work in isolation from each other. That is, regular education and special education supervisors tended to operate under dissimilar reporting structures and distribution systems. Their specific responsibilities differed significantly across programs, as did their client structures and actual school assignments. Even within a program area, one regular education supervisor rarely had the opportunity to draw upon his/her colleagues for ideas and support, let alone direct assistance. The outcomes associated with the traditional use of supervisors, in the views of individuals who served in these positions and researchers who studied them, included:

- ambiguity among supervisors and clients about the role;
- multiple clients and tasks served through a "circuit rider" model;
- fragmented planning process stressing the reactive rather than anticipatory mode;
- a sense of professional isolation (Bickel and Artz, 1984).

The school improvement program presented the supervisors on the consultant team with both the opportunity and the necessity of trying to redesign this role. The opportunity was present because this set of supervisors had a unified mandate and a shared set of schools and clients. The necessity was there because, early on in the school year, the team recognized that there were: (1) more instructional problems than could be adequately addressed by the project staff; (2) most of the problems required sustained attention in order to make significant progress; and (3) some problems affected every school in the program. In light of these difficulties, and given the opportunity to take initiatives in this area as a part of the school improvement program work, the consultant team gradually redefined the role of supervisor. Several key features characterized the new model:

- attempts were made to focus on key problem areas as defined with the director and principals;
- time was allocated to a problem area in relation to need;
- supervisors planned as a team and in specific situations worked as a team on-site where a particular issue so required;
- time was provided to allow supervisors to share data, ideas, etc.

Data-Based Instructional Planning

An important feature was the press to integrate the use of data at multiple levels in the program, to guide planning and instructional decisions. The role of documenter was an example of this feature at the program level. Examples at the school level included the introduction of the monitoring system and the supervisory process described above.

A fourth example was evidenced in a series of in-services held with individual principals over the course of the first two years of the program. The focus of the in-services varied, but each shared a structure which started with a review of data relevant to the issue at hand, and ended with the development of an action plan designed to meet the needs identified in the data. The underlying goal of these activities was to encourage principals to use data to guide their instructional leadership activities.

Additional Initiatives

A number of additional initiatives were developed and implemented during the early years of the program. These included a staffing process which was designed to systematize special education assessment practices and student discipline guidelines for each school.

The staffing process was a particularly interesting innovation. While the primary purpose was to review individual special education referrals, the meetings in some buildings also became a forum for discussing broader instructional issues. The meetings included the principal, social worker, school psychologist, regular and special education supervisors, and teachers specific to the student(s) being considered for special education placement. Data on the child's classroom instructional environment were collected, and modifications to meet his/her needs were recommended and implemented as first steps in the staffing process. Referral was no longer the start of a nearly automatic special education placement. This broader focus for the staffings also had the effect of giving the principal an opportunity to exercise real leadership in instructional matters (e.g., reassigning students, conducting and calling for classroom observations) with increased data and more coordinated staff support.

Program Documentation: Origins

The documentation of the school improvement program was an integral part of the program from the start. The earliest expression of the need for documentation was contained in the initial action plan passed by the school board in July 1981.

> As a plan is implemented, it will be important to document the implementation process and the progress that is made in each school. The documentation can

provide useful feedback to the building committees and support staff, as well as information useful to other school improvement initiatives in the district (PPS, 1981, p. 11).

In addition to the explicit functions of generating immediate feedback and shaping future improvement initiatives, a third function was implied in the phrase "progress in each school." This phrase suggested a link between documentation activities and summative-oriented evaluation. This linkage was unintended and was the source of some initial confusion about the role of documentation.

When documentation was first proposed, neither the prospective documenter nor the leadership of the district had a clear vision of what the task should entail. This type of research was unprecedented in the district. Indeed, little was available in professional research literatures that shed direct light on what a documentation design might look like.

Several initial steps were taken to define documentation further. First, two client groups were identified that would be the consumers of information produced through documentation activities. The formative feedback function designed to aid the development and implementation of the program served the needs of the director and the consultant team. The district oversite/ management group was primarily interested in the documentation of school improvement strategies that could be disseminated to other schools in the district. This represented a more long-range historical function of documentation, one that grew in importance during the third year of operation when the district began to consider an expansion of the program.

The documenter concentrated on the development of a research plan the first year to meet the needs of the consultant team. A preliminary plan was drafted for discussion (W.E. Bickel, personal communication, August 21, 1981). Six basic assumptions about documentation activities were identified in the plan:

1. They should reflect the views of a wide variety of participants.
2. They are related to, but distinct from, any summative evaluation design.
3. They should employ a variety of data collection techniques.
4. The methodologies employed should be influenced by participants.
5. They should sample rather than exhaustively attempt to record implementation activities.
6. Each collection activity should be specifically justifiable in terms of the goals of documentation.

Proposals for a number of types of data collection activities were also listed in the plan, including: observations of major meetings (eventually to be defined as those which included faculties or administrative staff across all seven schools); reviews of minutes of staff and steering committee meetings; reviews of logs of participants; and interviews with key participants. In addition, the documenter proposed that one of the seven schools be selected for an intensive case study in which essentially all activities related to the program would be documented. The primary purposes of this individual school case study were to: (1) describe the development of the program in detail in one site, and (2) provide a basis for hypothesis generation about critical developmental and implementation issues that could then be investigated further in the other schools. The case study approach also reflected a realization that documentation resources were limited (initially, 50 percent of the documenter's time plus 10 hours per week from one graduate student) and intensive observations at each site were out of the question.

The outcome of the discussions with the team was a slightly revised plan distributed by the director to the principals as part of a document describing the entire project (Venson, 1981). The major revision in the plan, made at the suggestion of the director, was the addition of specific purposes that justified each data collection activity. For example, the revised plan noted that the purpose of the surveys of principals was to provide uninhibited feedback from each school on in-school perceptions of the project.

Data Collection

Several data-gathering routines were implemented early in the documentation activities, and they remained in place during the course of the research. Observations were conducted of any program-wide meetings (e.g., in-services, principal cluster sessions, weekly team planning meetings). Extensive field notes that tracked major issues confronted by participants (and decisions made) were prepared from each observation and added to the archive. In addition, regular debriefings were held with individual members of the consultant team. These, in combination, formed a record of the evolution of issues, goals, and problems encountered in the development and implementation of the program, as viewed from the perspective of the team.

At the school level, sample observations were made of the various kinds of meetings that regularly occurred as a result of program initiatives (e.g., faculty steering committees, special education staffings involving principals, a school's support staff, and individual teachers). In addition, at the school chosen for intensive study, any meeting held as a result of or that might relate to the improvement activities was observed. Regular conversations of both formal and informal nature were held with the faculty and administration of this school. Problems that arose at this school were viewed as cautionary signals suggesting that similar ones might exist in other sites. When a problem was identified, specific investigations at other sites were conducted to verify whether similar difficulties were being encountered.

School level observations shifted in the second year from the use of a case school approach (supplemented by a sampling of all types of meetings across the seven buildings) to a concentration on several, specific improvement strategies being implemented across all sites. These strategies concerned a revision of the role of supervisor and the use of data for instructional leadership. Both of these initiatives had important implications for other schools in the district. The use of these themes to focus site observations reflected the responsibility of documentation activities not only to assist in the implementation of the program but also to learn from these experiences about improvement strategies that might be disseminated to other schools in the district.

The program of observations conducted during the first two years of the program was supplemented by two additional data collection strategies. These involved document collection and the querying of specific participant populations (e.g., principals, teachers) about either the overall status of the program or about some specific program initiative (e.g., the utility of the steering committee process). The inquiries were designed to give the consultant team feedback, as well as to provide a vehicle to elicit ideas about how to improve the implementation process. The summaries of these queries, along with the field notes, the debriefings, and the archive of related documents, formed the core database for the documentation activities and for the writing of this case history.

Results and Use of Documentation

Documentation research is decision-oriented. With the Leviton and Hughes (1981) scheme in mind (discussed in chapter 9) concerning evaluation use, documentation data have been used primarily in instrumental and conceptual ways. Several examples will illustrate.

The implementation of building-level steering committees as problem-solving devices was one area in which documentation activities influenced the team's work. An issue report written midway during the first year of the program identified a number of concerns about the steering committee (e.g., the quality of interaction between teachers and principals, and of the problem-solving process). These concerns were based upon the documenter's observations at the school chosen for intensive study. In response to the report, the director decided to change the schedule of steering committee meetings to enable him to attend meetings in all seven schools. Further, the director requested that the documenter conduct a survey of teachers participating on steering committees and interviews of principals to assess their views of the process and to obtain ideas for improvement. Based upon the observations of the director, the survey, and interview data, the school improvement team developed an intensive summer in-service program for steering committee members on communication skills, group dynamics, and problem-solving processes.

A second example of the use of documentation data occurred in the context of team planning for the second year of the program. The team developed a series of priorities designed to focus their work in each school. One priority was the identification of individual classrooms in need of intensive supervision. Part of the database used by the team in determining their set of target classrooms included analyses of standardized test scores by the documenter. These analyses tracked student growth in school improvement classrooms in reading and math over the two years prior to, as well as the first year of, the program. Classrooms were identified where little or no growth had occurred. This information was helpful to the team in setting priorities for the coming year.

It is important to note that the results of the analyses of achievement were one of many kinds of data the team used in making its decisions. This typifies the way research data are most often used. That is, rarely does a single piece of research drive a major decision. Rather, research information goes into a larger arena where other issues (e.g., other data, considerations about resources and politics) also influenced the final decisions. In this instance of analysis of classroom growth, the research data really provided a place to begin further diagnoses of problems uncovered. These additional diagnostic steps included consultation with principals and classroom observations on the part of the consultant team. The achievement analyses could not tell the team what the problem was, only that in these classrooms there possibly was something amiss. The need to follow-up initial indicators with closer inspection and diagnosis is discussed in detail in chapter 5.

Another example of a type of use involved data collected through a detailed questionnaire administered to principals and teachers at the close of the second year of the program. The basic goals of the questionnaire were to gather information about the quality of implementation of the program initiatives in each school and the participants' perceptions concerning what should be priority areas for the third year. Participant knowledge about and degree of use of program initiatives were measured. The findings were summarized in a variety of ways (e.g., by school, by program, by initiative, by comparisons of teacher/administrator responses).

Dissemination of the results of the questionnaire occurred in several stages. First, findings were reviewed with the consultant team during a one-day planning session prior to the beginning of the 1982–83 school year. Presentations of program level results were then made by the documenters to the seven principals at a workshop held prior to the opening of the school year. This group presentation was followed early in the fall of 1983 by presentations in each of the seven schools. These presentations stressed building level results as well as the location of a particular school on an issue relative to the others in the program. The within-school presentations had two components: (1) a review of building-level data with the principal and the consultant team; and (2) a discussion of the results with the entire faculty. The outcomes of the building presentations included the development of action plans in each school for the team, the principal, and the steering committee. The dissemination of the questionnaire results was noteworthy because it represented another example of the importance of researchers taking some responsibilty for insuring that findings become integrated into the decision-making process, a point discussed at some length in chapter 9.

Examples of use also occurred in relation to the long-range goal of documentation, namely, the identification of improvement strategies that might be disseminated to other schools in the district. For instance, this type of use occurred when the data produced by documentation activities were used as a basis for developing plans to expand the district's school improvement efforts. This expansion occurred through two mechanisms, the middle-school needs assessment process (see case 7) which included in its summary report descriptions of improvement strategies found useful in the school improvement program, and the development of plans for the involvement of a second wave of elementary schools that occurred after the third year of operation of the program.

The examples of use discussed thus far have generally fallen into the instrumental category. Documentation data at times also had an effect on the participants' thinking about the program. Such conceptual effects most often occurred as a result of the researchers using data to frame planning issues for consideration by the team. One example of this occurred during the first year of the work in relation to the use of supervisory time. As a result of numerous observations of team planning meetings, as well as meetings involving the participating principals and the team, it became increasingly clear that new methods for allocating supervisory time had to be developed.

First, through some structured conversations with the supervisors, the fundamental issues were clarified. These concerned the fact that needs for supervisory time outstripped resources, all needs were not equally important (especially in relation to program goals), and some fundamental needs required sustained attention if there were to be a reasonable change for impact.

With issues clarified, the next step taken by the documenter was to write down in a coherent way the ideas expressed by team members over time about how various aspects of these problems might be addressed. What emerged was the notion or model of focused team supervision (Bickel and Artz, 1984) that eventually became one of the team's program initiatives.

It is important to stress that the roots of the "model" were in the thinking of individual team members as they tried to address the disparate needs of seven schools. The role of documentation involved helping to clarify the team's own understanding about the problems and to summarize systematically (and in some cases sharpen) their ideas about how the use of supervisory resources might be changed. It is worth noting that aspects of the focused, team supervisory model have since been extended to other district schools.

Relationships to DOER

This case illustrates, first of all, the potential utility of district managers building a research capability into an innovation process. Documentation can directly improve the quality of the program being implemented, and it can provide useful information for future innovative efforts. Both outcomes also are related to the improvement orientation of DOER.

Case 5 provides further evidence of the kind of interaction that can take place between researcher and client in order to shape the direction of a research effort. This case also provides ample evidence for supporting the position taken in chapter 4 that information needs of clients are diverse and that one must use a variety of methods to respond to changing information needs. School improvement documentation also illustrates concepts discussed in chapter 5 on monitoring and tailoring. In effect, documentation activities represented a modest "program-level" application of several concepts discussed in chapter 5. Data collection activities were continuous, and feedback mechanisms were linked to "action systems" (i.e., the management group and the consultant team). Finally, case 5 exemplifies the kind of ongoing and interactive dissemination process discussed in chapter 9 of this book that can help to insure the utilization of research results.

CASE HISTORY 6
TITLE I PROGRAM
FOR SECONDARY STUDENTS

Introduction and Background

In the spring of 1980, the Pittsburgh public school (PPS) district decided to expand the remedial reading programs offered under the federal compensatory education program (Title I) into the high schools. At that time, having demonstrated a need for such services at the high school level, the Pittsburgh schools implemented a small pilot reading program for eligible students in three high schools. The ensuing fall, the program was to be further expanded to include all 10 of the eligible secondary schools in the district.

A committee was formed to select the reading program or programs to be implemented in this expansion of Title I. This group consisted of administrative staff, teachers, and members of the Parents' Advisory Council. After considering 10 curricular programs, three were judged to be capable of addressing the needs of the eligible Pittsburgh high school students. As a result, the district contracted with those three separate companies to provide the equipment, materials, and support services necessary to implement their respective reading programs in 10 high schools in the fall of 1980.

While each of these programs was unique in many respects, all were considered by the PPS to be an appropriate response to the goals established for the Title I secondary reading program. Specifically, that responsibility was stated in the agreement approved by the school board: ". . . to provide instruction in reading to a group of students who are most likely to drop out of school unless some effort is made at finding remedies for their reading difficulties. . . . The laboratories serve as one of the attempts at the secondary level to remedy the students' reading problems at the level at which the students can succeed."

All three programs emphasized individual instruction. The student was placed into the program at a point in the curricular sequence appropriate for his/her level of ability and needs with respect to remediation. This was accomplished through the administration and scoring of placement tests. Then, depending upon the specific program, the student completed a set of lessons at his or her own pace. The individualization of the instruction was to be enhanced by the staffing of the reading programs. Each laboratory was to have a certified reading specialist as the primary teacher, with an educational assistant present in all classes as well.

LRDC Evaluation Activities

In March 1980, as the first reading laboratories were beginning their operation, the district contacted LRDC concerning the conduct of an evaluation of the program in the upcoming school year (1980–81). The initial request was that we do a study that would allow them to pick the best program. At our first meeting, the form and substance of possible research activities were discussed. It was generally agreed that at this point we would not try to conduct an evaluation concerned with selecting a single "best" program from among the three. The reasons for this were essentially four in number.

First, it was noted that the 1980–81 school year was the first full year of program operation. Thus, it would involve new personnel working with these laboratories for the first time. The inevitable problems that beset programs in their "start-up" phase would be expected to mask the effectiveness of the various programs.

The second consideration was that the manner of selecting and placing students into the laboratories was such as to make each of the programs vastly different from one another in terms of their participants. This would make it difficult, if not impossible, to attribute any effects to the programs themselves. A study that addressed such issues would require an understanding of the ways in which these groups differed. Acquiring such an understanding was thought to be one worthwhile goal of any initial research effort.

Third, it was realized that most students did not participate in the reading labs on a full-time basis. They were pulled out of and shared class time with an English With Emphasis on Reading (EWER) class. Because of this, any possible effects attributable to the reading labs will necessarily be confounded with the EWER instruction.

A fourth problem concerned the potential damage that could result from a premature (and possibly invalid) judgment concerning the "best" of the three laboratories. In the event that such a decision is to be made, program performance in terms of achievement is an important factor to be considered. It must, however, be assessed as accurately as possible. A decision based on results that are questionable for the reasons cited is itself suspect.

For the reasons outlined above, it was decided that LRDC would not engage in a summative evaluation designed to select a best program. Rather, the LRDC research would be primarily oriented toward program improvement. This approach is also supported by the fact that such a formative evaluation is of greatest value to a program in its early stages of implementation.

Meetings between the district and LRDC staff in the fall of 1980 further defined the questions to be addressed by the work, and eventually led to the development of a research plan. LRDC personnel visited every site at which reading labs had been installed. They observed classroom activities and interviewed each of the reading specialists. In addition, the plan called for the collection of a variety of data describing the characteristics and performance of program participants.

The interviews, classroom observations, and data collection were carried out in the interest of addressing the following general issues/questions:

1. Can and should this program be coordinated with other programs serving a similar population?
2. How can the program participants be described (so that reasonable assurances are made of the appropriateness of the materials used, and so that the description might inform future research efforts)?
3. What are the abilities and needs of the students at their entrance into the program?
4. What growth can be observed in the students over the period of their participation in the program?
5. What other factors might be considered in improving the PPS programmatic efforts in this area? Note that a number of these questions parallel those raised in case 3 regarding the PASS program.

Results

At the school level, enrollments were fairly evenly distributed. Most schools served between 5 percent and 8 percent of the total school enrollment at that school. Two schools served about 11 percent of their school's population. District-wide, the grade placement of the students showed a predominance of ninth graders (65 percent). This was consistent with the program's goals of addressing the needs of students in this grade. However, within schools, the grade placement pattern varied considerably. Some had few or no upper class students, while others had a much more even distribution of grade levels. This difference in patterns is especially strong when examined for each of the laboratories.

One of the things we were asked to assess was the extent to which the needy populations of the respective schools were being served. An estimate of the proportion of a school's population which was "in need" was obtained from the number of students below PPS standard on the Basic Skills Assessment (BSA), a test given in the district at 11th grade. This was then compared to the proportion of the school's enrollment which was being served by the Title I reading labs. Since this latter proportion was greatly determined by the size of the reading labs, what was of interest was whether the variation in the two sets of proportions paralleled one another. Ideally, the greater proportions of students served by the labs should be at those schools with the larger number of needy students. Comparing these proportions, it was seen that for the most part, the program was doing that effectively. However, it was noted that a number of programs had enrollments far below their capacity. This was true despite indications (per the BSA results) that there were needy students who might fill those positions.

With respect to the participants' sex and race, we established the majority of the students were male (56 percent), and that two-thirds of those in the program were black.

In addition, data were collected on students' participation in the subsidized lunch program in order to obtain a proxy measure of socioeconomic status. While the data are incomplete because certain schools were unable to make information on free lunch eligibility available, it does show that the great majority (65 percent) of reading lab participants also participated in the lunch program.

For the PPS students, eligibility for entry into the secondary reading program was determined by their scores on their most recent standardized test of reading ability. For those participating in the school year 1980–81, that test was the Metropolitan Achievement Test (MAT).

The information which was available for the MAT was limited to a single total reading score. Furthermore, these scores were "from the most recent testing available." Since the PPS testing program was implemented only through the eighth grade, that was the most recent MAT testing for students in grades 10 through 12. Consequently, the MAT scores (some of them as much as three-and-a-half years old) were a better review of the eligibility determinations than they were a measure of the reading ability of the students as they enter the program.

These scores were provided as normative data in terms of grade equivalents. Two points were worthy of note with respect to these data. The first was that 10 percent of those entering the program had MAT scores above the established eligibility point of two years below grade level (in this case, 9.0 minus 2, or 7.0). The second point was that 39 percent of the participants entering the program did not have data available on this eligibility criterion at all.

A better indication of the level of ability of students entering the program was gained from the Gates-MacGinnitie scores from the pretest administered at the outset of the program. They revealed that the average student placed in the 4.6 to 6.5 grade equivalent range. Statistical analysis showed differences between the programs in terms of the entering ability of students. Generally speaking, performance on the vocabulary test was somewhat better than on the reading comprehension. In addition, the results corroborated an observation made above, as some 16 percent of the students scored above the eligibility criterion of two grade levels below grade level.

The secondary reading program represented an effort at the secondary level by the PPS at remediating reading deficiencies of low achievers. Therefore, student participation in such efforts was of critical importance. For this reason, a separate analysis of those who dropped out of the program (i.e., those with enrollment but no completion data) was carried out. It was hoped to shed some light on the retention problem in the secondary reading program.

We found that the dropout rate for the program varied considerably from school to school. This was especially true where the attrition was expressed as a percentage of the total enrollment of the program for that school. Those percentages ranged from 9 to 44 percent, with three programs losing over one-quarter of their students. The clients were cautioned about assigning cause to these attrition rates. Other reasons could have been refinement of eligibility criteria while the program was operating or incomplete recordkeeping yielding apparently high attrition. Nonetheless, an area of concern was indicated in these data, and it was felt that further inquiry might prove valuable.

Student achievement was assessed in the secondary reading labs through administrations of the Gates-MacGinnitie Standardized Reading Test as pretest and posttest instruments. The pretest and posttest results for vocabulary, reading comprehension, and total reading showed that at all schools, for all tests, the ability levels (in terms of grade equivalents) were higher following participation in the program.

An assessment was made of possible differences in impact of the three programs on student achievement. Since it was known that the entering abilities of students in any educational program are the primary determinants of end-of-program achievement, statistical methods (multiple regression and analyses of covariance) were used to adjust for the effects of entering abilities. This done, no differences were observed in the effects of the three programs.

Finally, the researchers collected and analyzed data on students' attendance at the various program sites. It was noted that the maximum amount of attendance that was possible varied from student to student. This was so because of a number of factors. For example, students entered the program at a number of points over the school year. In addition, students were scheduled into the programs for one to five days a week, and in this way could be expected to spend very different amounts of time in the labs. The extent of this variation was noted in the fact that the maximum possible attendance for students ranged from 11 to 165 class periods. Clearly, there was little uniformity to the amount of exposure received by the students. This issue was one of the major motivations behind the restructuring of the program which was proposed and is detailed in the following section.

In order to evaluate absenteeism in the reading program, an index was developed which compared the average number of absences to the average of the maximum possible attendance figures. These indices were computed for each school in the program and for each of the three labs employed in the district. At the school level, this index revealed four schools where the daily absentee rate was at 20 percent or greater. This same index computed at the laboratory level indicated no major difference among the laboratories in terms of attendance.

Recommendations for Program Improvement

In addition to working up student data in the ways described above, we also observed each school's reading lab and interviewed the reading specialist. Based upon reviews of all of these data, we offered the following recommendations for program improvement in a report to program administrators:

1. Integration of Title I Labs with English with Emphasis on Reading (EWER) Classes

In nearly all cases, the students who participate in the labs are enrolled also in EWER classes from which they are pulled out to attend the labs. This fact alone makes coordination of services between these components of major importance. At present there is minimal coordination of this type, while the interviews with the reading specialists do indicate support for such effort without exception. It would seem desirable then to work in this direction, and the following are some ideas to do so:

Restructuring of EWER.   At present the EWER program at each school is taught by a large number of English teachers, each of whom has one such class. This makes any attempt at coordination cumbersome. We might recommend structuring the program so that a single teacher is responsible for EWER. This would make further attempts at coordination possible.

Scheduling of Time in Lab.   Under the current scheduling arrangements, the students are rostered into the reading labs one period per day for either two or three days per week. Put another way, time in the lab is time lost from EWER. While the labs themselves are modular in curricular design, the EWER classes operate as self-contained classes attempting to maintian an established sequence for a group. The scheduling arrangement renders this nearly impossible. We recommend a more systematic schedule that would improve the implementation of the set of curriculum for EWER. One suggestion might be for students to alternate between the two (with all students spending an equal time in each). This might be done by alternating weeks in each, or perhaps alternating blocks of time within weeks.

Schedule of In-service Programs.   Adoption of the first suggestion above would immediately identify a small interested group of teachers likely to attend and benefit from a program of joint in-service meetings for EWER and reading lab teachers alike. Such a program is thought to be highly desirable, and we urge that the first (for introductory and planning purposes) be carried out as soon as the roster of teachers is known.

It should be noted that the suggestions listed above arise from a reconceptualization of remedial reading services as a single programmatic effort subsuming the two components (EWER/Reading Lab). Such an effort would permit the program to focus upon a set of objectives that may be met through a variety of curricula. The district might wish to develop and consider additional action consistent with this view.

2. Coordination of Remedial Reading with Regular Programs

Interviews with the reading specialists indicate little if any effort to coordinate the reading labs with other classes offered to the students. Some work in this area may lead to considerable benefits in terms of educational outcomes and even morale:

Visits from Other Faculty.   It might be suggested simply that the labs host a series of visits from other faculty. This would afford the opportunity for the reading specialists to explain briefly the nature of the program, the equipment, and the materials available at the lab. A considerable benefit may occur should other faculty find opportunity to draw on them.

Preparation of Materials.   Independently, or in connection with the above suggestion, the preparation and distribution of very brief content analyses and outlines of the materials in each program might be of great service. The labs are rich in materials, the contents of which are relevant to a number of other subjects.

The activities outlined above have direct educational benefits. They also serve to enhance the visibility and prestige of the reading labs within the schools. If this can be done, it may have the additional outcome of counter-manding the effects of labeling the students and the stigma which a number of teachers have strongly noted.

3. Rostering of Students in Reading Program

Many of the problems experienced by the program to date are no more than those expected with any first-year effort. A common problem has been un-certainty and delay in establishing rosters.

To the extent possible, criteria must be established now. Students to be enrolled should be identified and rostered into the program in the coming spring. In this way, things will be set to go (both from the perspective of the program and the students) at the point that school opens in the fall. This will eliminate classroom rosters in flux (and constant retracing of steps) over the first quarter of the school year (P. LeMahieu and W. Cooley, personal communication, March 31, 1981).

Relationships to DOER

Several points are worth noting about case 6 and DOER as we have discussed it in part II of this book. In some respects, this case suffers from the absence of a strong client orientation. Initial research tasks were defined through discussions with the director for secondary instruction, but these early conversations were not sustained. This case does illustrate the emphasis in DOER on improvement-oriented research. Further, the use of on-site observations, participant interviews, and analyses of various quantitative data underscore the emphasis in chapter 4 on being methodologically eclectic. Each kind of data collection strategy added to the breadth and quality of the research findings. Case 6, like case 11, serves to illustrate some of the problems one can encounter in the typical use of research resources in educational settings, particularly those requiring summative evaluation research. In case 6, such an approach could have been premature and problematic for the reasons noted in the text. Finally, this case serves as an example of what not to do on the dissemination issue. Without a deeply involved client, there was little opportunity to do the kinds of early dissemination we wrote about in chapter 9. Further, the dissemination of results relied heavily on the distribution of the memo reproduced in this text, with little further researcher/ client or user interaction.

CASE HISTORY 7
MIDDLE-SCHOOL NEEDS
ASSESSMENT

Introduction

This case describes a needs assessment of 10 Pittsburgh middle schools. The case is divided into five major sections. These include a description of the original context surrounding the district's request for a needs assessment, the methods used in the assessment, and examples of results generated by the research. The final sections contain discussions of the dissemination process and the use made of the results by the school district managers.

Background to the Assessment Request

The Pittsburgh schools moved to a new, more uniform, district-wide grade organization in the fall of 1980 as part of a plan to desegregate the schools. The change to a middle-school organization for all children in grades six, seven, and eight was a major feature of that desegregation plan. As was pointed out in case 2, prior to the reorganization, the district contained a wide variety of school grade organizations below the high school level.

It is worth noting that although the district's move to a uniform middle-grade organization was primarily the result of this desegregation pressure, the change was coupled with much discussion of educational philosophy. Prior to 1980, several middle schools had already been established in the district. A number of key central administrators were prominent figures in national associations involved in promulgating the middle-school concept as an important educational reform (Eichhorn, 1966). The public debate surrounding school board deliberations about the district desegregation plan included much discussion of the relative merits of the middle-school concept.

Of the 14 newly constituted middle schools that began operation in 1980, four were designed as magnet schools. That is, these four were to draw their enrollment from across the city, based on parent and student interest in the specialized programs they offered (e.g., centers for performing arts, foreign languages, etc.). The remaining 10 were desegregated by redefining mandatory attendance areas, and thus involved a significant amount of new, nonvoluntary busing.

In the fall of 1981, the second year of the new school organization plan, the board requested an assessment of the 10 desegregated middle schools. Although there was general satisfaction with the relative ease with which this new feeder plan had been implemented, the board wanted to assure itself and its constituents that "a high quality program was at the end of the bus ride." Further, they wanted to identify ways in which the quality of the middle schools might be improved. It is also fair to say that in spite of numerous positive aspects of the first year of implementation, some people felt that all was not well in the middle schools. For example, some parents reported to the school board at open hearings that the middle schools seemed out of control, the quality of school life was low, and associated transportation problems were severe. These negative perceptions (which had received considerable play in the media) were reinforced in the fall of 1981 when initial enrollment for the middle grades indicated a slight decline.

One additional factor is worth noting about the context for the assessment. The school district had just completed a major reorganization of the central office staff in the summer prior to requesting the assessment. This resulted from an organizational efficiency study conducted by an outside consultant firm. One major feature of the staff reorganization plan was the abolishment of three assistant superintendents charged with the management of elementary, middle, and secondary school programs. A single associate superintendent office with one deputy would be in charge of all school management issues. In the eyes of some, one important effect of this new management scheme was to reduce the organizational identity of middle-school programs; no single office was now closely identified with these schools. This added further impetus to the board's interest in inquiring about conditions in the middle schools.

The superintendent initiated discussions with LRDC researchers in October 1981. An initial proposal was submitted to the board in November. Unlike past work, the district directly contributed some of its own resources for the support of the assessment. The study was characterized by district leadership as part of the effort to attract and hold students in the public schools. This priority was one of the six that emerged in the earlier district-wide needs assessment (case 4).

The proposal stated that the purpose of the study was to examine the Pittsburgh middle schools in order to determine ways in which these schools can and should be improved. An examination of the quality of the middle schools was viewed as being particularly timely at this early stage in their implementation. Any shortcomings that would normally occur during a major new initiative could be identified and resolved before they became more difficult to correct.

A second purpose noted in the proposal concerned the possibility that some parents may have shifted children to private schools rather than attend the desegregated middle schools. Closer inspection of the data was required to establish whether such a shift was actually occurring. If so, it was important to understand why parents were taking this action and to identify what the district might do to correct the conditions or perceptions that were causing it.

Work on the assessment formally began in December 1981. Details on the methods used are contained in the following section.

Assessment Methods

The basic approach for the middle-school assessment was similar to that used in case 4 for the district-wide needs assessment. That is, the assessment had two major components. One involved gathering perceptions from a wide variety of middle-school constituencies about the conditions of the schools and how they might be improved. These stakeholder views were supplemented with analyses of a number of district databases for the purposes of identifying additional issues and for testing the validity of the perceptions collected.

In order to gather perceptions, various groups were surveyed using questionnaires, personal interviews, and telephone interviews. These survey data were then analyzed along with other data collected in the district (e.g., student achievement, demographics) in order to identify relative strengths and weaknesses in middle schools. A total of 1,200 adults were surveyed, including board members, bus drivers, cafeteria workers, counselors, custodians, deans, paraprofessionals, parents of fifth grade and middle school students, principals, psychologists, school clerks and secretaries, security guards, social workers, supervisors, teachers, and a sample of Pittsburgh residents. In addition, a questionnaire on the quality of school life (Epstein, 1981) was administered to the 7,000 students in these 10 middle schools.

In addition to establishing the perceptions of various middle-school constituencies, a number of district databases were analyzed. These included data on student achievement and attendance, class size, costs, enrollment, retentions, suspensions, and transportation patterns. When negative perceptions were found to be consistent with these other data, it suggested conditions in the schools which should be improved. Where negative perceptions existed that were found to be inconsistent with other evidence, it indicated attitudes that may be changed by the provision of better information. Further, both kinds of research strategies were useful in determining what seemed to be working particularly well in individual schools. This information was valuable because positive aspects found in some schools might be transferable to less successful schools.

A key feature in the design of the middle-school assessment process was the use of a special task force established by the district to advise the researchers in the design of the data collection efforts and the interpretation of the findings. The task force consisted of individuals knowledgeable about the middle schools: board representatives, administrators, counselors, deans, parents, social workers, supervisors, and teachers. This task force became an important resource to the assessment process, serving as a pilot group to develop and test survey instruments, and as a sounding board to critically analyze early results. The benefits of working with the task force outweighed the drawbacks, but it is worth noting that there were some of the latter. Because the task force was fairly representative of middle-school constituencies, it encompassed a diverse array of viewpoints on such critical issues as the need for the study, the central questions that should be addressed, and the likely use of results that would be produced. Two issues, survey respondent confidentiality and the ultimate use of assessment data, serve to illustrate the kinds of concerns that surfaced in task force meetings and their impact on the assessment.

A member of the task force who represented the teachers' union was very concerned about respondent identification, especially of teachers. He argued forcefully that if teachers provided too much personal demographic data, the identity of the teacher could be easily established. Implicit in this concern was the belief that teachers who were openly critical of their own school, or of the district as a whole, might face aversive sanctions from administrators. He predicted that teachers in such circumstances would not provide their honest views of middle-school conditions. The researchers, on the other hand, wanted to specifically identify teachers so that a followup study would make it possible to adjust for nonrespondent bias. The compromises worked out among researchers and task force members regarding this confidentiality issue exemplify the kinds of tradeoffs between scientific methodologies and practical data collection realities that are often required in such research. The final survey instruments carried school codes, broad areas of teaching responsibility, areas of certification, grades taught, and number of years teaching experience (total experience as well as in middle schools). Specific subject area assignments were not included. Further, the completed surveys were mailed directly to the LRDC office, thus avoiding the possibility of the responses being viewed by building level administrators. Although the potential to do followup surveys to establish the extent of nonrespondent bias was eliminated by respondent anonymity, the overall effect was to increase task force confidence in the perceptions that would be collected.

A second issue that surfaced in task force discussions concerned the ultimate use of data produced through the assessment. Most members of the task force were drawn from district personnel directly involved in middle schools. While diverse positions were represented, most of the members expressed strong support for the middle-school concept. Given the fact that middle schools were part of a controversial desegregation plan, there was strong concern among several vocal task force members that any negative data that might be uncovered "would be used to harm the middle-school program." The most important factor that helped to ease this concern was the emphasis in the research on an improvement, rather than a summative approach, to the assessment. This was so, despite a general consensus that no one could control the use of data once they were made public.

The above two vignettes help to illustrate the impact the presence of the task force had on the assessment process. As a result of task force interactions, the knowledge shared about the goals of the assessment was increased, the survey instruments themselves were piloted and shaped, and the commitment to work on the dissemination of results were heightened among middle-school personnel. Perhaps most importantly, the task force provided a forum in which key middle-school personnel could express their concerns and anxieties about the organizational status of middle schools, and the relationship of the assessment to this status. These benefits outweighed the drawbacks of the task force approach which included a slowing down of the research process and a buffeting of the researchers and the research design by the various and sometimes conflicting viewpoints held by middle-school personnel. It should be noted that some insulation from the buffeting was provided by the superintendent's and board's commitment to the study. While task force members expressed many initial doubts, they did not seriously consider dropping the assessment.

Assessment Results

A preliminary report was presented to the board in June 1982. A final report was issued in January 1983. The findings in the final report were organized into three major components involving: (1) aspects of the middle schools viewed most positively; (2) aspects in need of improvement; and (3) a suggested strategy for improving middle schools in the future.

In general there was a consensus among parent groups surveyed that the middle schools were doing a good job. Parents with children in the middle schools were particularly positive. Some of the features they rated most positively included: providing a program of extracurricular activities; providing an appropriate building for the middle school students; concentrating on instruction in reading, writing, and mathematics; and expecting students to achieve. Although parents of fifth grade children tended to be far less knowledgeable about the middle schools than parents of middle-school children, those who were familar with the middle schools identified these same four features as the most positive aspects. Teachers and administrators cited features such as the successful integration of students, team teaching, extracurricular activities programs, and the quality and breadth of instructional programs when noting successful aspects of middle schools. Findings in areas of desegregation, team teaching, and extracurricular programming will serve to illustrate the kinds of results generated by the assessment.

Desegregation

A very significant finding of the assessment was that desegregation seemed to be working relatively smoothly in the middle schools. Pittsburgh residents, parents, teachers, and other professional staff members indicated that the middle schools provided students with the opportunity to interact with individuals different from themselves in an integrative environment. Principals reported that extracurricular activities served an important integrative function. Principals uniformly took the position that desegregation was working and that children were benefiting from the experience. Most principals indicated that they deliberately mixed homerooms by race, sex, and ability.

With the implementation of the desegregation plan, most schools were considered desegregated under state regulations. However, one school had experienced change since the implementation of the plan. At the time of the assessment, the school's percentage of black students was out of compliance with the Pennsylvania Human Relations Commission guidelines. It was noted in the assessment that if this had occurred because white families were tending to send their children elsewhere, it was ironic since this school was among the best in the district on various indicators of quality. These indicators included positive attitudes toward the school on the part of white students, as well as the amount of growth in achievement that was being realized in the instructional program.

The data available at the time of the assessment did not allow the researchers to determine if the disproportionate decrease in the number of white students attending that school was simply a function of a decreasing number of white children in its attendance area. It was noted that a new student information system being planned for the district would make such a study possible in the future. Meanwhile, it seemed important that the district make sure parents realized that a high quality program existed in this school, just in case this enrollment trend was being caused by a negative misperception of the school.

Transportation, an area that was linked to desegregation, also did not emerge as a major issue in the middle schools. Relevant groups surveyed (parents, principals, support staff, bus drivers) reported that transportation for the most part was adequate. However, a few transportation recommendations were given: improve discipline on the buses through more bus monitors; review distance requirements for transportation eligibility; and maintain bus schedules on time.

Teaming

The teaming of teachers was seen as a very positive force in the middle school by all groups surveyed. It was viewed as an organizational structure that facilitated school operations and as a mechanism to promote interdisciplinary teaching. This definition of teaming was at the heart of the middle-school philosophy. Team leaders saw it as a mechanism for sharing ideas and responsibilities, and as an effective way of increasing teacher morale.

Although the team concept was supported across all middle schools, the specifics of its actual implementation varied by school. The middle school organization was divided into three components: the school administration, the house and the team. These components were led by the principal, the dean, and the team leader, respectively. The number of houses, and teams within each house, depended on student enrollment, but there was at least one academic team in a house and one related arts team per school (with the exception of one school which sent its students out for vocational education).

Where teaming was implemented in a manner consistent with the middle-school philosophy, team leaders saw their role as coordinators of both instructional and noninstructional aspects of the team. Where teaming moved away from implementing the original concept, team leaders saw themselves as administrators. Some team leaders had reservations about this trend and felt that the supervision of other teachers was best served by the dean or supervisor.

According to team leaders, there were a number of reasons why the concept of teaming had undergone changes, but a major reason involved the emphasis on a newly developed criterion-referenced testing program in the district. Teachers were turning to their content area meetings for curriculum and instructional planning. The focus was no longer on an interdisciplinary curriculum but a specific content curriculum. This had the effect of undercutting the team concept since teams were organized on an interdisciplinary model.

Discipline was another area where the teams' operational strategies differed. Some teams developed their own rules and regulations for students to follow, while others did not. There was also variability in handling discipline problems. Some teams handled as many of their discipline problems as possible, while others always referred them to the principal.

Extracurricular Activities

Extracurricular activities were considered to be very important aspects of the middle school by all groups surveyed. Activities in this category included clubs, intramural sports, and all other events held outside the regular academic curriculum (e.g., assemblies and field trips). The clubs covered a wide range of activities (e.g., aerobics, crocheting, chess, model making, and candle making). Activities took place either during the school day or after the school day was over.

For the most part, activities were open to all students. Some schools did have an academic criterion students needed to meet in order to participate in intramural sports teams. A criterion of "no outstanding discipline problems" was also imposed on the student at the time of participation in some schools. The clubs were well attended by students, and all students participated in activities held during the school day (i.e., movies and dances).

The extracurricular activities served many important purposes, including the integration of the students. Activities also served to promote student-teacher interaction on a nonacademic level. This type of interaction was considered to be important in helping students see their teachers as individuals and not just as authority figures. Activities also served to enhance cooperation among students. Students learned to work together in a relaxed setting.

Areas in Need of Improvement

The second major set of results from the assessment involved the identification of a number of "improvable conditions." For example, there appeared to be a lack of understanding or awareness of many positive features of the middle schools among people not directly connected with them. There was a very large percentage of "don't know" responses to the survey items among fifth grade parents. The importance of providing this group a better orientation to the middle school was noted.

Only 23 percent of the teachers indicated that parents were productively involved in the middle schools. Principals felt that the geographically extended feeder patterns hindered parent participation in the schools. Parents of middle school children gave the middle schools one of their lowest ratings on "providing programs for parent involvement." Seventy-nine percent of middle school parents reported that they seldom or never visited their child's school. Improving parent involvement was thus clearly an important need.

Teachers cited teacher morale as one of the three areas most in need of improvement. Only 29 percent of the teachers felt that teacher morale was high, whereas 61 percent of other professional staff reported that teacher morale was high in their building. An analysis of relationships among teacher responses suggested that low teacher morale was primarily a function of how discipline-related problems were handled in their building, as well as the perceived leadership capabilities of the principal. Another factor influencing morale involved the fact that one-third of the middle-school teachers indicated that they would rather be teaching in elementary or high schools. It also appeared to be the case that many teachers seemed to have been assigned to these new middle schools without adequate orientation to the middle-school philosophy and structure.

Another issue concerned the fact that there were many large discrepancies between what the teachers perceived to be true of their school, and what the other professional staff in that same building perceived to be true. Within buildings, a greater effort was needed to achieve a consensus about what was happening in that school and what the priorities for school improvement should be.

The two areas of greatest concern involved student discipline and support staff functions. A more detailed discussion of the findings on discipline will illustrate the kinds of results generated by the assessment.

Discipline

There was a consensus among all groups surveyed (except principals) that discipline in the middle schools was an area in need of improvement. Sixty percent of the teachers and other support staff targeted discipline as a major area of concern. It was also clear that when discipline problems were perceived by teachers as not being handled well in school, teacher morale was very low. The primary concerns of school staff were that school rules and regulations needed to be more consistently enforced and that teachers and staff needed more options for punishing unruly students. These two concerns, plus the in-house suspension policy, were examined more closely in followup interviews in order to describe better the discipline process in the middle schools.

Consistency of discipline policy can be thought of in terms of rules used as well as in their enforcement. All middle schools appeared to follow the district's general code for discipline. This code consisted of nine regulations governing student behavior. A written copy of this code was given to the teachers, students, and parents at the beginning of each school year. Eight of the 10 schools had an additional set of rules pertaining only to their school. These rules were more detailed versions of the district's code (often in the student's language) as well as rules that covered more minor aspects of student behavior.

Each house within a school, each team within a house, and each teacher on a team could have a unique set of rules. More schools had team rules than house rules. Nine of the 15 team leaders indicated the existence of team rules, with the remainder leaving this option for the individual teacher. Although each set of rules could differ, the staff interviewed did not feel they were necessarily inconsistent. Rather, they felt that these sets governed different levels of student behavior.

Consistency in punishment of rule breakers appeared to be a greater concern than consistency in rules per se. The majority of deans interviewed indicated they were aware that teachers thought of this as a problem. As a group, deans were committed to uniformity in identifying students who were unruly; however, they felt the punishment should be decided on an individual basis. That is, consideration should be given to student's background, school history, or circumstances surrounding the event when determining the appropriate discipline option. The deans suggested that more open communication among all staff involved in administration of discipline policy would foster a more consistent policy.

The deans were the major disciplinarians in the middle schools. The amount of time a dean spent on discipline, however, varied a great deal from school to school. This range was the result of the referral process (the process by which a discipline case leaves the classroom and ends up in the dean's office), as well as the number of discipline problems the school routinely handled. In 8 of the 10 schools, the referral process was identical. That is, the teacher identified a problem and then contacted the student and the parent in an attempt to resolve it. If unsuccessful, the teacher brought the problem to the attention of the team. The team then tried additional methods to modify the student's behavior. Options open to the teacher and team included detention hall, lunch, extra homework, and denial of privileges. If the misconduct continued, the team referred the student to the counselor or the dean. Although the process was the same in eight schools, the amount of time and success at each step was different.

In one school, the dean reported that the teams completely handled 90 percent of its discipline problems, while in other schools the reverse was true. Some deans reported spending up to 99 percent of the day handling discipline problems, while others said it was as little as 10 percent. The role of the counselor in handling discipline problems also varied from school to school. In at least three of the schools, the counselors' defined role as student advocate prohibited them from taking a major role in disciplining students. In other schools, the counselor was viewed more as an assistant to the dean, and therefore handled the same type of problems the dean handled. These problems typically included students with repeated minor offenses or major offenses such as fighting, and drug or alcohol problems. The dean's options included all of those previously mentioned plus in-house suspension.

In-house suspension received positive ratings from all staff interviewed. All 11 deans reported it had resulted in fewer out-of-school suspensions and was viewed by teachers, students, and parents as a good alternative to out-of-school suspensions. In all but the most serious offenses, in-house suspension was tried first as a method of changing student behavior. If this failed, out-of-school suspension procedures were initiated. The process of assignment to in-house suspension, and the description of the in-house room and rules were similar across all schools. In most schools, the deans and principal were the only ones who assigned this punishment. Over 60 percent of the teachers surveyed indicated that more options were needed in dealing with the unruly students.

Student truancy was also a problem in the middle schools. Average daily attendance dropped from 91 percent in the elementary schools to 86 percent for middle schools. (It then dropped only one percentage point in the high schools.) Records of students who have failed a grade indicated that absenteeism was a major reason for failure. A followup of students who were chronic truants revealed that many had not had a home visit by a social worker. More effort in this area was clearly needed.

A Recommended Improvement Strategy

The third section of the final report spelled out a possible improvement strategy for middle schools. The researchers stressed the fact that each of the 10 schools had different strengths and weaknesses. Although some schools had several problem areas, and some problems were common to more than one school, the problems tended to be scattered among the schools. This suggested a targeted school improvement effort, where specific problems are worked on in specific schools. A profile for each school was developed that described the main findings for that school with respect to areas in need of improvement. Table C7-1 shows how the various problems were distributed among the 10 schools. Each row in the table represents a school, and each column identifies a possible problem. An asterisk (*) appears if a given school seemed to have a particular problem. The table illustrates the fact that different schools had different problems. This finding had important implications for the school improvement strategy recommended by the researchers to district leadership.

The problem-solving school improvement approach recommended to the district was based upon both specific findings generated by the assessment process, the experiences gained from the documentation of the elementary school improvement program (case 5), and the literature describing school improvement efforts elsewhere in the country. The approach had five key features or assumptions:

1. A single improvement program cannot be applied to all 10 middle schools. Except for a few issues that were identified as problem areas in every school, each school's profile was different. The number and kinds of problems, as well as the groups of people who considered each issue to be a problem, varied greatly from school to school. Only an individualized improvement approach could meet such various needs.

2. One improvement strategy cannot be applied to all problem areas. The kinds of problems identified in the middle schools involved instructional, school climate, and personnel issues. Clearly, solutions in a particular

Table C7-1. Distribution of Problems Among the 10 Schools

Problem Area / School ID Number	Teacher Survey				School Data						Quality of School Life (Stud. Attitudes)		
	Discipline	Staff Functions	Parent Involvement	Teacher Morale	Suspensions	Teacher Attendance	Attendance	Achievement	Staff-Teacher Difference	Home Room Segregation	School	Teachers	Classwork
1	*							*					
2	*	*		*	*	*	*			*	*	*	*
3			*			*						*	
4	*	*											
5	*	*											
6	*				*								
7	*	*		*							*		
8								*	*				*
9								*					
10	*	*	*				*	*	*		*	*	*

*Indicates a problem area for that school.

problem area required different configurations of people and resources within each building and at the district level. For example, a specific personnel issue could only be addressed by those directly charged with that responsibility.

3. Any improvement strategy must involve the participants in its planning and implementation. The school improvement experience and the literature supported the concept that ownership of the improvement plan by those responsible for making it work in their schools was crucial to the improvement effort. Teachers and principals must feel involved in the plan and committed to its success. The suggested problem-solving approach was founded on the idea of direct principal and teacher involvement.

4. All improvement strategies must be designed with certain common elements. Although an individualized problem-solving approach implied that the improvement plan for every middle school will be unique to that school to some extent, the literature described some basic components that must be part of any successful improvement strategy.

5. Existing district resources should be used where feasible. A problem-solving approach to school improvement should not require the development of a program totally new to the district. Instead, this approach to improvement should permit an emphasis on the use of appropriate existing resources to focus on problems in a systematic way.

The recommended school improvement strategy envisioned a basic sequence for each school staff as they began their improvement efforts. These included: (1) the review of the data from the assessment that indicated the existence of a particular school problem; (2) the conduct of further diagnoses to define and measure the problem specifically; (3) the development of objectives and an implementation plan to meet the needs; (4) the identification of the resources necessary to implement the plan; and (5) the monitoring and assessment of the implementation of the plan, revising it as necessary.

The problem-solving strategy also assumed that some problems uncovered in the assessment could not be addressed at the building level. For example, teacher concern about ambiguity in the roles of middle-school support staff would be a matter for central administrative attention, as it affected all schools and was manifested in district personnel job descriptions.

The above represent a sample of the kinds of results and recommendations that were developed. In the following sections the process used to disseminate these results and the subsequent use made of them are described.

Dissemination

Dissemination began on May 21, 1982, when the researchers met with the superintendent and several key central administrators to review preliminary results of the data collection activities. This meeting had the dual purpose of presenting early findings and planning future dissemination activities.

A great deal of the discussion at the May 21, 1982, meeting focused on how school level data should be disseminated. Of special concern were the implications of publicly identifying specific schools that seemed to have more problem areas than others, and the issue of data related to personnel performance that could be linked to individuals in the system (e.g., negative comments from teachers about their social worker's performance). More will be said about these issues later in this section.

The dissemination plan that was developed included a presentation to the task force of preliminary tabulations of survey data in early June and an overview of results to the board later that same month. The goal of the task force presentation was to offer an opportunity for members to develop their own interpretations of the data and to share them with the research group. The board meeting was designed to give a sense of the progress made to date and to identify areas requiring further data collection that could address issues of concern to board members.

As it turned out, a number of questions for clarification did surface at the June meeting. These included interest in more details about school level variations in policies related to teaming, student discipline, and use of support staff. Interviews of numerous school personnel were undertaken in the fall of 1982 to gather additional data in these areas. The final report was issued in January 1983 incorporating all of the findings of the research as well as the recommended strategy for a middle-school improvement program.

The report issued in January 1983 represented the end point and final summary of assessment data. Numerous reports had been developed prior to that month, designed for targeted audiences or focused on specific issues or populations. For example, summaries of the interviews of middle-school principals were prepared as a separate report, as were data relevant to specific policy areas such as transportation, and team teaching.

Perhaps the most interesting issue that emerged during the dissemination process involved problems associated with the public release of school level and, to a lesser extent, personnel level data. As noted earlier, the concern about school level data first surfaced in the May 21, 1982, meeting to plan dissemination activities. It continued throughout the dissemination process. For example, great interest was expressed by board members over which schools were "winners" or "losers" in the problem area matrix (see table C7-1) presented at the June meeting. While there was no question that all data generated by the study should be available in some form to the board, there was eventual agreement that school level data should not be identified in public reports.

There were two reasons for this decision. First, most of the data represented what might be termed a preliminary diagnosis. More detailed, building level data collection and analyses were required by school personnel to illuminate fully what the nature and, most importantly, what the root causes were of a specific school's problem areas. Second, a public display that rank ordered the quality of middle schools could seriously damage a school's morale and thus reduce the effectiveness of future improvement efforts.

The release of data concerning specific personnel groups (e.g., support staff) was equally sensitive, although agreement about what to do with such data was much more easily reached. District leadership made these data available to departmental heads responsible for support staff role groups with the proviso, again, that the information could only be considered as preliminary indications, with more detailed diagnosis required.

Use of the Study

A discussion of utilization in this case must make a distinction between use of specific data generated by the study and use of the assessment process itself. At the specific level, school profiles generated through the assessment provided an initial basis for individual school improvement efforts. In the spring of 1983, a district person was identified to work with building principals in assisting them in understanding their own school's data, in communicating the findings to their staff, and in developing plans for either further data collection or for taking action to address improvable conditions. Again, at the specific finding level, data relevant to personnel problem areas such as the role of middle-school support staff or data relevant to specific district-wide policy areas (e.g., transportation) were made available to appropriate departmental heads. This information provided the basis for a number of review processes that occurred during the year subsequent to the issuance of the final report.

At the broadest level, the assessment process seemed to be useful to the system in several ways. First, reflecting one of the initial goals of the study, the assessment process appeared to be useful in sustaining public confidence in the middle schools. This was probably so because many of the findings were quite positive, in some instances surprisingly so (e.g., the fact that a majority of middle-school parents were so positive contrasted with the image that had been built up by public testimony at board hearings). In addition, those still concerned about improvable conditions could now take some comfort in the fact that many of these were receiving the system's attention through the various improvement efforts underway.

The public confidence utility was paralleled by board impressions. Members who were advocates of the middle-school programs were reassured in their positions. Members with concerns about the middle schools had more detailed data that could be helpful in marshaling political support for improvement efforts.

The assessment process also seemed to serve an important function for middle-school personnel in the system. Various role groups had the opportunity to speak out on middle-school conditions. Clearly there was concern about "misuse" of data (where misuse could range, depending upon the individual's perspective, from covering up conditions in need of improvement, to using specific negative data to attack the broader middle-school concept). However, these concerns notwithstanding, there was evidence in many of the survey and interview responses that people were pleased to have had an opportunity to be heard. This appreciation was probably further reinforced by anxiety over the loss of a specific office for middle schools in the new reorganized central administration of the district.

Relationships to DOER

It was in the process of conducting this middle-school assessment that many of the features of monitoring and tailoring described in chapter 5 were formulated. It seemed to us that what we were doing should be part of a continuous process of system improvement, and not a "one-shot" study that started with collecting new data and ended with writing a final report. As we looked at distributions, we kept seeing outliers in need of attention. Different schools stood out in different distributions. Different indicators suggested that different kinds of attention were needed in different schools.

There was also an important lesson in the followup activities. As the previous section indicates, there were several examples of district-wide uses of these results. The primary client was the superintendent, with the school board running a close second. So they ended up getting the information they wanted from the study.

Where the lack of use was disappointing was in the school level followup activities. We essentially abandoned the study with the issuing of the final report. (Other demands from the district became a higher priority.) The results were in the form needed to conceptualize the improvement effort, but the data were not worked up in ways that were adequate to guide the school level improvement efforts. Nor were the school principals, who would have to lead such improvement efforts, considered to be clients in the analyses that were done. We moved on to other studies, and the school level efforts never really materialized. Had we begun with the school principals as clients, we may have missed our primary target. What was needed was a reworking of the data with each principal and school improvement committee, helping them to see what the data suggest regarding their individual schools. As far as school improvement was concerned, this study did not have the impact it might have because the necessary school level effort got diverted.

CASE HISTORY 8
COMPUTER-BASED INFORMATION
SYSTEMS

This case is a little different from the rest. It does not examine a specific request for information, but represents a summary of why and how we went about building computer-based information systems. This story extends over the entire period of our work with the school district. It describes our attempts to be more responsive to district requests for information through the establishment of computer files that would facilitate our ability to work up data relevant to district policy questions and management needs. This case illustrates the general principles outlined in chapter 6.

Recognition of several factors led to the computerization of data files: the importance of timeliness; the recurring need for the same data to shed light on different problems; and the critical need to bring data from different sources together in one place. We began to establish a computer-based information system for the Pittsburgh public schools by establishing a school level file. That is, we created a data file that described each of the 90 schools in the district, pulling together information relevant to each of the schools. Table C8–1 lists the variables we included in our first school level file. The file was begun in the context of case 1 (the elementary school achievement study) and was extended as we moved into a study of the different grade organizations in the district (case 2). The expanding database became a critical component of our district-wide needs

Table C8-1. Variables Included in School Level File

School ID number
Grades included
Number of blacks
Total number of students
Number of special education students
Average class size
Number of suspensions
Number of students transported
General fund per pupil cost
Supplemental fund per pupil cost
Total per pupil cost
Average daily free lunches served
Adjusted total cost
School achievement indicator fall (pre-)
School achievement indicator spring (post-)

---

assessment (case 4), and subsequently provided the basis for looking at differences among schools for the selection of schools to participate in the school improvement program (case 5). Similarly, data relevant to the middle schools were the basis for our initial tasks in the middle-school assessment (case 7).

Having demonstrated the value of a school level file, we began to construct a student level file. It is, of course, one thing to establish a relatively clean set of data on 90 schools. It's quite another to construct a data file representing 45,000 students. We began with two existing files. One was the standardized achievement test results which the district had been receiving from the test publishers in the form of a magnetic tape, containing test results for all of the students who had taken the California Achievement Test (CAT) (grades 1-8). The other file was something the district called the CAPAS (Computer Assisted Pupil Accounting System) file, which was a student tracking file with basic information regarding student home background. Fortunately, both the CAT file and CAPAS file contained the same student identifying number, so we merged the two files in an effort to get a single file with the linked information. Because of extensive student mobility and inaccuracy of identifying numbers, we were only able to achieve an 80 percent merge for the grades for which we had both CAT and CAPAS data. We then had another sobering experience. We went into one of these schools on another project and tried to use the student file for that school from this merged file. We found another 20 percent inaccuracy, in the sense that some of the students in the school were not in the file, and students in the file were not in the school. So it became quite clear that something else had to be done in order to try to establish a student level file that was current and accurate.

Meanwhile, the district had begun to build a new computer system of its own. One of the outcomes of the district-wide needs assessment was a recognition of the need for a management information system. To guide its development, the board created a new position, director of management information and planning, and in the spring of 1981 brought in someone from outside the district to fill that position.

The director's first task was to develop a plan for designing and implementing such a system. A plan was created which became one of the seven action plans submitted to the board in July 1981 as a result of the needs assessment that was conducted in the fall of 1980 (case 4).

A key paragraph in that plan was:

> A major underlying assumption of the Management Information System is that the most important element in the delivery of the educational services of the District is the individual school, and the main focus of the MIS is to provide services and assistance to the administrators within the schools to allow them to manage the school and function as educational leaders.

Then in December 1981, the board voted to provide the district with a computer system that would be linked to each school building via computer terminals in each school.

A Data General MV8000 Computer System was purchased for this purpose. The plan was very ambitious. The system was to include all central administrative functions (budgeting, accounting, payroll, personnel, etc.), as well as support such within-school functions as scheduling, attendance, grade reporting, transportation, federal and state reporting, and student achievement.

As far as helping schools and principals were concerned, the results were disappointing. As was being learned in school districts throughout the country, the central administrative functions are so overwhelming and so proximate to the central computer that they tend to dominate the attention of computer system developers. The part about helping schools and principals seldom comes to pass. Implementation of the central administrative functions not only tends to absorb all of the energy of the programming staff but it also saturates the computer's capabilities.

A conclusion we have come to after several years of working on this problem of creating current and accurate central files is that a computer file will only be accurate to the degree to which those data are actually used in the schools. It is unrealistic to expect principals, school secretaries, counselors, etc., to exert the care and effort needed to maintain a complete and accurate central district file in the hopes that some central officer might find it useful. Also relevant is the fact that a computer file that would be functionally useful within a school requires a level of detail about students that would place an excessive load on the central computer. Further, it would be at a level of detail that is unnecessary at the central district level.

At the time those notions emerged, the potential of the micro-computer began to be apparent, together with the possibility of transferring files between a school-based micro-computer and a central computing facility. Thus, we went back to the drawing boards with a different concept, that of distributed processing. What has emerged is a micro-computer system able to operate at the level of detail that is useful for helping educators in the school building. The balance of this case history describes how and why we are developing such a school-based micro-computer system. This project is still in progress as our book goes to press.

A School-Based Information System

The elementary school principal is under a great deal of pressure to be the instructional leader of the school. When coupled with the various administrative tasks a principal has, the instructional leadership role adds a tremendous amount of responsibility. Such leadership requires the principal to participate in instructional decisions that will increase teacher effectiveness and student learning. Therefore, the principal must be informed of what teachers are teaching and how well students are learning. The principal must be able to monitor important indicators of instructional processes and outcomes, and then help teachers to tailor curriculum or instruction as needed. (The monitoring and tailoring concepts discussed in chapter 5 applied at the school level.)

In a search for clues as to how this achievement monitoring might be done, Durant (1984) conducted a review of the effective schools and school improvement literatures. The main generalizations from that literature that are relevant here are:

1. effective schools are defined as schools serving students from low socioeconomic background that exhibit high student achievement;
2. effective schools tend to have principals who exhibit certain qualities called instructional leadership;
3. monitoring student achievement is an important characteristic of an effective instructional leader;
4. very little is said about the specifics of such monitoring;

5. very little is said about how to get principals who do not exhibit instructional leadership qualities to do so.

In an effort to explore how this achievement monitoring might be facilitated by computer support, we launched the Computer-Assisted Professional (CAP) project. The objective was to design an instructional information system that will facilitate the instructional leadership responsibility of the elementary school principal and improve student achievement. The information system is designed to include both classroom and student level data, and provides written and graphic displays at the level of detail necessary for principals and other professionals in the school to identify and help diagnose possible problems at either the classroom or student level.

Development of a Prototype

In the fall of 1984 we began working on the design and development of such a system in the context of one of the Pittsburgh elementary schools. This was done by establishing an extensive database for that school and then working up displays of these data in ways that the principal and other professionals in the school find useful.

The school is one of seven schools participating in Pittsburgh's school improvement program (case 5). This program has been testing a "paper and pencil" instructional monitoring system in each of these seven schools (Venson, 1981). Program staff developed forms which monitor a student's reading progress, failing report card grades, failing teacher-made test grades, and the retesting of all failed tests including reading mastery tests. The school improvement system was designed to help principals identify students in need of extra help. The program's experience indicated that the principal has difficulty in "processing" all these data and integrating the classroom information with achievement test scores and other data available in the school.

However, the school improvement program's experience also indicated that decision making was a prominent part of the principal's role as instructional leader, and that data were necessary for making informed decisions. In this role, the principal was involved in such decisions as the proper placement of students in the curriculum, or deciding when a student was in need of extra compensatory services, or determining particular classrooms in which the instructional supervisors might focus teacher development efforts. As we noted, reports of other school improvement projects mention the need to monitor student progress, but none has described precisely how that might be done. How can the data be effectively captured? What data should be monitored? At what level of detail? Displayed how?

We decided to work on answers to these questions by first establishing an extensive school database that errored in the direction of overinclusiveness, and then began working with the principal in the school, identifying the types of problems that come up on a day-to-day basis, and trying to work up the available data in ways that would be helpful.

The establishment of this initial database took advantage of data already available in school district files. Thus, from the standardized test file, we pulled off test data for the students in this school. Similarly, from the student tracking file, we pulled student records relevant to this school. Data being collected from the classrooms for the school improvement program monitoring were hand-entered.

We begin this work on a mini computer (the LRDC Vax). This made it possible to establish a larger database than was possible on a school-based micro. This approach offered us the initial flexibility we needed for this exploration. It also made it easier to transfer files from the University of Pittsburgh computer and the district computer to the LRDC Vax for producing an integrated database for the school. This prototype was developed as a doctoral dissertation (Durant, 1984).

We then shifted to an IBM XT micro-computer located in the school. The system has been implemented with a very flexible database management software package called Knowledge Manager developed by Micro Data Base Systems, Inc. Its data-management language is much like natural language programming and uses free-form text similar to English sentences. Knowledge Manager is a relational database management system that allows the user to combine data from different files within the database and create tables and graphs of this information. It greatly simplifies the tasks of data retrieval and report generation.

As this work continues, one of the things we are exploring are alternative ways of displaying data, whether through tables, bar garphs, scatterplots, histograms, etc. The book by Tufte (1983) on *The Visual Display of Quantitative Information* is helpful in this regard.

One of our objectives is to develop displays that signal various kinds of achievement difficulties that might be emerging that will suggest priorities for corrective action. For example, at a recent staff meeting the principal and supervisors were discussing a third grade classroom in which reading progress seemed to be at a standstill. The lack of progress was noted in data from the school improvement program's monitoring system. The next task was to work up data that might help the principal and supervisors plan an improvement strategy for that classroom. This analysis was guided by our own abilities to display and interpret data, but once we developed procedures that seemed relevant to this particular type of question, they became a part of what automatically was done with these data when that type of question came up in the school.

Our approach has been to try to make available to principals the procedures that an expert data analyst would use to generate useful information from the school database. Eventually, this expertise would be available to the principal in the form of computer routines which would be automatically invoked when principals ask particular questions. We do not expect principals to learn how to program computers, nor do we expect principals to learn different ways of analyzing and displaying data. What we are doing is building into the software available to the principal a menu which will make the connections between different types of problems and the resulting displays of data that might help principals work toward solutions to those problems.

In addition to designing ways of being responsive to types of questions that principals and staff are raising in the school, we are analyzing the data in ways that reveal possible instructional problems, a kind of early warning system. As particularly revealing displays are found, they are being incorporated into procedures that will become part of the principal's monitoring routines.

For example, simply monitoring what is being taught to a class may be misleading. A principal may see that a teacher has covered 88 percent of the curriculum by mid-year. At first glance one might think that the teacher is doing very well, but if the principal examines how well the students are mastering the material, that might tell another story. The principal may find that even though a teacher claims that 88 percent of the curriculum has been taught, only 18 percent of the students have mastery of that material, as was noticed in one of our classrooms.

The school-based micro system that has been implemented has the following features. It has a data management software package as the core program. It is able to download files from the district's central computer that are relevant to that school. It is able to send summaries of school level data back to the district files, at the level of detail the district needs for system-wide purposes. It has attached to it a scanner that enables data collected in the school to be added quickly to the school-based files. It is menu-driven by the principal and other professionals in the building. It allows the user to make ad hoc inquiries when the menus fail to anticipate a type of information need. In addition to CRT displays, it is capable of producing printouts that the principal can easily share with other professional staff in the building when CRT displays are found that seem relevant and appropriate for current planning functions.

What is critical is that the design of the school micro system has build-in incentives for the school personnel to use the system. The local school micro must offer the kinds of data that principals need in order to effectively provide the kind of instructional leadership that schools require. It must provide classroom level diagnostic information able to guide the supervisory talent available in the schools for staff development. It must include test scoring services that teachers are willing and able to use; it must provide information to the social workers regarding chronic truance and attendance patterns; and it must provide information to the teachers directly as to the available instructional materials that would be particularly helpful for the students in that classroom given recent test results.

There are several commercial systems that are currently available that perform some of these functions, but none of them seems to provide the kinds of flexibility needed to adapt to local differences in how education is conducted. Given the availability of sophisticated application packages for database management, we think it is highly advantageous to develop and adapt these systems to local differences, such as the types of criterion-referenced tests being used, ways in which student tracking and attendance accounting is conducted, the types of special services available in the building for students, etc. It also makes it easier to be adaptive to the current central computer's file structures and methods of handling data.

The school improvement "bandwagon" developed as an attempt to apply the findings from the research on effective schools through implementing effective schools characteristics in less effective schools. That is turning out to be a very difficult task. Two conclusions from the research in these two areas are that: (1) strong instructional leadership is important for schools to be effective; and (2) monitoring student progress is important for principals to be effective instructional leaders. As a result of the impact of these two findings on schools, there is a lot of pressure on the principal to be an instructional leader. How can a principal become a better instructional leader, and what is an efficient way of monitoring student progress? These are the questions that are being addressed in this project.

CAP is being developed for the professionals in the school as the primary users. This is being done by generating, manipulating, and reporting data using an established school database. The data derive from data files at the district level and from data being collected in the school building. We are now working with the principal and other professionals in the school on a routine basis, providing information for their instructional activities and decision making. In this way we are determining what information is clear and useful to them and how it should be presented. From this experience, the system requirements of CAP for the elementary school are being specified.

Current Applications of CAP

One way of getting a sense of how this system is being used is to read what the users in the school have said at the end of their first year of using the system. Here is how they described the utility of the system as of May 1985.

Student and Teacher Schedules

Printouts of schedules are produced and distributed to administrators, clerks, and support personnel. These are used many times daily to locate students or teachers. Previously, the entire school shared one master copy of the schedule which was kept in the main office. Now, as the schedules change, revised printouts are easily made and copies distributed.

Emergency Information.

Before the CAP system was introduced in the school, student emergency information was difficult to keep updated. Student address changes were made if parents notified the school, but phone numbers were constantly changing and were very difficult to keep current. Several attempts were made by the school to update the emergency information, but it still was inadequate. A computerized form letter was created which included the current information on each student and an area for updating the information. This individualized letter was sent home with each student. The response was tremendous. The emergency information is now current, and the CAP system allows the information to be easily updated.

Student Address and Phone Lists

Using the updated home data from the emergency form update, homeroom lists are created with student's address, home phone, parents' work numbers, and emergency phone numbers. These are distributed to all the teachers and support staff. These listings are a part of the menu options and when changes have been made, new listings can be made.

Alphabetized Student Listing

A listing of all students in the school alphabetized by name including their grade assignment, homeroom, home address, and home phone is one of the most used listing generated. This is used by the clerical staff, nurse, social worker, lunch room aides, support staff, principal, and assistant principal. Recently the use of this listing cut the task of checking student addresses against transportation bus lists from a two-to-three-day job in previous years to a one-half-day job.

Homeroom Listings

An alphabetized list of homeroom members which includes name, grade, CAPAS number, sex, race, and homeroom has been a valuable printout. This printout has been used primarily as a homeroom membership verification and as a method to follow student homeroom membership tracking. This is used by CAP staff, attendance clerk, social workers, Chapter I teachers, and the parent–teacher organization.

Attendance Data

Included in the attendance data are cumulative days absent, tardy suspensions (in-house and out-of-school) and excused and unexcused absences. This is most useful in monitoring student attendance. Using ad hoc inquiries, the social worker is able to tailor a worksheet for pertinent information based on attendance outliers. He is able to identify student attendance problems, as well as include addresses and phone numbers for future parent contacts.

Attendance data are extremely helpful in relation to student achievement monitoring. By including attendance and disciplinary actions as a variable in ad hoc inquiries, important patterns emerge. This is important in determining the monitoring of achievement and future instructional leadership of supervisors, principals and assistants, teachers, and special teachers (Chapter I and itinerant support staff).

MAP Testing

One of the most important functions of the CAP system is to scan and score the MAP criterion-referenced tests for reading, math, and grammar. Prior to the CAP system, tests were administered and sent to the central office for processing, and the results were returned two weeks later. Now test results are available the same day the tests are given. This is extremely important to guide classroom instruction. Also, because the tests are scored within the school, errors in coding can be detected and corrected. After each scanning and scoring, teachers receive a classroom report for each level tested and the principal receives a school summary. In addition, other reports are generated in conjunction with student monitoring. A brief description of various reports and displays follows:

1. Teacher's report — a report which includes student's name, objectives incorrect, total number of objectives correct for each student within a given test level. The report also indicates which objective has been taught by the teacher and a classroom summary of the percentage correct.

2. Principal's report — an aggregate report of all classrooms and levels tested on a given test administration. It lists whether an objective has been taught and the percentage of students getting the objective correct for each classroom.

3. Classroom report — a predefined report within the CAP menu which gives student's name, test scores (percent correct), test levels for all MAP tests within a subject area. There are two such reports (one includes data for the classroom, the other only students with complete data that correlate with a graphic display).

4. Classroom objectives report — a classroom level report that shows each objective, whether it was taught, and the classroom percent correct for each objective.

5. Graphic displays — two different ones are available in the CAP menu: graphic display showing student's percent correct across tests by level within subject area; and graphic display showing percent objectives correct across tests by level within a given subject area.

Teacher-made Tests

With the use of machine scoreable general purpose answer sheets, teachers are now able to machine score any teacher-made tests which have been adapted to the answer sheets. By following a simple menu, tests results can be obtained in a few minutes. Although this is one of the most recent CAP developments, it has proven to be quite a successful and valuable option. Not only is it a time-saver for teachers but, more important, it is a great motivator for students. The immediate feedback of test results has motivated students to improve on subsequent tests.

Focus on Reading

Student individual reading pacing schedules are a part of the CAP database. These include monthly reading levels and units for each student. Also available are predefined reports.

1. School Reading Progress Report — this report is organized by grades within a grade level. It includes CAT results for reading, beginning of year pacing schedule, the most recent pacing schedule, a student's most recent reading grade, and MAP test results, and levels.

2. Individual Student Progress Report — this report includes reading pacing schedules, reading grades, MAP tests results, MAP levels, Chapter I eligibility, CAT reading national percentile, CAT reading grade equivalent, and days absent.

CAT (California Achievement Tests)

Individual standardized achievement test results are a part of the database. These data are used in many different reports and the ad hoc inquiries. Reports containing CAT data are as follows: (1) Chapter I eligibility report; (2) student achievement monitoring report; (3) individual student reading progress report; and (4) school reading progress report.

Using ad hoc inquiries reports based on CAT data have been generated for use by the principal in planning instructional supervision and planning for: (1) Chapter I reading and math; (2) scheduling computer- assisted instruction; and (3) administrative reports.

Classroom Level MAP Monitoring

Classroom level reports comparing each objective tested across tests for MAP reading, math, and grammar is an option on the CAP menu. These consist of predefined reports and graphs.

1. Classroom predefined report — this report is broken down to the objective level for each classroom. Each objective is listed as is the total percentage of students getting the objective correct, and whether the objective has been taught. This is done across tests for each subject tested.

2. Classroom level graph — this is a bar graph that depicts the above classroom level predefined report and the percentage of students getting the objective correct across tests. With the use of the predefined report and graphic display, the teacher and principal are able to get a better idea of how a class is performing on the objective level, whether the class is improving with further instruction, where reteaching needs to occur, and whether a given test is much harder than others.

Middle-school Assignments

By designating a field in the database for middle-school assignments, fifth grade students' middle-school assignments were entered. Printouts were produced and sent to the middle schools, listing each student's name, address, zip, and home phone that will enter there in 1985–86. This will also be used to send student achievement data to the middle schools for the following school term.

Ad Hoc Inquiries

By using ad hoc inquiries as an option on the menu, many reports have been generated. Listed below are a few not listed previously.

1. School retention report — a report was generated that listed students in all grade levels that have failing grades in reading, math, and language. This was generated for each homeroom and included information on attendance, reading national percentile, math national percentile, language national percentile, all grades to date for reading, math, and language, the most recent MAP score for reading, math and language, and the student's date of birth. The teachers, supervisors, and principals will use the report to screen for possible retentions for the following school year.

2. The principal needed a report for the central office which focused on students with CAT reading national percentile between 20–50 percent. This was easily done in minutes with the ad hoc inquiry feature. Prior to the CAP system, he would have had to hand sort through all of the CAT data and compile a list of students and then have it typed.

3. Grade summaries — in order to get a more concise picture of grades and grading practices in the school, the principal has used ad hoc inquiries to obtain reports on students' grades (e.g., which students received A's in math or what were the individual reading grades for the fourth grade).

4. A parent of a first grader with a new baby at home was unable to walk her frightened child to school each day. She called the school for a list of names of other children in her neighborhood that walked to school that her child could walk with. By selecting for a certain street address, a list of students was sent home to her.

5. In order to prepare a transportation schedule for the following school year, an alphabetical listing of fifth graders was prepared to remove them from the schedule.

Ad hoc inquiries are used daily for individual data retrieval (student addresses, student phone numbers, parent's name, emergency information, CAT scores, MAP scores, grades, pacing schedules for reading, absentees). This capability is one of the most important options of the CAP system.

CASE HISTORY 9
DOCUMENTING THE
DEVELOPMENT OF A SECONDARY
TEACHER CENTER

Introduction

This case describes the documentation of the development of a major staff development program for secondary teachers, the Schenley High School Teacher Center. The case is divided into six main sections: the background of the teacher center; its basic structure; the origins of the management request for program documentation; the methodologies employed in documenting the center; examples of research results produced; and the use made of documentation information by system managers.

Background

The district began the development of a teacher center for high school teachers in the fall of 1981. Several factors influenced the origin of this program. Through a district-wide needs assessment in 1981 (case 4), the board had established two broad policy objectives: to improve instruction and to develop more cost effective management in the district. Enrollment had been declining in the schools for some time. The reduced grade level cohorts were now reaching the high schools. District leadership was faced with, on the one hand, the need to reduce staff and close schools and, on the other hand, the recognition that secondary instruction, like other levels in the district, was in need of improvement.

The response to these potentially conflicting needs was a proposal by the superintendent in the fall of 1981 to keep Schenley High School open. It had been one of the schools proposed for eventual closing. Schenley could be used as a site for a high school teacher renewal program to begin in the fall of 1983, the substance of which was yet to be defined.

The basic concept of the program was to bring teachers from their home high schools to work with specially selected and trained teachers at Schenley for what amounted to an eight-week mini-sabbatical. Schenley would continue as a fully operational comprehensive high school. The teachers visiting Schenley would be replaced in their home schools by a cohort of specially trained teachers for the period of their stay at the center. About 50 visiting teachers would participate in each session. This represented approximately 7 percent of the high school teachers, which was the projected surplus. Thus, in 16 eight-week sessions over four years, the entire secondary teaching staff would have an opportunity to come to the center.

The board of education gave the superintendent the approval to develop the concept further. A steering committee of central administrators, teachers, and community and university representatives was established to mount what was essentially a feasibility study. Input from a wide spectrum of district constituencies was elicited. By June of 1982 the district was in a position to request private support for a year of formal planning of the Schenley High School Teacher Center (Pittsburgh public schools, June 1982). External funding was obtained from the Ford Foundation. From September 1982 to August 1983 the district undertook a broadly based planning process under the direction of a newly appointed principal for Schenley and a center director.

Numerous committees of teachers, administrators, and community representatives were established during the formal planning year. Each committee focused on a specific aspect of the center's program. By the spring of 1983, these committees submitted reports to the principal and director of the center.

The Teacher Center Program

Four major strands of activity for teachers coming to Schenley emerged from the planning process. The first of these involved instructional skills.

Using an approach based on the work of Madeline Hunter (1984), visiting teachers spent a significant amount of their eight-week schedule working with central staff and Schenley resident teachers learning, practicing, and discussing instructional skills. This component of the program was heavily oriented toward clinical experiences. Visiting teachers had the opportunity to observe instruction, demonstrate their own instructional skills in real classroom settings, and confer with peers and staff development professionals about what they were learning and doing.

The second major strand of the center's program emphasized growth in one's content area of teaching. Visiting teachers spent time with their content area supervisor (i.e., social studies teacher with their social studies supervisor) learning more about their own discipline. Reviews of new developments in the field, new strategies for teaching specific subject area concepts, visitations to other classrooms, and short internships in the community were examples of the kinds of activity employed in this area.

The third strand involved increasing teacher awareness and understanding of the adolescent. Typical activities included a range of seminars, taught in many instances by resident Schenley teachers, on subjects related to the psychlogical, emotional, and physical development of adolescents.

The fourth major program strand involved a potpourri of activities that visiting teachers participated in based on their own areas of particular interest. Personal growth seminars, externships, and individual research/study projects were some of the options made available.

It should be noted that as the program completed its initial year of operation, managers began to plan for followthrough activities to take place in the home school once a teacher had completed a cycle at Schenley. Followthrough plans became increasingly formalized during the second year of operation, to the point where each teacher was expected to develop a set of objectives and activities to be pursued when she/he returned to the home school. As this book goes to publication, the center leadership is planning to supplement individual followthrough plans with school-wide activities in each high school. While the details of these followthrough activities have yet to be worked out, what has emerged is the growing conviction that such activity will be essential to the continuing impact of the program.

Finally, the program established an outside board of visitors as part of its overall structure. This board consisted of prominent educators and researchers from across the country, served as critics of the program through annual, formal site visits, and informal contacts throughout the life of the program.

Management Request for Documentation

Two factors influenced the original request for the documentation of the center. The district sought external support in June 1982 for a year's planning process from the Ford Foundation. The positive response made by the Ford Foundation was in part based on the perception that the Pittsburgh center potentially could develop into a model for other districts across the country. Thus, the foundation was interested in documenting the evolution of the center in detail so that others might learn from the Pittsburgh experience (E. Meade, personal communication, April 1985).

A second factor involved the experience the district already had with documentation through the school improvement program (case 5), and the utility of having a documenter observe a complex planning and development process. The documentation of the school improvement program had been underway for a year by the time the request for planning support for the center was submitted to the Ford Foundation. Many of the formative evaluative functions discussed in case 5 were well established and known to district leadership. This experience, coupled with the foundation's interest in developing a resource with the potential for national impact, provided the basis for the district's request that a research and documentation component be developed as part of the center's planning process.

A third factor emerged later that underscored the value of the original decision to document the center. This involved the district's decision to begin planning a similar effort for elementary teachers. Having a detailed chronicle of the center's development facilitated planning for an elementary initiative which began in the fall of 1984.

Given the initial request for documentation, activities for the center followed a pattern similar to that in case 5. The researcher spent a significant amount of time in dialogue with center leadership. This dialogue had the twofold purpose of clarifying immediate information needs as well as developing an understanding on the part of the principal and director of both the potential and the limitations of documentation research.

The dialogue to define center documentation activities at the program level benefited from the prior (and indeed ongoing) experience accrued through the school improvement work. For example, the principal of Schenley personally knew the director of school improvement program and was able to draw upon the director as an additional source of information about the benefits/drawbacks of this approach to research.

Research Strategies

Several general research strategies were employed in documenting the center's planning activities. First, a detailed archive was constructed that contained a comprehensive collection of the "paper trail" of program development activities. Procedures were set in place that enabled the documenter to readily obtain copies of any written material relevant to the program.

Second, observations were made of key planning meetings, meetings of various subcommittees, and community meetings related to the development of the center. The observations were recorded in detailed field notes and became an important resource in understanding the evolution of the program. The observations were exploratory in nature and served to enhance the awareness of the documenter about various issues influencing the planning process. In addition, the field observations provided valuable, informal opportunities for dialogue with a wide variety of participants. Observations were planned in ways that sampled planning activities at multiple levels in the program.

Third, the researcher acted as participant observer in a number of planning sessions. This most often occurred in, but was not restricted to, meetings where feedback was being given to planners on some data collection activity. The center's planning sessions were remarkably open and relatively unstructured. Perhaps because so much of what was being developed was new, participation was widely encouraged.

Fourth, specific, targeted research inquiries were conducted from time to time in order to develop a more fine-grained picture of the evolving program than could be obtained otherwise through document reviews and observations. These ranged from regular, informal debriefings with center leadership to more structured interviews and questionnaires with a variety of program participants. The more structured inquiries often focused on specific components and were addressed to targeted role groups. For example, questionnaires with open and close-ended questions were administered at the end of each cycle to all 50 visiting teachers. These questionnaires addressed such areas as what participants felt they had accomplished through their experiences, what aspects of the program were not working well, and how such components might be improved.

Another example of targeted research activity was the use of a panel study design in tracking perceptions about the program's status over time as seen by a number of role groups. The panel research consisted of repeated interviews or surveys with targeted sets of participants using a structured set of questions about the program's goals and the procedures employed to meet these goals. The panel design methodology was particularly useful in identifying changes in perceptions of key role groups and in isolating probable causes for these changes.

Documentation Results

A variety of products were generated through documentation activities. These ranged from a detailed archive of field notes and program documents to presentations and reports that summarized what was learned at specific points in time as the program was planned and implemented. A few of the results of these research activities from the first year of program implementation are described below to provide a flavor of the kind of information that can be developed through documentation research. The results are classifiable into comments on specific program operation issues and those involving the more basic structure of the center.

The research activities during that initial year focused on two broad concerns: the overall planning process, and the clinical teaching experiences of resident and visiting teachers. Of the center's activities examined that year, clearly one of the most interesting was the process of clinical resident teacher/visiting teacher interaction. Visiting teachers spent a significant amount of their time planning, teaching, observing, and conferring under the guidance of clinical resident teachers who were part of the resident staff at Schenley. This process of peer teaching spoke directly to the professional isolation that so dominates the teaching field once the classroom door closes.

From the data collected through observations, interviews, and questionnaires it was clear that most teachers found the one-to-one teacher interaction generally quite rewarding. Numerous comments by teachers from both groups expressed the view that this process of peer interaction and reflection about one's craft established a tone of professionalism that was often missing in education. In fact, the value of collegiality and professionalism was mentioned often in both groups' feedback about this aspect of the program.

It was also noteworthy that the clinical resident teachers worked hard at trying to avoid the image of "master teacher." The data clearly showed that the learning experience went in both directions, with clinical teachers learning much from visiting teachers coming through the center.

A number of issues about the clinical teaching process were identified through the research. Clinical resident teachers raised concerns in three main areas. First, there was the problem of personal stress which came from the need to wear several professional "hats" during a given day (e.g., teacher of adolescents, teacher of adults, seminar leader) and the related intensity of the schedule of activities. Second, there was some uncertainty about how to deal with visiting teachers who had uncooperative attitudes. Third, there was some feeling of professional isolation from other resident staff (nonclinical resident teachers). Clinical teachers lacked the time to have much interaction with their Schenley colleagues; and the resident staff not serving as clinical resident teachers or as seminar leaders were relatively uninvolved in ongoing center program activities.

Visiting teachers cited somewhat different concerns about the clinical process. Although many clinical resident teachers found it difficult to confer with visiting teachers about a lesson which didn't go particularly well, many visiting teachers expressed the desire for less positive reinforcement and more critical analysis of their teaching. One suspected, however, that this readiness for frank interchange was, in part, a product of confidence produced by earlier, positive feedback experiences of teachers during the cycle. It was also probably true that clinical resident teachers became better prepared to provide critical feedback when needed as they gained more experience. Some visiting teachers also expressed dissatisfaction with the intensity of activities. The primary concern was that their teaching experiences at Schenley were unrealistic because the schedule of events forced them to conduct teaching episodes in isolated segments without opportunity to follow up a lesson the next day or to teach an entire unit. Finally, a few visiting teachers experienced difficulties because they were not matched to a clinical resident teacher in precisely their same content area specialty (e.g., a particular foreign language or science concentration). It should be noted that the size of the clinical resident teacher group limited the number of subject areas and specialties that could be directly paired with incoming teachers.

Turning to concerns of a more fundamental nature, documentation research uncovered several issues that, in effect, represented critical factors in determining the course of the program that first year. One of these concerned the need to balance the various interacting components in the program. Balance emerged as an important condition for the successful development of the program in three respects. First, there was the need to strike an appropriate balance among the four major strands of program activity: improvement of instruction, content update, understanding the adolescent, and individual study. Given the overall goals of the center, how much time and emphasis should be allocated to each one of these? Was one component more "basic" than the other?

Second, the individual needs and interests of visiting teachers had to be balanced with the broad goals of the program. This was rather easily managed when many teachers expressed an interest in the same type of activity. It was more difficult in areas such as teaching skills and content area knowledge, where both the spread of needs and the program's ability to identify them were problematic. How to tailor the program to better meet individual strengths, interests, and needs, and how to identify those characteristics were important issues that influenced center planning for the second year of operation.

Finally, a balance had to be struck between the teacher renewal efforts at Schenley and the need to run a healthy, complex, comprehensive high school. Insuring the continuity and quality of education at Schenley ultimately had to take precedence over the center program's function. An awareness of all three of these balancing requirements was significant to understanding the first year of implementation. And some of the program adjustments that were taken should be understood as attempts to "strike a better balance."

Another fundamental theme that emerged from the research involved visiting teacher concerns about conditions in the district and how these concerns affected teacher participation in center activities. As expected, teachers came to Schenley with a mixture of feelings that ranged from apprehension and anxiety to enthusiasm and high expectation. Somewhat unanticipated, however, was the fact that a number of teachers came with additional concerns that were focused on their own schools or on the district as a whole.

This presented an interesting dilemma for center planners. The program was essentially focused on encouraging individual growth in teachers. Some teachers were saying, in effect, that this exclusive focus on teachers was unfair. If secondary education were to be improved, then everyone had a part to play, and conditions perceived to be undesirable in the district and in their home schools must also be addressed (e.g., antiquated scheduling procedures, perceived lack of administrative support, etc.).

The dilemma had two aspects to it. One concerned how the program could respond, short-term, to the issues raised. This was addressed during the first year by providing time for teachers to share their concerns directly with the superintendent in open forums. The discussions that occurred were frank and potentially productive, and they continued through subsequent cycles.

A second more fundamental issue concerned the focus of change implicit in the initial center structure. To draw a rather simplistic trichotomy, should the center's focus of change be on the individual teacher, the individual high school organizations in the district, or the "process of secondary education?" Documentation data suggested that most center planners thought that all three were important, but that changing teachers' attitudes and behaviors was most critical. Yet, as some visiting teachers suggested, to expect a "renewed" teacher to return to the same home school or district conditions was potentially self-defeating.

A third major issue that surfaced in documentation data collected during the first year of operation concerned differences in goals among participants. In observing and listening to planners and teachers, one had a sense that there were a number of competing visions of what constituted teacher renewal. At the core, should the eight weeks have the flavor of diagnosis and prescription, where teachers' needs are identified and experiences designed to address them? Or, should a cycle primarily be an opportunity to step back from the rigors of daily classroom instruction to permit teachers to reflect on their profession and their own place in it? In other words, was knowledge and skill attainment or intellectual stimulation the crucial goal?

The various models of what constituted renewal distributed themselves along several continuums. One continuum might be thought of as having a training program concept on one end and a sabbatical leave concept on the other. Another continuum might have self-directed experiences versus other-directed experiences at the polarities. Conceptions of renewal held by individual teachers and district managers ranged all along these continuums.

The initial program of the center had aspects of all of the models of renewal noted above. Clearly, there were expectations from the district that each teacher should have certain experiences; there were also opportunities for choice and independent study in other areas of the program, based on teacher-defined needs or interests. The primary issue underlying the early implementation process wasn't whether one model was more correct than another. Rather, what was significant was that these competing models caused differing expectations about how the eight weeks should be spent, and these differing expectations had important effects on the direction of the program.

The above comments are a sample of the kinds of information that were provided to planners by documentation research during the first year of implementation. Examples of how documentation data were used by planners are given in the following section.

Management Use of Documentation Information

Several examples will be drawn from the first year of implementation to illustrate how the documentation data assisted managers in making midcourse corrections. In addition, the institutional memory function of documentation data will be discussed in the context of the plans to develop an elementary teacher center.

Before beginning the discussion of use, it is important to state again the caveat that research data represented only one kind of data used by managers in making decisions. While it is fair to say that the information provided planners through documentation research was important to the decision process, such information was one of a variety of factors that influenced mid-course corrections taken in the program.

With the above caveat firmly in mind, it is still quite possible to note numerous instances where planners made significant changes in the operation of the program, primarily as a result of information gathered through documentation activities. Four examples of instrumental use will serve to illustrate how documentation data can be helpful to a planning process.

As one method for assessing the status of implementation, center planners and the researchers structured a mid-cycle feedback session with visiting teachers during each cycle. Teachers worked in small groups, reflecting on how various components of the center's program could be improved. A consensus was developed, and recommendations were presented to the center's planners. A major concern expressed by one cycle of teachers involved the fragmented nature of the eight-week schedule resulting from the fact that every week had activities from each of the four strands of the program. As a result of this feedback from teachers, center planners dramatically changed the structure of the schedule for subsequent cycles. In essence, the changes meant that each of the eight weeks had a central activity focus. Feedback from teachers in subsequent cycles indicated that the changes helped to facilitate learning and scheduling processes in the program.

A second example of the use of research generated information involved an issue that emerged over several cycles. Through end-of-cycle questionnaires and site observations, it became clear that many visiting teachers wanted more flexibility in the program to individualize the activities in relation to their own needs. Recalling one of the results reported in a previous section of this case, there was considerable disagreement among participants over how much of the center's activities should be district-mandated or self-selected by teachers. This trend in the data, presented to planners through informal conversations and written reports, had several interesting effects on the program. By the third cycle of the first year, the center's leadership was clearly convinced of the importance of the individualization concern on the part of the teachers. However, as a preliminary step to, in the words of the director, "loosening up the program," it was essential that the planners decide what the core expectations or "givens" were in the program that each teacher should participate in, and what aspects were less fundamental. The debate touched off by the individualization issue had three important effects. First, it clarified for all concerned what constituted the "heart of the program" from the district's point of view. Second, it clarified what areas and opportunities should be optional yet available to help meet individual teacher needs and interests. Third, this debate indeed resulted in an increased number of choices for visiting teachers. Perhaps the most interesting of these involved the option of independent study made available to teachers in subsequent cycles.

Another example of use involved the recognition among center leadership, based on documentation reports, that there were "a number of competing visions of what constituted teacher renewal" among all levels of center participants. This diversity of perspectives on renewal was especially evident as core planners debated what should be thought of as fundamental or optional in program offerings. The problems caused by divergent visions was further exacerbated by the fact that most of the major components of the program had been developed and were implemented by discreet entities in the district's organizational structure (e.g., the instructional skills component by the staff development team, the content area update by instructional supervisors, etc.). There was a natural tendency, given the work load and demanding schedule, for each organizational unit to focus almost exclusively on their own area of responsibility. To the extent that this was so, and that this organizational fragmentation was coupled with differing perspectives on renewal, program components were in danger of being seen by visiting teachers as unconnected to each other. Further, the issue of quality control in program offerings was made more difficult under these conditions. During the fourth cycle of year one, the center management responded to these problems by forming an ad hoc committee with members who represented each major program component. The committee was given the charge of sampling a range of program activities with a view toward assessing strengths and problems in current program offerings. One of the conditions set for the committee was that members must sample outside their own immediate area of responsibility. The director had several goals in this exercise, namely, to develop data on the quality of programming and, through the discussion of quality, to stimulate a greater convergence in the thinking of participants about what should be the central purposes of the center.

Relationships to DOER

Like case 5, this case illustrates the value of assigning research resources to study and document the development of complex educational innovations. Documentation as an on-line research resource aided program managers in improving the implementation of the program. The documentary record that emerged from the research was useful as the district planned similar initiatives at other grade levels. This case illustrates the nature and value of researcher–client dialogue, the necessity of being methodologically eclectic, and of taking an interactive view of research and dissemination processes.

This case also further illustrates the complexity of this type of field research. One important difficulty concerned focus and selection for the research activities. This was an essential concern for managers and researchers alike. Given finite resources, where should research activities concentrate? The dialogue that occurred with clients provided the mechanism for addressing such issues. The criteria used for deciding where to focus included program areas that contained the most uncertainties for managers, and program initiatives (such as the clinical teacher) that were both unprecedented and potentially generalizable to other schools in the district and to other districts in the nation.

CASE HISTORY 10
THE USE OF
ACHIEVEMENT TEST RESULTS
IN PERSONNEL EVALUATION

Early in 1984, a concern arose regarding the results on the district's standardized achievement test, the California Achievement Test (CAT). The concern stemmed from two phenomena. One was the appearance of a few schools that were showing phenomenal achievement growth. The other had to do with the increasing pressure which the board and central administration were placing on increasing CAT scores.

This concern reached a climax in January 1984 when the board dismissed a principal for not having demonstrated instructional leadership and replaced him with someone who had "turned around" one of the low achieving elementary schools in the district. What was played up in the newspaper was the fact that the high school principal was replaced because the school's standardized test scores were too low, and the one who replaced him had demonstrated an ability to produce high test scores.

At a hearing for the dismissed principal, the president of the local teachers' union was quite outspoken in his rejection of the use of standardized test scores in personnel evaluation, to the point that some of his remarks were interpreted by board members as a threat. He seemed to imply that if the board used CAT scores for personnel evaluation, teachers can and would produce artificially inflated results, since the use of standardized tests was inappropriate for that purpose.

In this climate, we were asked to address the board on the issue of standardized tests and personnel evaluation. The following is the statement of the major points made to the school board, including some of the overhead transparencies that were used.

Use of Achievement Test Results
Presentation to Pittsburgh Board of Public Education
March 7, 1984

How to Raise CAT Scores?

The district certainly has reason to be proud of the very dramatic way in which student achievement in Pittsburgh has improved over the past three years. The results in the three areas tested (mathematics, language, and reading) are clearly an important accomplishment (figure C10-1). But as more and more pressure is placed on this particular test (for example, if they were used in personnel evaluations) it seems important that you look at the many different ways in which CAT scores can be raised.

One way, of course, is to actually produce general improvement in students' abilities in mathematics, language, and reading. There are two ways of doing that. One is to have more efficient instruction, and the other is to have more instruction in these three subjects at the expense of other subjects. The latter might be a problem if you believe that schools have a broader mission than the improvement of student skills in math, language, and reading, which is all that CAT covers.

Another way to raise CAT scores is to produce specific improvement in the particular CAT objectives, as illustrated in figure C10-2. There is never a perfect fit between, for example, the mathematics objectives that were in the curriculum and the mathematics objectives that are incorporated in the CAT test. Over time, as teachers become more and more familiar with the CAT, they will tend to shift their emphasis from type C objectives to type A objectives, resulting in higher CAT scores, but not necessarily reflecting a general improvement in mathematics. Having the test determine the curriculum is not necessarily bad, except that the test was not built to provide a logical curriculum; it was built to sample what is common across typical curricula for a particular grade. It does make sense to examine objective level results on a district basis. If district-wide performance is unusually low on an objective that is clearly an important part of the curriculum as it is

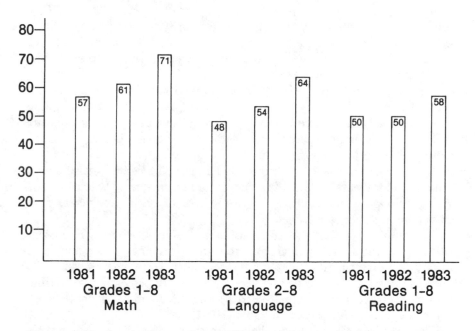

Figure C10-1.   Percent of Students Scoring at or Above National Median

structured, that then suggests an area in which more effective instructional materials might be identified and made available. However, a mindless following of CAT objectives could produce a curriculum scope and sequence that does not facilitate student learning.

Another way to improve CAT scores is to drill on specific questions known to be in the text. In a district as large as Pittsburgh, it is not really possible to have a completely secure program of standardized testing. (Or at

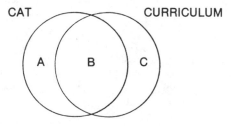

Figure C10-2.   Curriculum Shifts from Type *C* Objectives to Type *A* Objectives, with Same Amount Being Taught

least you won't want to pay the cost of such security.) Therefore, it is clearly possible for teachers to identify and drill on specific items and produce higher test scores that are completely misleading with respect to the resulting normative information.

For example, drilling on five pairs of words with opposite meanings that are in the test would greatly enhance a student's performance on the reading test. The five pairs then no longer represent a random sample of opposite meaning words that a student might know, but is a very biased sample of word pairs they just happen to know.

A fourth way in which test scores can be raised is to administer the tests in nonstandard ways. Giving the students more time during a timed test or giving help and hints during the test can easily produce increases in classroom and school averages.

Part of understanding the score-raising possibilities is to notice how sensitive the norms are to small changes in test performance. For example, in third grade mathematics, there are 85 questions. If a student answers 30 questions correctly, that is below average work (45th percentile). By getting four more correct (from 30 to 34 correct), the student moves from the 45th percentile to the 55th percentile (table C10–1).

Thus, you can see that small changes in the number correct can make a large difference in classroom and school level results, particularly when they are described in terms of the percentage of students who score about the 50th percentile, which is the way the district tends to display these results.

Now the district is planning to administer a second standardized test this spring to a sample of students to try to determine whether the increases in CAT results "are real." In anticipating the possible outcomes for this validation study, it is important to notice what produces differences in outcomes of this type. If the results of the second test are different from the CAT results, it is probably going to reflect the difference in overlap between

Table C10–1.   How Test Norms Relate to Number of Correct Answers

| National Percentile | Number of Questions Correct (Grade 3) | |
	Reading (73 questions)	Math (85 questions)
60	50	36
55	48	34
50	45	32
45	42	30
40	39	28

what is currently taught in the district, and what is tested in the test. So the second testing cannot detect whether or not "cheating" is going on, since it can also reflect differences in curriculum overlap, as illustrated in figure C10-1.

As we began to notice unusually large growth results on the part of some classrooms and some schools, my first temptation was to pursue the possibility that these were not just the result of some real, intensive effort to improve student performance, but were the result of unethical behavior on the part of teachers and principals. It may be that we could have found such cases, but that seemed to be the wrong concern. The more important question was to examine why professionals may feel compelled to behave in unethical ways and work at trying to change the incentive system that seemed to be operating.

Why Not Use CAT Scores for Personnel Evaluation?

Probably the most important thing to remember in thinking about standardized test results is that current measures of student achievement are very dependent upon prior achievement. A lot can be done to improve student achievement, but the fact remains that what a student is able to learn today is very dependent upon what has been learned to date. This is particularly true of standardized achievement tests, which represent broad samplings of what students might know. They are not intended to be examinations of what students have just been taught. That is a very important difference. If you use the standardized test as an examination and teach what it measures, then you invalidate the normative information. If you do not teach what it measures, then it is extremely difficult to make dramatic improvements in student performance. If teachers begin to suspect that some teachers are teaching the test, and if principals and teachers begin to suspect that test scores are being built into personnel evaluation, then it is very easy to see what principals and teachers are going to do. They sense that it is unfair to be judged by student outcomes without taking into account entering student achievement, and they know that comparing school achievement averages tells you nothing about the quality of the present educational program in those schools and classrooms. So it is not surprising if principals and teachers respond in unethical ways if they feel that the board and central administration are behaving in irresponsible ways.

Even if you were to incorporate CAT results into the formal evaluation of principals and not do it for teachers, that "principal pressure" is going to get passed on in the principal's evaluation of the teachers in his or her building. So it will amount to the same thing.

Another important consideration is that if you begin to use CAT results in ways for which they were not intended (e.g., personnel evaluation), you will soon find that they no longer are useful for other functions for which they are perfectly valid. It is important for the board to have reliable information on how Pittsburgh's students compare with students elsewhere, and standardized test results have been useful for that purpose. That will not continue to be true if the norms have been corrupted through unethical practices. Similarly, the use of tests to measure progress toward achievement goals and district-wide efforts to diagnose curriculum weakness will no longer be possible if the scores are not to be trusted.

There are other unintended side effects of too much pressure being put on a single test. One such phenomenon that seems to be happening is that there is an increase in special education referrals. Principals are putting pressure on the referral process because they want children into special education and out of their school averages, since special education students are not included in school-wide achievement results. Another is the possibility that students who need extra help, from such programs as federal Chapter I Compensatory Education, have become ineligible because of artificially inflated test scores (since CAT results are used to determine student eligibility).

But What About Accountability?

All of these considerations result in a very large dilemma. One could argue that the real increases in student achievement that have been occurring in the district have been the result of putting increased pressure on standardized achievement test results. There certainly has been increased attention given to CAT results, but that may have been due to the excitement generated by recognizing how a refocusing of the district's energies on improving student achievement has resulted in higher CAT scores. As you incorporate those CAT results directly into personnel evaluation, the district will just be deceiving itself because the results will become meaningless since they are so easily corrupted, and since using them is viewed as patently unfair by those who would be responsible for administering the tests.

But then, what about principal accountability? Can a principal be accountable for the achievement of students in his or her building? When addressing that question, four other questions come quickly to mind.

1. Can initial student differences be taken into account?
2. Do principals have adequate resources to monitor and correct ineffective teaching?

3. Do principals have adequate options for dealing with disruptive students?
4. Do principals have any control over the instructional resources (e.g., budget, personnel selection) available to the school?

It seems hard to expect principals to be accountable for student achievement unless these questions can be answered in the affirmative. It is important to note that great progress has been made in the district, particularly with respect to question number 2. Thanks to Monitoring Achievement in Pittsburgh (MAP) and Pittsburgh's Research-based Instructional Supervisory Model (PRISM), the district has made great strides in providing principals with tools to monitor achievement progress and to provide more effective instructional leadership, including specific techniques for improving inadequate teaching. But there is still a lot to be done even in that area, as well as other areas that are relevant to this concern.

There remains a very real and very legitimate concern: How can the board be reassured that incompetent practice is being detected and corrected in the district? One recommendation is that the board not try to perform this very complex task of evaluating professionals in a direct way. That is not only a very complex professional task; it is also critical that such evaluations not become more of a political process.

Figure C10-3 is a schematic that identifies levels of accountability for different role groups. In such a scheme, test scores can help professionals identify where ineffective practice may be occurring, but they can only suggest where to look. If a variety of indicators are examined, that can *suggest* where ineffective practices *may* be occurring, but then someone capable of doing so has to spend time observing those practices and determine more precisely the nature of the problem. Such observational mechanisms, to be considered fair, must first have a strong system of corrective feedback, so that people can be made aware of possible shortcomings and given an opportunity to correct them. That is what PRISM is all about.

What can reassure the board that sensible accountability is taking place in the district is to first be assured that you have a strong program for staff development in place. Then if, in particular cases, staff development does not help, that same effort of staff development can produce documentation that can be the basis for more dramatic action. When you begin to receive well-documented cases of incompetent practice, you will know you have an effective system of personnel evaluation in place in this district.

ACHIEVEMENT PROGRESS: ACCOUNTABILITY:

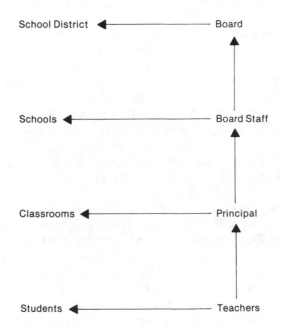

Figure C10-3.   Who Monitors What?

Relationships to DOER

The presentation reported in the foregoing section seemed to go well. There was a lively discussion during the question and answer period. The reporters who cover education for the two major Pittsburgh newspapers were present, and articles covering the meeting appeared the next day. Also, points made during the presentation appeared in a special feature in the Sunday newspaper that was entitled, "Tests Reshape City Schools Teaching" (*Pittsburgh Press*, March 11, 1984).

This case is an example of DOER trying to enrich an ongoing public debate. The client here was the board itself. The presentation was at the request of the board president, and the negotiations regarding the specifics were conducted with the chair of the education committee, at whose meeting the presentation was made.

The only relevant pending legislation was the request from the testing office that the board approve the funding for a validation study that was referred to in the presentation. The board did grant that request and the study was conducted. The subsequent results did reassure the board that the gains in test scores over the past three years were real.

It must be admitted, however, that the accountability model (figure C10–3) was considered quite naive and was ignored. The board continued to insist upon school level results. The task of finding valid ways to do that remains a big challenge.

What this case illustrates, particularly, is the importance of timeliness. Sometimes this refers to the need to have information in time for a big vote, but occasionally timeliness means taking advantage of a current, hot debate in the continuous effort of making policy boards and the general public better informed about technical issues like test bias, norm-referenced tests, accountability mechanisms, etc. Issues run hot and cold. When they are hot, the researcher has to be ready, willing, and able to contribute critically needed technical information to the debate.

CASE HISTORY 11
SELECTION OF A
NEW READING PROGRAM

Our notion of client orientation involves considerable initial dialogue so that the client's needs for information can be clarified and possible ways of producing useful information can be defined. Out of that dialogue some useful research can usually be agreed upon.

After we agreed to work on a particular project, we tried to behave as though we were the district's research office. In that way we could come as close as possible to understanding the dynamics and subtleties of conducting research within an educational system. One important difference, however, was that we could say "no" to a potential undertaking more easily than an actual employee of the system could. This case is an example of our having said no. However, it represents a good example of what the in-house researchers ended up doing when faced with a request to do a summative evaluation. They expanded the initial request, which seemed to be a non-productive use of time, into a useful piece of DOER.

The Research Task Emerges

During the 1981–82 school year, the district began to search for a new reading series for the K–8 reading program. The current reading program had been in use for 10 years; some of the material had 1969 copyright dates, and it was beginning to get difficult to obtain replacement material. Also, the basal reader in use did not have a phonics emphasis and phonics was "in the air."

In January 1982, this call for a new reading program increased in intensity when a new board member assumed the chairmanship of the education committee. She was determined to get the board to adopt a strong phonics program as soon as possible. At a meeting of the education committee in February, it was agreed that there would be a pilot testing of a number of reading programs in selected schools for the school year 1982–83.

A committee of teachers, supervisors, and parents reviewed the vast array of options. Their deliberations included publisher presentations, published textbook reviews, testimony by reading experts, and lots of home study. Then in the summer of 1982, they selected two reading series for this tryout. It was to be conducted in six of the elementary schools and three of the middle schools. On September 1, at a meeting of the education committee, the committee chairperson criticized the selection committee's choices and said that neither of the selected series was analytic in its approach to phonics. Several of the board members seemed to join in with that notion and one of them even commented that the teachers probably selected these two because the phonics method requires more time and effort on the part of teachers. At the board's request, then, two more programs were quickly added to the pilot, both of them with "phonics first"; and six more elementary schools were added for the tryout of these two additional series.

Parallel to these board deliberations, the director of testing had several meetings with us to discuss whether or not we might help in conducting this comparison. The notion was that the district's standardized test results would be used as a dependent measure in a straightforward comparison of outcomes. Given that these schools had volunteered to be the tryout schools for each of the selected reading series, and given our general notion of the futility of such quasi-experimental contrasts (Cooley, 1978), we respectfully declined to help.

As the pressures on this tryout kept building, however, we were asked to consider one more time. On September 21, 1982, we met with the director of this reading tryout and a new staff member who had just joined the testing office. They did not have the option of not doing the study because it had been mandated by the board, and they wanted to discuss some notions they had so that something useful might be done.

We reviewed the reasons why there would probably be no differences in standardized test outcomes after properly controlling for initial student differences, but we went on to discuss some of the factors that would be important to examine. It seemed critical to obtain data on the implementability of these various programs, obtain expert reviews of the relative merits of the various approaches, and conduct an analysis of the degree to which the various curricula were consistent with the reading objectives for each grade, as defined by the new MAP reading objectives. Also, costs needed to be analyzed — not only costs of the materials themselves but staff development costs that the different programs might require.

The Study is Conducted

The experimental contrast of the achievement impact of these seven reading programs — four for the elementary schools, and three for the middle schools — involved 12 elementary schools and 4 middle schools, with a total of 6,800 students and 200 teachers. The in-house researchers made several important additions to the achievement outcomes comparisons that helped to sort out their relative merits. They added teacher and student surveys, classroom observations, and analyses of test and curriculum overlap.

The analyses of covariance that were conducted using the standardized achievement test results as a dependent variable, produced the expected results. There were no significant achievement differences among these programs after entering abilities were statistically controlled. Fortunately, the selection committee had lots of other data to help them make their choice. Particularly helpful was a teacher survey that was administered to all participating teachers which provided ratings of the quality of the curriculum materials, the effectiveness of the teacher-learning strategies that were built in, the utility of the teachers' editions, workbooks, student assessment procedures, and other supplementary materials, as well as specific questions on the implementation problems that were encountered. Also, a student survey was conducted which allowed student views to be incorporated into the deliberations. Classroom observation data were also helpful in sorting out implementation differences and in helping the committee to see how the different programs "worked."

In early May of 1983, the committee recommended that the board adopt the strong phonics program for grades K-2, but change to a different reading series for grades 3-8. According to the project director, the 3-8 program selected offered a better program for developing comprehension skills and incorporated better balance of fiction and nonfiction in the literature selections. When forwarding the committee's recommendations to the board, the superintendent emphasized the fact that the committee used a multipronged attack on this question, which included attitudinal surveys, literature reviews of other research on these programs, cost data, etc.

On May 23, 1983, one of the local papers had a major article on the vir-
tues of the two reading programs, with pictures and quotes of teachers ex-
pressing their satisfaction with the programs that were being recommended
to the board. The board did not act at its May meeting, but postponed the
decision to the June meeting. As late as June 15, 1983, the chairman of the
education committee was still strongly objecting to the switch in programs
at third grade. In the board discussion on that date, the objecting board
member insisted that the results of the pilot test were not being honored by
the selection committee, and she called for another review of the results.
But finally, in a 6 to 2 vote (with one member absent), the board adopted
the committee's recommendations, and the two selected programs were implemented in the fall of 1983.

Relationships to DOER

This brief case history is particularly important in seeing how the client-oriented
approach might work when the dialogue between client and researcher is unable
to reconcile notions of what might be done. As was pointed out, we were able to
decide not to conduct such a quasi-experiment, but the in-house research office
did not have that option. What it did was to expand the effort so that a broader
range of data could be brought to bear on the issue. These other data turned out
to be extremely valuable, particularly in light of the fact that the achievement
contrasts that the board insisted on in the first place did not produce any significant differences among the programs.

It also shows that there are clear cases when summative-type evaluations
must be done by the research office. Not every request can be turned into a
formative, improvement-oriented exercise. There was a definite decision to
abandon the old program, not to try to improve it, and there was a definite
decision to field-test several versions and pick the most effective and most
appropriate series for the district. By casting a broad net for a wide range of
data, it was possible to produce information that the selection committee
found quite useful and which most of the board members found acceptable
as a basis for choosing that new reading series.

REFERENCES

Alkin, M.C. (1975). Who needs it? Who cares? *Studies in Educational Evaluation* 1: 201–212.

Alkin, M.C., Daillak, R.R., and White, P. (1979). *Using evaluation: Does evaluation make a difference?* Beverly Hills: Sage.

Alkin, M.C., Jacobson, P., Burry, J., Ruskus, J., White, P., and Kent, L. (in press). *A handbook for evaluation decision makers.* Beverly Hills: Sage.

Anderson, S.B., and Ball, S. (1978). *The profession and practice of program evaluation.* San Francisco: Jossey-Bass.

Anderson, S.B., Ball, S., Murphy, R.T., and associates. (1975). *Encyclopedia of educational evaluation: Concepts and techniques for evaluating educational and training programs.* San Francisco: Jossey-Bass.

Artz, N. (1982). *Promoting a change in schools: Implementation issues.* Unpublished manuscript, University of Pittsburgh, Learning Research and Development Center.

Baker, F.B. (1978). *Computer managed instruction: Theory and practice.* Englewood Cliffs, NJ: Educational Technology Publications.

Banks, W.C., McQuater, G.V., and Hubbard, J.L. (1978). Toward a reconceptualization of the social-cognitive bases of achievement orientations in blacks. *Review of Educational Research* 48:381–397.

Berk, R.A. (1981). *Educational evaluation methodology: The state of the art.* Baltimore: The Johns Hopkins University Press.

Berman, P. (1980). *Toward an implementation paradigm of educational change.* Santa Monica, CA: The Rand Corporation.

Bickel, W.E. (1983). Effective schools. *Educational Researcher* 12(4):3–31.

————— . (1984). Evaluator in residence: New Prospects for school district evaluation research. *Educational Evaluation and Policy Analysis* 6:297–306.

Bickel, W.E., and Artz, N. (1984). Improving instruction through focused team supervision. *Educational Leadership* 41(7):22–24.

Bickel, W.E., and Cooley, W.W. (1981). *A utilization of a district-wide needs assessment.* Unpublished manuscript, University of Pittsburgh, Learning Research and Development Center.

Bickel, W.E., and Cooley, W.W. (1985). Decision-oriented educational research in school districts: The role of dissemination processes. *Studies in Educational Evaluation. 11,* pp. 183–203.

Bloom, B.S. (1976). *Human characteristics and school learning.* New York: McGraw-Hill.

Bond, L., and Glaser, R. (1979). ATI but mostly A and T, with not much I. *Applied Psychological Measurement* 3:137–140.

Borich, G.D., and Jemelka, R.P. (1982). *Programs and systems: An evaluation perspective.* New York: Academic Press.

Bouchard, T.J., Jr.(1976). Field research methods: Interviewing, questionnaires, participant observation, systematic observation, unobtrusive measures. In M.D. Dunnette (ed.), *Handbook of industrial and organizational psychology,* pp. 363–413. Chicago: Rand McNally.

Boulding, K.E. (1985). *The world as a total system.* Beverly Hills: Sage.

Brandt, R.S. (ed.) (1981). *Applied strategies for curriculum evaluation.* Alexandria, VA: Association for Supervision and Curriculum Development.

Bronfenbrenner, U. (1976). The experimental ecology of education. *Teachers College Record* 78:157–204.

Brookover, W.B., and Lezotte, L. (1979). *Changes in school characteristics coincident with changes in student achievement.* Unpublished manuscript, Michigan State University, The Institute for Research on Teaching, East Lansing.

Bryk, A.S. (1983). *Stakeholder-based evaluation.* San Francisco, CA: Jossey-Bass.

Burstein, L. (1984). The use of existing data bases in program evaluation and school improvement. *Educational Evaluation and Policy Analysis* 6:307–318.

Campbell, D. (1979). Degrees of freedom and the case study. In T.D. Cook and C.S. Reichardt (eds.), *Qualitative and quantitative methods in evaluation research,* (vol. 1, pp. 49–67. Beverly Hills: Sage.

Carter, A.E. (1982). *The homes of truants: Parents' perception of the problem of truancy.* Unpublished doctoral dissertation, University of Pittsburgh, Pennsylvania.

Carter, L.F. (1984). The sustaining effects study of compensatory and elementary education. *Educational Researcher* 13:4–13.

Churchman, C.W. (1979). *The systems approach and its enemies.* New York: Basic Books.

Ciarlo, J.A. (ed.) (1981). *Utilizing evaluation.* Beverly Hills: Sage.

Coleman, J., Campbell, E., Hobson, C., McPartland, J., Mood, A., Weinfield, F., and York, R. (1966). *Equality of educational opportunity.* Washington, D.C.: Office of Education, U.S. Department of Health, Education and Welfare.

Commager, H.S. (1965). *The nature and the study of history.* Columbus, OH: Charles E. Merrill.

Conant, J.B. (ed.) (1950). *Robert Boyle's experiments in pneumatics.* Cambridge, MA: Harvard University Press.

Cook, T.D., and Reichardt, C.S. (1979). *Qualitative and quantitative methods in evaluation research,* vol. 1. Beverly Hills: Sage.

Cooley, W.W. (1978). Explanatory observational studies. *Educational Researcher* 7:9-15.

————— . (1984a). Improving the performance of an educational system. *Educational Researcher* 12:4-12.

————— . (1984b). *Reflections upon a grand tour.* Unpublished manuscript, University of Pittsburgh, Learning Research and Development Center.

Cooley, W.W., and Glaser, R. (1969). The computer and individualized instruction. *Science* 166:574-582.

Cooley, W.W., and Leinhardt, G. (1980). The instructional dimensions study. *Educational Evaluation and Policy Analysis* 2(1):7-25.

Cooley, W.W., and Lohnes, P.R. (1976). *Evaluation research in education.* New York: Irvington.

Cronbach, L.J. (1982). *Designing evaluations of educational and social programs.* San Francisco: Jossey-Bass.

Cronbach, L.J., and associates. (1980). *Toward reform of program evaluation.* San Francisco, CA: Jossey-Bass.

Cronbach, L.J., and Snow, R.E. (1977). *Aptitudes and instructional methods.* New York: Irvington.

Cronbach, L.J., and Suppes, P. (eds.) (1969). *Research for tomorrow's schools: Disciplined inquiry for education.* New York: Macmillan.

Cuban, L. (1976). *Urban school chiefs under fire.* Chicago: University of Chicago Press.

Datta, L. (1979). *O thou that bringest the tidings to lions: Reporting the findings of educational evaluations.* Paper presented at the meeting of the National Symposium on Educational Research, Baltimore, MD.

————— . (1981). Communicating evaluation results for policy decision making. In R.A. Berk (ed.), *Educational evaluation methodology: The state of the art,* pp. 124-125. Baltimore: The Johns Hopkins University Press.

David, J.L. (1981). Local users of Title I evaluations. *Educational Evaluation and Policy Analysis* 3:27-39.

Denzin, N.K. (1971). The logic of naturalistic inquiry. *Social Forces* 50:166-182.

Dillon, J.T. (1984). The classification of research questions. *Review of Educational Research* 54:327-361.

Durant, D.M. (1984). *The development of computer assistance for elementary school principals to facilitate instructional leadership.* Unpublished doctoral dissertation, University of Pittsburgh, Pennsylvania.

Ebert, M.K. (1980). *An investigation of the causal relationships among loans of control, environmental motivators, engaged reading time, and reading ability.* Unpublished doctoral dissertation, University of Pittsburgh.

Edmonds, R.R. (1979). Some schools work and more can. *Social Policy* 9:28–32.

Edmonds, R.R., and Fredericksen, J.R. (1978). *Search for effective schools: The identification and analysis of city schools that are instructionally effective for poor children.* Unpublished manuscript, Center for Urban Studies, Cambridge.

Eichhorn, D.H. (1966). *The Middle School.* New York: The Center for Applied Research in Education.

Ein-Dor, P., and Segev, E. (1978). Organizational context and the success of management information systems. *Management Service* 24:1064–1077.

Eisner, E.W. (1975). *The perceptive eye: Toward the reformation of educational evaluation.* Stanford, CA: Stanford Evaluation Consortium.

Epstein, J.L. (1981). *The quality of school life.* Lexington, MA: Heath and Company.

Evaluation Unit. (1981). *A needs assessment of the Pittsburgh Public Schools.* Unpublished manuscript, University of Pittsburgh, Learning Research and Development Center.

Evaluation Unit. (1983). *An assessment of the Pittsburgh middle schools.* Unpublished manuscript, University of Pittsburgh, Learning Research and Development Center.

Fisher, C.W., Filby, N.N., Marliave, R., Cahen, L.S., Dishaw, M.M., Moore, J.E., and Berliner, D.C. (1978). *Teacher behaviors, academic learning time and student achievement: Final report of Phase III-B, Beginning Teacher Evaluation Study.* (Technical Report V-1). San Francisco, CA: Far West Laboratory for Educational Research and Development.

Flexner, A. (1910). Medical education in the United States and Canada. *Carnegie Foundation Bulletin* 4.

Glaser, R. (1963). Instructional technology and the measurement of learning outcomes: Some questions. *American Psychologist* 18:519–521.

Gold, N. (1981). *The stakeholder process in education program evaluation.* Unpublished manuscript, National Institute of Education, Washington, D.C.

Goodlad, J.I., O'Toole, J.F., Jr., and Tyler, L.L. (1966). *Computers and information systems in education.* New York: Harcourt, Brace & World.

Green, T.F. (1971). Equal educational opportunity: The durable injustice. *Philosophy of Education*:121–156.

Green, T.F. (1980). *Predicting the behavior of the educational system.* New York: Syracuse University Press.

Guba, E.G. (1969). The failure of educational evaluation. *Educational Technology* 9:29–38.

Guba, E.G., and Lincoln, Y.S. (1981). *Effective evaluation.* San Francisco: Jossey-Bass.

——————— . (1983). Epistemological and methodological bases on naturalistic inquiry. In G.F. Madaus, M. Scriven, and D.L. Stufflebeam (eds.), *Evaluation models: Viewpoints on educational and human services evaluation,* pp. 311–333. Boston: Kluwer-Nijhoff.

Gustafsson, J. (1980). *Matching aptitudes and treatments: The ATI-paradigm in research on individualization of instruction.* Unpublished manuscript, University of Goteborg, Sweden.

Hill, P. (1980). Evaluating programs for federal policy makers: Lessons from the NIE compensatory education study. In J. Pincus (ed.), *Educational evaluation in the public policy setting,* pp. 48–76. Santa Monica, CA: Rand.

Hoaglin, D.C., Light, R.J., McPeek, B., Mosteller, F., and Stoto, M.A. (1982).*Data for decisions.* Cambridge, MA: Abt.

Holley, F.M. (1983). Of tugboats and local education agency evaluation units. In R.G. St. Pierre (ed.), *Management and organization of program evaluation,* pp. 49–57. San Francisco, CA: Jossey-Bass.

Holzner, B. (1978). The sociology of applied knowledge. *Sociological Symposium* 21:8–19.

Hunter, M. (1984). Knowing, teaching and supervising. In P.L. Hosford (ed.), *Using what we know about teaching,* pp. 169–192. Alexandria, VA: Association for Supervision and Curriculum Development.

Johnstone, J.N. (1981). *Indicators of education systems.* London: Kogan Page.

Joint Committee on Standards for Educational Evaluation. (1981). *Standards for evaluations and educational programs, projects, and materials.* New York: McGraw Hill.

Kennedy, M.M. (1982). *Working knowledge: and other essays.* Cambridge, MA: The Huron Institute, 1982.

————— . (1984). How evidence alters understanding and decisions. Educational Evaluation and Policy Analysis 6:207–226.

Kennedy, M., Apling, R., and Neumann, W.F. (1980). *The role of evaluation and test information in public schools.* Unpublished manuscript, The Huron Institute, Cambridge.

Kent, S. (1967). *Writing history.* New York: Meredith.

King, J.A., and Pechman, E.M. (1984). Pinning a wave to the shore: Conceptualizing evaluation use in school systems. *Educational Evaluation and Policy Analysis* 6:241–251.

King, J.A., and Thompson, B. (1981). *A nationwide survey of administrators' perceptions of evaluations.* Paper presented at the meeting of the American Educational Research Association, Los Angeles, CA.

Krathwohl, D.R. (Chairman). (1975). *Educational indicators: Monitoring the state of education.* Proceedings of the 1975 ETS Invitational Conference, New York.

Land, K.C., and Spilerman, S. (eds.) (1975). *Social indicator models.* New York: Russell Sage Foundation.

Leinhardt, G. (1978). Coming out of the laboratory closet. In D. Bar-Tal and L. Saxe (eds.), *Social psychology of education: Theory and research,* pp. 83–110. Washington, D.C.: Hemispher.

————— . (1983). Overlap: Testing whether it is taught. In G.F. Madaus (ed.), *The courts, validity, and minimum competency testing,* pp. 153–170. Boston: Kluwer-Nijhoff.

Leinhardt, G., Bickel, W., and Pallay, A. (1982). Unlabeled but still entitled: Toward more effective remediation. *Teachers College Record 84* 391:422.

Leinhardt, G., and Seewald, A. (1981). Overlap: What's tested, what's taught? *Journal of Educational Measurement* 18:85–96.

Leinhardt, G., Zigmond, N., and Cooley, W.W. (1981). Reading instruction and its effects. *American Educational Research Journal* 18(3):343–361.

Leviton, L.C., and Hughes, E.F.X. (1981). Research on the utilization of evaluations: A review and synthesis. *Evaluation Review* 5:525–548.

Lindblom, C. (1972). *Strategies for decision making.* Urbana: University of Illinois.

Lofland, J., and Lofland, L.H. (1984). *Analyzing social settings: A guide to qualitative observation and analysis.* Belmont, CA: Wadsworth.

Love, A.J. (1983). *Developing effective internal evaluation.* San Francisco, CA: Jossey-Bass.

Lyon, C.D., Doscher, L., McGranahan, P. and Williams, R. (1978). *Evaluation and school districts.* Unpublished manuscript, Center for the Study of Evaluation, Los Angeles.

Lytle, J.H. (1984). *From compliance evaluation to proactive research and development.* Paper presented at the annual meeting of the American Educational Research Association, New Orleans.

MacRae, D. Jr. (1985). *Policy indicators: Links between social science and public debate.* Chapel Hill: The University of North Carolina Press.

Micro Data Base Systems. (1984). *Knowledge manager.* Lafayette, IN: MDBS.

McCall, G.J., and Simmons, J.L. (eds.) (1969). *Issues in participant observation: A text and reader.* Reading, MA: Addison-Wesley.

McLuhan, M., and Leonard, G.B. (1967). The future of education. *Look* 31:23–25.

Meyers, W.R. (1981). *The evaluation enterprise.* San Francisco, CA: Jossey-Bass.

Meehl, P.E. (1957). When shall we use our heads instead of the formula? *Journal of Counseling Psychology* 4:268–273.

Murrell, S.A., and Brown, F. (1977). Judging program evaluations. In R.D. Coursey et al. (eds.), *Program evaluation for mental health.* New York: Grune and Stratton.

Nelson, R.R. (1977). *The moon and the ghetto.* New York: Norton.

Nevins, A. (1962). *The gateway to history.* Garden City, NJ: Doubleday.

Odden, A., and Dougherty, U. (1982). *State programs of school improvement: A 50-state survey.* Denver: Education Commission of the States.

O'Reilly, C. (1981). Evaluation information and decision making in organizations: Some constraints on the utilization of evaluation research. In A. Bank and R.C. Williams (eds.), *Evaluation in school districts: Organizational perspectives,* pp. 25–65. Los Angeles: University of California, Center for the Study of Evaluation.

Overstreet, H.A. (1927). *About ourselves: psychology for normal people.* New York: Norton.

Patton, M.Q. (1975). *Alternative evaluation research paradigm.* Grand Forks, ND: University of North Dakota Press.

————— . (1978). *Utilization focused evaluation.* Beverly Hills: Sage.

————— . (1980). *Qualitative evaluation methods.* Beverly Hills: Sage.

Pittsburgh Public Schools. (1981). *An action plan for increasing the effectiveness of individual schools.* Unpublished manuscript.

————— . (1982). *Prism III: Schenley high school teacher center.* Unpublished manuscript.

Provus, M. (1971). *Discrepancy evaluation.* Berkeley, CA: McCutchan.

Purkey, S.C., and Smith, M. (1983). Effective schools — A review. *Elementary School Journal* 83:427-452.

Raiffa, H. (1968). *Decision analysis.* Reading, MA: Addison-Wesley.

Rawls, J. (1971). *Theory of justice.* Cambridge, MA: Harvard University Press.

Redfield, R. (1973). A contribution of anthropology to the education of the teacher. In F.A.J. Ianni and E. Storey (eds.), *Cultural relevance and education issues,* pp. 201-214. Boston: Little, Brown.

Redlich, J. (1914). The common law and the case method. *The Carnegie Foundation Bulletin* 8.

Reichardt, C.S., and Cook, T.D. (1979). Beyond qualitative versus quantitative methods. In T.D. Cook and C.S. Reichardt (eds.), *Qualitative and quantitative methods in evaluation research,* pp. 7-32. Beverly Hills: Sage.

Resnick, D.P., and Schumacher, C. (1980). *The Pittsburgh research and measurement bureau, 1918-1939.* Paper presented at the meeting of the American Educational Research Association, Boston, MA.

Rich, R.E. (1977). Use of knowledge by federal bureaucrats. In C.H. Weiss (ed.), *Uses of social research in public policy making.* Lexington, MA: Heath.

———— . (1981). *Social science information and public policy.* San Francisco: Jossey-Bass.

Rossi, P.H. (1972). Booby traps and pitfalls in the evaluation of social action programs. In C.H. Weiss (ed.), *Evaluating programs: Reading in social action and education.* Boston: Allyn and Bacon.

Rossi, P.H., and Freeman, H.E. (1982). *Evaluation.* Beverly Hills, CA: Sage.

Sanders, J.R. (1981). Case study methodology: A critique. In W.W. Welch (ed.), *Proceedings of the 1981 Minnesota Evaluation Conference,* pp. 41-49. Minneapolis: Minnesota Research and Evaluation Center.

Schatzman, L., and Strauss, A.L. (1973). *Field research: Strategies for a natural sociology.* Englewood Cliffs, NJ: Prentice-Hall.

Schuetz, P. (1980). *Truancy in urban elementary grade students.* Unpublished manuscript, University of Pittsburgh, Learning Research and Development Center.

Scriven, M. (1967). The methodology of evaluation. *AERA Monograph Series in Curriculum Evaluation,* No. 1. Chicago: Rand McNally.

———— . (1973). Goal-free evaluation. In E.R. House (ed.), *School evaluation: The politics and process.* Berkeley, CA: McCutchan.

Smith, N.L. (1984). *Evaluation units in state departments of education: A five-year update* (Research on Evaluation Program Paper and Report Series, No. 96). Portland, OR: Northwest Regional Educational Laboratory.

Sproull, L., and Larkey, P. (1979). Managerial behavior and evaluator effectiveness. In H.C. Schulberg and J.M. Jerrell (eds.), *The evaluator and management,* pp. 89-104. Beverly Hills: Sage.

Sproull, L., and Zubrow, D. (1981). Performance information in school systems: Perspectives from organization theory. *Educational Administration Quarterly* 17 (3):61-79.

Stake, R.E. (1967). Toward a technology for the evaluation of educational programs. In R.W. Tyler, R.M. Gagne, and M. Scriven (eds.), *Perspectives of*

curriculum evaluation. AERA monograph series on curriculum evaluation.
Chicago: Rand McNally.

Stake, R.E. (1981). Case study methodology: An epistemological advocacy. In
W.W. Welch (ed.), *Proceedings of the 1981 Minnesota Evaluation Conference,*
pp. 31-39. Minneapolis: Minnesota Research and Evaluation Center.

————— . (1983). The case study method in social inquiry. In G.F. Madaus, M.
Scriven, and D.L. Stufflebeam (eds.), *Evaluation models: Viewpoints on educational and human services evaluation,* pp. 279-286. Boston: Kluwer-Nijhoff.

Stevenson, J.F. (1981). Assessing evaluation utilization in human service agencies.
In J.A. Ciarlo (ed.), *Utilizing evaluation,* pp. 35-57. Beverly Hills, CA: Sage.

Stevenson, J.F., and McNeill, D.N. (1979). Meta-evaluation in the human services.
In H.C. Schulberg and J.M. Jerrell (eds.), *The evaluator and management,* pp,
37-54. Beverly Hills, CA: Sage.

Stufflebeam, D.L. (1971). The relevance of the CIPP evaluation model for educational accountability. *Journal of Research and Development in Education*
5:19-25.

————— . (1977). *Working paper on needs assessment in evaluation.* Paper presented at the meeting of AERA Evaluation Conference, San Francisco.

Stufflebeam, D.L., Foley, W.J., Gephart, W.J., Guba, E.G., Hammond, R.L.
Merriman, H.O., and Provus, M.M. (1971). *Educational evaluation and decision-
making.* Itasca, IL: Peacock Publishing.

Sumner, W.G., and Keller, A.G. (1927). *The science of sociology.* New Haven, CT:
Yale University Press.

Taylor, F.J. (1977). *Beyond ATI to ILD: A new approach to media research.* Unpublished manuscript, University of London, Department of Child Development
and Educational Psychology.

Tufte, E.R. (1983). *The visual display of quantitative information.* Cheshire, CT:
Graphics Press.

Tyler, R.W. (1949). *Basic principles of curriculum and instruction.* Chicago: University of Chicago Press.

van Geel, T. (1976). John Rawls and educational policy. In S.K. Gove and F.M.
Wirt (eds.), *Political science and school politics,* pp. 121-143. Lexington, MA:
Lexington.

Venesky, R.L., and Winfield, L.F. (1979). *Schools that succeed beyond expectations
in teaching* (Tech. Rep. No. 1). Newark: University of Delaware.

Venson, L. (1981). *School improvement program.* Unpublished manuscript. (Available from the Pittsburgh Public Schools, 341 S. Bellefield Avenue, Pittsburgh,
PA 15213).

Wax, R.H. (1971). *Doing fieldwork: Warnings and advice.* Chicago: University of
Chicago Press.

Webb, E.J., Campbell, D.T., Schwartz, R.D., and Sechrest, L. (1966). *Unobtrusive
measures: Nonreactive research in the social sciences.* Chicago: Rand McNally.

Weber, G. (1971). *Inner-city children can be taught to read: Four successful schools.*
Washington, D.C.: Council for Basic Education.

Webster, W., and Stufflebeam, D. (1978). *The state of theory and practice in educational evaluation in large urban school districts.* Paper presented at the meeting of the American Educational Research Association, Toronto, Canada.

Weiss, C.H. (1972). Toward comparative study. In C.H. Weiss (ed.), *Evaluating action programs: Reading in social action and education.* Boston: Allyn and Bacon.

————— . (1977). *Using social research in public policymaking.* Lexington, MA: Lexington-Heath.

————— . (1979). The many meanings of research utilization. *Public Administration Review* 39:426–431.

————— . (1980). An EEPA interview with Carol H. Weiss. *Educational Evaluation and Policy Analysis* 2(5):75–79.

————— . (1981). *Measuring the use of evaluation. In J.A. Ciarlo (ed.), Utilizing evaluation,* pp. 17–33. Beverly Hills, CA: Sage.

————— . (1983a). The stakeholder approach to evaluation: Origins and promise. In A.S. Bryk (ed.), *Stakeholder-based evaluation,* pp. 3–14. San Francisco, CA: Jossey-Bass.

————— . (1983b). Toward the future of stakeholder approaches in evaluation. In A.S. Bryk (ed.), *Stakeholder-based evaluation,* pp. 83–96. San Francisco, CA: Jossey-Bass.

Weiss, C.H., and Bucuvalas, M.J. (1980). Truth tests and utility tests: Decision-makers' frames of reference for social science research. *American Sociological Review* 45(2):302–313.

Williams, R.C., and Bank, A. Assessing instructional information systems in two districts: The search for impact. *Educational Evaluation and Policy Analysis* 6:267–282.

INDEX